To build a button

1. Create the button:
   - Choose the Button tool.
   - Select New Button from the Objects menu.

2. Customize the button:
   - Double-click on the new button (or select Button Info... from the Objects menu).
   - Type a name for the button (optional).
   - Choose the button style (for invisible button, click Transparent with Show Name clicked off).
   - Click on Icon... if desired, select an icon, click OK.
   - Drag the corner of the button to change its shape; drag the center to move it.

3. Add a visual effect (optional):
   - Double-click on button again, click on Effect....
   - Click on an effect and (optionally) click on a speed; then click OK.

4. Link the button:
   - Double-click on button again; click on LinkTo....
   - If linking to an existing card, go to that card and click on This Card button.
   - If linking to another stack, open that stack and click This Stack.
   - If linking to a new card with the same background, select New Card from the Edit menu and click This Card.
   - If linking to a new card with new background, select New Background from the Objects menu and click This Card.
   - If linking to a new card with a previously used background, go to a card with that background, select New Card from the Edit menu, and click This Card.

5. Script the button (optional):
   - Double-click on button again; click on Script... button.
   - Add to or modify existing script.
   - Click the close box of the script window.

To build a field to contain editable text

1. Create the field:
   - Choose the Field tool.
   - Select New Field from the Objects menu.

2. Customize the field:
   - Double-click on the new field (or select Field Info... from the Objects menu).
   - Type a name for the field.
   - Choose the field style (Transparent for invisible).
   - Drag the corner of the field to change its shape; drag the center to move it.
   - Click on Font...; select desired font and style (use a common font such as Geneva if your stack will be used on other computers).

3. Fill the field:
   - Select the Browse (hand) tool (*not* the *A*), position it over the field, and type text.
   - Use standard editing techniques, including Cut Text, Copy Text, and Paste Text.

HyperCard 2 in a Hurry

GEORGE BEEKMAN

OREGON STATE UNIVERSITY

Wadsworth Publishing Company
Belmont, California
A Division of Wadsworth, Inc.

This book was created on Macintosh computers using HyperCard 2, Microsoft Word, PageMaker, MacPaint, SuperPaint, DeskPaint, SnapJot, Image Grabber, QuicKeys, OmniPage, and Word Finder. The camera-ready copy for the text was printed on a Linotronic 300 Imagesetter.

Computer Science Editor: Frank Ruggirello
Editorial Assistant: Rhonda Gray
Editing and Production: Scratchgravel Publishing Services
Print Buyer: Martha Branch
Signing Representative: Tamy Stenquist

Printed in the United States of America

2   3   4   5   6   7   8   9   10—96 95 94 93 92 91

Library of Congress Cataloging-in-Publication Data
Beekman, George.
    HyperCard 2 in a hurry / George Beekman.
            p.   cm.
    ISBN 0-534-16422-6
    1. Macintosh (Computer) —Programming. 2. HyperCard (Computer program)   I. Title.
QA76.8.M3B42   1991
005.265—dc20   91-13650
                                                                    CIP

CONTENTS

Foreword   **xii**

Preface   **xiv**

Introduction   **xix**

What Is HyperCard?	xix
HyperCard, Hypertext, and Hypermedia:	
Beyond Books	xxi
HyperCard Essentials	xxi
Charting a Path through This Book	xxii

Session 1
HyperCard for Browsers: Making Tracks through Stacks   **2**

Objectives	2
The Problem	3
Introduction	4
Customizing This Session	4
If You're New to the Macintosh . . .	4
If You're a Macintosh Veteran . . .	4
Which HyperCard?	4
Which System?	5
Tips for Hard Disk Users	5
Tips for File Server Users	5
Tips for Floppy-Disk-Based System Users	6
Tips for Everybody	7

Meet Mac   **8**
Booting the Mac   *8*
Mousing Around   *9*
Opening Windows   *10*
Changing the View in a Window   *11*
Closing Windows   *12*
Ejecting a Disk   *12*

Stacks, Macs, and Backups   **13**
Initializing a Disk   *13*
Copying Files   *15*
Organizing with Folders   *16*
Backing Up a Disk   *17*
Using the Trash   *18*
Customizing Your Work Space   *18*

Hello, HyperCard   **19**
Launching HyperCard   *19*
Opening via the File Menu   *21*
Locating a File in a Folder   *22*
Taking a Tour   *24*

HyperCard Navigation Tips   **28**
Browsing with Buttons   *28*
Navigating with the Go Menu   *29*
Navigating by Keyboard   *29*
Using the Navigator Palette   *31*
Using the Scroll Window   *33*
Hiding and Showing the Menu Bar   *34*
Finding Hidden Buttons   *34*
Asking for Help   *34*
Ending a HyperCard Session   *36*
Shutting Down   *36*

Summary   **37**
Key Words   **37**
Self-Testing Exercises   **39**
Projects   **40**

Session 2
The Dynamic File Cabinet: Information Storage and Retrieval   42

Objectives   **42**
The Problem   **43**
Introduction   **44**
HyperCard as a Database   *44*
Home Base   **44**
Starting at Home   *44*

Changing the User Level and Name	*44*
Changing the Home Memory	*45*
Locating a Stack	*47*
Browsing through the Appointments Stack	*48*
HyperCard's Text Fields	**50**
Entering Text into a Field	*50*
Editing Text	*51*
Using the Clipboard	*53*
Basic Database Operations with HyperCard	**55**
Browsing through the Addresses Stack	*56*
Adding and Deleting Cards	*57*
Sorting a Stack	*59*
Using the Find Command	*59*
Using the Phone Dialer	*61*
Marking Cards	*61*
Printing Card Images	*64*
Printing a Report	*66*
Creating a Report Template	*67*
Customizing Cards	**70**
Resetting the User Level (with Magic)	*71*
Saving a Copy	*73*
Going into the Background	*73*
Deleting Buttons and Fields	*73*
Copying a Field	*74*
Labeling the Field	*75*
Shutting Down	*77*
Summary	**77**
Key Words	**77**
Self-Testing Exercises	**78**
Projects	**78**

Session 3
Stacks from Scratch: Building with Buttons

80

Objectives	**80**
The Problem	**81**
Introduction	**82**
Stack Construction Toolbox	**82**
Creating a New Stack	*82*
Tearing Off the Tools Menu	*84*
Drawing Lines	*85*
Using the Eraser	*86*
Drawing Polygons	*86*

Pouring Paint Patterns	*89*
Using Paint Text	*91*
Instant Buttons, Instant Cards	**95**
Creating a Button	*95*
Linking the Button	*96*
Adding a Visual Effect	*97*
Using the Clipboard	*98*
Painting Passages	*100*
Drawing Rooms	*102*
Drawing Labels	*104*
Creating an Invisible Button	*106*
Drawing One Last Card	*108*
Introducing Stackware Engineering	**109**
Software Engineering Simplified	*109*
Adding Emergency Exits	*109*
Borrowing a Button	*111*
Summary	**114**
Key Words	**114**
Self-Testing Exercises	**115**
Projects	**116**

Session 4
Hypercard's Hidden Layers: Backgrounds and Backtracking   118

Objectives	**118**
The Problem	**119**
Introduction	**120**
Some Background on Backgrounds	**120**
Examining Home's Background	*120*
A HyperCard Adventure	**121**
Starting a Stack	*122*
Drawing in the Background	*123*
Creating Titles	*128*
Borrowing a Background Button	*131*
Creating a New Background	*133*
Shaping Doors and Windows	*136*
Creating a Two-Way Link	*140*
Building Portable Furniture	*143*
Moving Furniture	*146*
Stackware Engineering Revisited	**148**
Uncovering a Bug	*148*
Planning a Network	*149*
Remembering the User	*150*

Secondhand Art   **151**
Copying a Card   *151*
Deleting and Rearranging Graphics   *152*
Borrowing Clip Art   *153*
Borrowing an Old Background   *155*

Loose Ends   **159**
Changing Links   *159*
Finishing the Game   *161*

Summary   **162**
Key Words   **162**
Self-Testing Exercises   **163**
Projects   **163**

Session 5
Behind the Buttons: Introducing HyperTalk   166

Objectives   **166**
The Problem   **167**
Introduction   **168**
HyperTalk Revealed   **168**
Sending HyperTalk Messages   *168*
Eavesdropping with the Message Watcher   *170*
Looking under a Button   *173*
Examining the Script of a Linked Button   *177*
Checking the Script of a Relative Link   *178*

Building a Dynamic Presentation   **180**
Outlining the Problem   *180*
Creating a Starry Background   *181*
Creating a Bullet Chart Background   *182*
Creating a Dynamic Bullet Chart   *185*
Building a Background Button   *186*
Rearranging Layers in the Background   *189*
Creating More Bullet Charts   *189*
Adding a Card Layer Illusion   *191*

Moving Pictures   **192**
Creating an Earth Icon   *192*
Spraying Away Life as We Know It   *196*
Scripting an Animated Sequence   *201*
Linking the Introduction to the Presentation   *203*

Animating with Icons   **203**
Creating a Spinning Planet   *203*
Creating Cards for a Finale   *207*

  Finding the Mouse   *207*
  Scripting a Moving Button   *208*

Using the HyperTalk Debugger   **210**
  Stepping through a Script   *212*
  Tracing a Script's Actions   *213*

Singing Stacks   **215**
  Making a Musical Card   *215*
  Hiding and Showing the Menu Bar   *217*
  Bringing It Home   *218*

Summary   **218**

Key Words   **218**

Self-Testing Exercises   **220**

Projects   **221**

Session 6
Creating Hypertext: Nonlinear Writing   222

Objectives   **222**

The Problem   **223**

Introduction   **224**

Designing Hypertext   **224**
  Defining the Problem   *224*
  Breaking the Problem into Pieces   *225*
  Fleshing Out the Pieces   *226*
  Designing the User Interface   *228*

Building a Background   **228**
  Painting the Background   *228*
  Building a Button Bar   *229*
  Adding Fields to the Background   *230*

Headlines and Footnotes   **231**
  Filling in the Blank   *231*
  Painting a Title   *231*
  Creating a Pop-Up Field   *231*
  Hiding Buttons with Buttons   *233*

Stacking the Deck   **233**
  Making the Main Menu Card   *233*
  Creating Reference Cards   *235*
  Scripting the Sequence Buttons   *237*
  Creating a Dead End   *238*

Planting a Hypertext Tree   **239**
  Automatic Backtracking   *239*
  Providing Many Happy Returns   *240*
  Creating Hot Text   *241*

Buttons That Talk Back 245
 Scripting the Find Button 245
 Adding an Interactive Exit 247
Modifying the Menu Bar 249
 Designing the Stack Script 250
 Writing Menu Manipulation Scripts 252
 Writing Custom Functions and Handlers 253
 Covering Our Tracks 254
 Putting the Stack Script Together 255
 Adding a Temporary Script 257
Missing Links 257
 Keeping Track of Loose Ends 257
 Critiquing Our Stack 258
 HyperTalk Housekeeping 259
 The Endless Stack 262
Summary 262
Key Words 262
Self-Testing Exercises 263
Projects 266

Appendix A
HyperCard Sources and Resources 269

Appendix B
Ask Doctor Hyper: A Beginner's HyperCard
Troubleshooting Guide 288

Appendix C
HyperCard Menus 292

Appendix D
HyperCard Keyboard Commands and Menu Equivalents 300

Appendix E
A HyperTalk Dictionary 304

Glossary 317

Index 322

FOREWORD

As personal computers become easier to use, they become increasingly more difficult to program. Hardy "early adopters" of personal computing had to learn and remember complex keyboard command schemes, sometimes working harder than the computer to perform a simple task. For most users today, however, getting a particular job done is the prize, not trying to figure out how to respond to a cryptic screen prompt. Users' expectations are high. The programmer's job is enormous.

Until recently, the formidable job of programming a personal computer dissuaded all but the most dedicated technical types. Professional and part-time hackers, nerds, and computer science students spent hours learning computer languages like BASIC, Pascal, and C to produce the Next Great Program. But every year the barrier to programming, especially in graphical environments like the Macintosh, climbed higher and higher.

When the Mac first arrived in 1984, Apple had prepared a three-volume set of programmer's manuals, called *Inside Macintosh*. These books documented all the built-in tools that were to make the programmer's job easier. That three-volume set has now grown to six, and, in hard cover, weighs something akin to a stereo component. So, if you want to program for the Macintosh in "traditional" languages, first you must master a language (Pascal or C), then *Inside Macintosh*.

While professional programmers were learning all the tricks, Apple continued to enhance the Macintosh's powers, and the nontechnical, would-be programmer was left in the dust. Those of us especially in the arts and humanities had to rely on software developed by what I call the Programming Priesthood. I don't mean that as a pejorative term, because the priests are the ones who give us useful general purpose tools, such as word processors and spreadsheets. But there has always been need for "little" programs—special purpose programs that meet the needs of an individual or small group. Unfortunately, the wall between the machine and those with the expertise worth computerizing became insurmountable.

Until, that is, I had the rare opportunity as an Apple outsider (a freelance writer, actually) to see an early prototype of what was to become HyperCard. John Sculley (whom I had just interviewed for *Playboy*) introduced me to HyperCard's creator, Bill Atkinson, in March of 1986. Bill showed me a few examples of applications he had made with his own new software tool—applications that I could easily create as well. I describe my reaction to this demonstration as feeling my brain expand to the size of the room and flooding rapidly with ideas.

Watching HyperCard's features solidify, and seeing Dan Winkler's implementation of the HyperTalk scripting language take shape over the next several months, made it clear that programming's barrier walls were to come tumblin' down. Creating screen items like scrolling text fields and clickable buttons no longer took dozens of lines of Pascal or C code—they were choices in menus and dialog boxes.

In addition to writing *The Complete HyperCard Handbook*, I also started working on two HyperCard-based applications that would eventually become commercial products. *Business Class* (a world traveler's guide) and *Focal Point* (a personal organizer). Within a short time, I went from an author of books and articles to software author.

I wasn't alone. Around the world, businesspeople, academicians, and students applied their expertise to HyperCard programs. People who would staunchly proclaim themselves nonprogrammers were creating multimedia training presentations, interactive cultural libraries, social science and historical simulations, student housing guides, and thousands more. HyperCard has touched thousands of lives.

As stepping stones to further computer language study, HyperCard and HyperTalk offer fine introductions to concepts of object orientation. The programming world is heading in this direction, with many professional programmers advancing to object-oriented Pascal and C++. If you progress to these levels, you will instantly see how simple and elegant the HyperCard environment is. Like many professionals, you may even continue to use HyperCard as a prototyping tool to test program flow and user interfaces.

Importantly, you don't have to be a computer science major to appreciate how HyperCard empowers you. If you can transform but one idea into a working HyperCard application, then consider yourself successful. It may open your eyes to even more possibilities. That is the beauty of HyperCard.

Danny Goodman

PREFACE

This book is designed to deliver what it promises: *HyperCard 2 in a Hurry*. Rather than exhaustively describing every feature and nuance of HyperCard and HyperTalk, *HyperCard 2 in a Hurry* systematically introduces the fundamentals of HyperCard, version 2.0 and beyond, through a series of self-study, hands-on sessions. The first two sessions introduce HyperCard as a tool for information storage and retrieval. The four remaining sessions illustrate essential techniques and tricks for building a variety of HyperCard stacks.

HyperCard 2 in a Hurry is not *Instant HyperCard*. Learning a complex and powerful tool takes time. But by focusing on the essentials of HyperCard and stack design, *HyperCard 2 in a Hurry* minimizes the amount of time it takes to become a competent, confident HyperCard stack designer. After a few hours with this book, a student with little or no computer experience should be able to design, build, and customize visually impressive and conceptually complex stacks to perform a variety of tasks. This statement says as much about HyperCard as it does about this book. Before HyperCard, it simply wasn't possible for a computer neophyte, with an investment of a dozen hours, to build sophisticated graphic presentations with complex logical structures. With HyperCard, beginners turn into programmers every day. This book is designed to facilitate that process.

The material in this book has been tested by hundreds of students (as well as several instructors and a few innocent bystanders). Most of the students were university students in a freshman computer literacy class, where they learned how to use computers mostly through hands-on experience with Microsoft Works and HyperCard. Junior high students in two-week summer math camps sponsored by the American Indian Science and Engineering Society provided the greatest inspiration in shaping the book. After being led through an abridged version of the Dungeon project in Session 4, these students applied what they learned to produce visual recreations of classic native American legends.

Their creations, completed in just a few hours, should convince even the most jaded skeptic that HyperCard *can* be learned in a hurry.

From Zero to HyperCard in Six Sessions

This book can be used by anyone who's interested in learning Hyper-Card. It assumes no computer experience but provides time-saving shortcuts and bypasses for Macintosh veterans. Each session guides students step by step through the process of using or creating stacks, pointing out the important concepts along the way. Projects are drawn from a variety of subject areas, so students with different backgrounds and interests can see by example how they can put HyperCard to work in practical and provocative ways.

Each session of the book adds another layer to the student's understanding of HyperCard. It's not necessary to complete all six sessions to learn HyperCard; many students may find it more appropriate to stop at the end of Session 2, 3, 4, or 5.

Sessions 1 and 2 lay the groundwork for the rest of the book by providing a guided tour of the Macintosh and HyperCard. Session 1 focuses on Macintosh basics and HyperCard fundamentals. Session 2 shows how to use HyperCard as a personal database; it includes a short section on modifying an existing database stack, giving students a preview of HyperCard's authoring tools. (Instructions are included for modifying the Apple version of HyperCard 2 that is bundled with new Macintoshes so that it can be used for stack authoring and scripting.) These sessions are designed so that Macintosh veterans can bypass review material.

In Sessions 3 and 4, students learn the basics of stack construction in the process of creating a dynamic multilayer map/display and a complex maze game. Graphic tools, cards, buttons, links, and backgrounds are introduced gradually as these projects unfold. Aesthetic and technical design principles are illustrated and explained along the way, so students have a conceptual framework to guide their use of HyperCard's tools.

Sessions 5 and 6 explore HyperTalk, the programming language that hides underneath HyperCard's friendly point-and-click interface. Session 5 uses sound effects and animation in a presentation graphics stack. Session 6 builds a nonlinear hypertext term "paper." In these sessions, students are guided through the design process that precedes the actual hands-on construction work. With the background the last two sections of this book provide, students can explore scripts created by others, expanding their HyperTalk knowledge as they do.

For those students who aren't satisfied with what they learn in these six sessions, Appendix A provides links to other sources and resources, including books, software, and hardware. This section is designed for readers who want answers to such questions as "What's a good way to learn more about HyperTalk?" and "How can I put my own pictures and sounds in HyperCard?"

The remaining appendices are designed to make this book a useful reference tool. These appendices answer the most common HyperCard questions, organize and annotate all the important HyperCard menu and keyboard commands, and define the essential HyperTalk terms.

In the process of writing this book, I've become even more convinced of the importance of HyperCard as an educational tool. HyperCard unlocks the door that used to say, "Programmers only beyond this point!" There's an exciting world full of creative computing behind that door. *HyperCard 2 in a Hurry* is a guidebook to that world.

What's New in Version 2?

The release of version 2.0 of HyperCard marks a significant change in the product. In addition to changing the basic look of many standard HyperCard screens, the HyperCard development team added several important features to make HyperCard even more powerful and friendly, including:

- Variable card sizes—stacks can be created with custom card sizes.

- Multiple windows—more than one stack can be open at one time.

- Text styles—a single field can contain multiple styles of text.

- Hot text—new HyperTalk functions make it easy to create true hypertext documents.

- Better printing—more printing options make HyperCard more useful for database applications.

- More powerful HyperTalk—dozens of new HyperTalk commands make it easy for beginning programmers to build sophisticated user interfaces, complete with interactive dialog boxes and pull-down menus. Some operations that used to require scripting, such as visual effects, can now be done via dialog boxes. In addition, a built-in icon editor, a powerful script editor, a convenient debugging environment, and a transparent run-time compiler are all available for the first time in HyperCard 2.

HyperCard 2 in a Hurry is designed to help first-time HyperCard users make the most of these new features. While retaining the basic hands-on structure of the original *HyperCard in a Hurry*, this edition has been rewritten to reflect the most important changes in HyperCard and to better meet the needs of the next generation of HyperCard users. Specifically, *HyperCard 2 in a Hurry* includes several significant enhancements and improvements:

- Because many HyperCard 2 users are working with the version bundled with new Macintoshes, whereas others are using the complete Claris package, *HyperCard 2 in a Hurry* has been written to work equally well with either version. All six sessions use stacks that are shipped with *both* versions, and Session 2 has specific instructions for turning the bundled version into a full-featured HyperCard that supports scripting.

- Step-by-step instructions have been improved to help keep readers on track. In addition to the check boxes for marking progress through instructions, the text includes a striped bar to make it clear when instructions are to be completed in the background layer. For readers who find the sessions too long to complete in a single sitting, break points are included to mark logical stopping places.

- The introductory Macintosh material has been condensed into a few optional pages in Session 1 to make room for more HyperCard-specific material while still allowing Macintosh neophytes to get started with just this book.

- Sophisticated new navigation tools such as the scroll window, the navigation palette, and stack-specific menus are covered in detail in Session 1.

- Session 2 includes detailed instruction for taking advantage of Hyper-Card 2's powerful new printing and report-generation features. In addition, Session 2 includes instructions for modifying an existing database stack, so users with specific business interests can start right away to create custom stacks.

- The projects in Sessions 3 and 4 have been enhanced with striking visual effects, now available to beginning stack builders without scripting.

- Scripting is introduced in Session 5, rather than Session 6, so the last two sessions can cover more advanced scripting concepts. Session 5 introduces scripting via sound and animation and includes a section on HyperCard 2's icon editor. The HyperTalk debugger is used to illuminate the message-passing process that commonly confounds beginners. Session 6 has been completely rewritten to take advantage of HyperCard's powerful new hypertext commands and functions. In addition, Session 6 provides instructions for creating a custom user interface complete with dialog boxes and custom pull-down menus. Session 6 concludes by developing a complex modular stack script through stepwise refinement. Both scripting sessions include clear definitions and examples of every HyperTalk command and function introduced. Most HyperCard stack builders will find that these two sessions tell them everything they need to know about HyperTalk. For those who need more, these sessions provide the background necessary to understand *HyperCard Script Language*

Guide, the official Claris handbook for HyperTalk (Santa Clara, CA: Claris, 1990).

Feedback on the original *HyperCard in a Hurry* has been overwhelmingly positive. Every change made in this new edition is designed to improve on the original while staying true to the original mission: to help readers master HyperCard in a hurry.

Acknowledgments

This book would not be what it is without the mental, physical, and spiritual contributions of many, many people. To all of you who helped me with a kind word, a thoughtful suggestion, an open ear, and/or a warm heart, I thank you—you know who you are, even if you don't find your name here. Specifically, a heartfelt thank you to Frank Ruggirello, Carol Carreon, Rhonda Gray, Hal Humphrey, Anne Draus, Greg Draus, Danny Goodman, Rebecca Smith, Larry Beekman, charles chesney, Alice Trinka, Sarah Lillie, Brian Crissie, Rajeev Pandey, Jeannie Holmes, Mary Ann Dengler, Jeff Hino, Mike Quinn, Kevin Hurst, Pam Meyer, Ken Tubbs, Paul Ritter, Gail Sanders, Shannon Whitmore, Bryan Miller, Phil Brown, Jack Dymond, Phil (Mouse Droppings) Russell, Neal Gladstone, Don Poole, Mike Massey, Walter Rudd, Liza Weiman, Loretta Reilly, Shoobedebop, the students and staff of the 1989 AESIS Math Camp, the hundreds of CS 101 students who beta-tested this material, the OSU Computer Science Department office staff, and the consultants and support technicians in the CS Department. I owe a special thank you to Linda Fernandes for her help in organizing and improving version 2 of this book. A note of appreciation goes to the representatives of Apple and Claris who helped with this book. I am also grateful to the following who reviewed the material while it was still in manuscript form: Sherry Francis, University of Akron; Paul W. Ross, Millersville University of Pennsylvania; Mary Anderson, Gonzaga University; Susan Wilkins, California State Polytechnic University; and Scott Kronick. Most of all, thanks to my family—Ben, Johanna, and Susan—whose sacrifices and support made this book possible.

INTRODUCTION

 If you're *really* in a hurry to get started with HyperCard, you may safely bypass the first two sections of this introduction, skipping directly to "HyperCard Essentials." But if you're totally unfamiliar with HyperCard, the material in those two sections will provide you with a background for understanding the ideas behind HyperCard.

What Is HyperCard?

HyperCard is one of the most interesting and influential pieces of software to be released in recent years. It's also one of the most difficult to describe. The question "What is HyperCard?" has several answers:

- **HyperCard is a tool for accessing information.** There's no shortage of information in today's world; the problem is finding the right piece of information when you need it. It's easy to spend hours scanning reference books for an elusive fact, quote, or idea, following footnotes and bibliographies that may lead toward other promising sources. There's no easy way to seek out particular facts quickly with conventional printed references.

    When you're looking for information with HyperCard, it's much easier to cut your own trails through the information. Unlike a conventional book or article, a typical HyperCard document contains links that can lead you quickly to other parts of the document—or to other related documents. If you're researching logging practices in the Pacific Northwest, you might choose to jump from reading a card about the Douglas fir to perusing a detailed entry on the spotted owl that lives in old-growth canopies, perhaps clicking a button that plays a recording of the owl's call. The possibilities are nearly limitless.

- **HyperCard is a tool for managing information.** Like a standard computer database, HyperCard allows you to store all kinds of information, from phone numbers to phonetic spellings, in organized packages that can be expanded and changed to meet your needs. But because HyperCard documents can be linked, it's possible to jump instantly from a calendar reminder of a friend's birthday to a phone book that can automatically dial your friend's phone number for you.

  Many people use HyperCard simply to access "canned" information; others use it to store their own personal information in an easy-to-access form.

- **HyperCard is a software construction kit.** The Macintosh has long held a reputation for being the most user friendly of computers. With its intuitive, graphic user interface and its consistent command structure, the Macintosh has become the computer of choice for millions of people who don't want to be bothered with memorizing cryptic commands like CHDIR SYS3825 or DEL *.BAS.

  Ironically, the user-friendly interface makes the Macintosh programmer-hostile when compared with other machines. Traditional Macintosh programming is incredibly difficult, in large part because the programmer has to anticipate the needs of the user in so many ways.

  HyperCard has changed all that. With HyperCard, it's possible for nonprofessional programmers to create original working software applications in hours rather than months. In the same way that MacPaint makes child's play of computer graphics, HyperCard can make a game of building software applications. Bill Atkinson, HyperCard's creator, calls it a "software erector set."

  Like any programming tool, HyperCard has strengths and weaknesses. Although it's not designed for building industrial-strength word processors or spreadsheets, it's nearly ideal for building customized personal information managers, educational tutorials, and user interfaces to other, less friendly programs.

- **HyperCard is a medium for publishing information in nonsequential form.** By simplifying the program-construction process, HyperCard has opened up the world of programming to thousands of people who consider themselves nonprogrammers. Most of these nonprofessional programmers are creating programs that are more like documents than applications. Engineers, teachers, and other professionals are using HyperCard as a medium for making their expertise available to others in a dynamic, interactive form.

- **HyperCard is a gateway to multimedia computer applications**. The user interface is often the weak link in a new piece of hardware or software. Because HyperCard shines as a user interface construction kit, it's being used to create friendly "front ends" for other software packages, hardware peripherals, and multimedia devices. With a well-constructed HyperCard front end, an otherwise complex technological device, such as a videodisc player or a CD-ROM drive, can become as easy to control as a child's toy.

HyperCard, Hypertext, and Hypermedia: Beyond Books

While HyperCard is a relatively new software product, it's based on ideas that go back to the earliest days of computing. In 1945, Vannevar Bush, science advisor to President Roosevelt, wrote about his vision of a system for tracking and using scientific literature. The **memex**, as he called it, would link together articles, sketches, and photographs in a comprehensive, cross-referenced research tool.

The technology of the time made it difficult, if not impossible, to actually create a memex. But over the years, Bush's ideas inspired Doug Engelbart, Ted Nelson, Alan Kay, and other computer visionaries to push the technology toward that end. These early efforts were generally referred to as **hypertext** because they allowed mostly textual information to be linked in nonlinear ways. Conventional text media such as books are linear, or sequential: They are designed to be read from beginning to end in one particular order. Hypertext media, or **hypermedia**, invite readers to cut their own trails through information.

If you're reading about Beethoven's life, for example, you might want to learn more about his hometown, the disease that caused his deafness, the composers who most inspired him, or the culture that spawned him. If you decide to explore the culture of the time, you might be fascinated by a discussion of religious festivals and decide to focus on those. That might start you wondering about the primitive rituals that predated those festivals, and so on. With a large, all-encompassing hypertext reference, you can follow your curiosity wherever it might lead you.

You're not likely to find HyperCard stacks that give you the kind of absolute intellectual freedom hinted at here; that kind of multidimensional, cross-disciplinary information source requires an investment of time and hardware that goes beyond what most of us would consider reasonable. But because HyperCard is the first software tool to popularize the concepts of hypermedia, it's rapidly pushing us toward the visions of Vannevar Bush.

HyperCard Essentials

When you work with a Macintosh, or any computer, you use **applications**—software tools—such as word processors and graphics programs to create **documents** such as letters, research papers, and posters. In the same way, you'll use HyperCard to create documents. A HyperCard document is known as a **stack**, and it's made up of identically-sized **cards**.

Like a 3 x 5 note card, a HyperCard card can contain any combination of graphics or text. Depending on the size of the card and the size of your monitor screen, a card might occupy a window on your screen, exactly fill the screen, or be so large that it's only partially visible on your screen.

It's possible to **browse** through the cards in a stack in sequential order, from the first card to the last. But in most stacks you aren't restricted to this kind of sequential access. **Buttons** on each card allow you to jump to other related cards in the stack—or to another stack—with a click of the mouse. For this kind of direct access to other cards, it's necessary to **link** the buttons to those cards. But as you'll see, it's a simple process to create a button that links one card to another.

Buttons can do far more than take you to another screen. HyperCard buttons can play music, open dialog boxes, launch other Macintosh applications, rearrange information, perform menu operations, dial telephones, send messages to hardware devices—do just about anything that you can do with your Macintosh. Programming a button to perform many of these tasks requires mastery of **HyperTalk**, HyperCard's hidden programming language. But as you'll see in the first four sessions of this book, it's possible to accomplish a surprising amount without learning a word of HyperTalk. In later sessions you'll see how a few carefully chosen HyperTalk words can enhance the stacks that you create.

Charting a Path through This Book

Learning HyperCard is like learning to ride a bicycle: Reading about it just isn't enough. This book is designed to give you hands-on experience so you can start using HyperCard productively as quickly as possible. It's divided into six sessions. Each session provides a new way of working with HyperCard. The more sessions you complete, the deeper your understanding of HyperCard. This kind of layered structure is possible because of HyperCard's multileveled nature. HyperCard can be just about as powerful a tool as you choose to make it.

To clarify, let's compare HyperCard to television. When you read an instruction manual for a new TV set, you learn how to turn it on, adjust the volume, and navigate the channels—but not how to make your own TV shows. In Session 1 of this book, you'll use HyperCard like a TV set: as a medium for receiving information packages created by others. Session 2 treats HyperCard more like a VCR; you'll learn how to capture and customize information sources. In Sessions 3 and 4, you'll master HyperCard as a video camera, so you can actually create your own programs. In the remaining sessions, you'll learn to work with Hyper-Card scripts, which have no analogy in the world of consumer video today. It's as if you could teach your video camera or television to do things that they couldn't do when they left the factory.

During a typical session of *HyperCard 2 in a Hurry*, you'll use Hyper-Card to solve a real-world problem, learning several new concepts and techniques as you do. Each session can be completed in roughly an hour or two. (If you're a rank beginner and/or very thorough, some sessions may take longer. If you have lots of experience with Macintosh computing, you can probably zip through two sessions in the time it takes a Macintosh neophyte to complete one.)

> Each session assumes you've mastered the material in the previous session, so resist the temptation to skip ahead. There may be times, though, when skipping ahead is the right thing to do. This book is designed to meet the needs of a widely diversified audience: seasoned Macintosh users, experienced programmers, and (especially) rank beginners—in short, anyone who wants to learn HyperCard in a hurry. Because different readers have different needs, this book has road signs in boxes like this to steer you around material that may be unnecessary or inappropriate for you.

In each session, you'll be asked to perform a number of tasks to complete a project. A typical task might look like this:

Resetting the User Level

The steps to perform a given task are preceded by check boxes, like this:

☐ **Point to the button labeled Cancel and click the mouse.**

Follow each instruction *carefully,* checking it off when you complete it. The paragraphs that precede and/or follow the instructions give you more details about why you're doing what you're doing. If you skip a step or don't do exactly what it tells you to do, you may take a wrong turn and stray from the path described in this guidebook.

Illustrations along the way show you what your screen should look like. Don't worry if your screen doesn't *exactly* match the ones in the book; when you're working in HyperCard's visual environment, there are all kinds of variations that have no effect on the end result.

Starting at the end of the second session, you'll be regularly switching back and forth between HyperCard's transparent card layer and opaque background layer. Because these two layers often look alike, it's easy to forget where you are and perform some operation in the wrong layer. HyperCard reminds you that you're in the background by putting candy stripes on the menu bar. Similarly, this book includes a striped bar next to all instructions that apply to the background layer, just like the bar you see here.

Even if you follow every instruction, check every screen shot, and monitor every background switch, you may feel hopelessly lost at some point when things don't match. When that happens, you can either (1) panic or (2) accept your disorientation as an opportunity to do some creative detective work. If you're here to learn, go with the second approach. Retrace your steps looking for the wrong turn. Read ahead to see if you made any incorrect assumptions about where the book is leading you. Uncertainty is a wonderful catalyst for learning; make the most of it!

Break Point

You may want to take a break in the middle of a session. This icon will let you know when it's a good time to quit. If you have to quit before completing a session, be sure to (1) quit HyperCard, (2) back up the files you have created or modified, and (3) shut down the computer. When you return, (1) start up the computer and (2) open the stack you were working on.

As you proceed through a session, don't try to memorize every step of every process. If a piece of information is crucial, this book will tell you.

> Boxes like this one contain facts, concepts, and pointers worth remembering. It's not necessary to memorize every detail in these boxes. They're easy to scan when you're reviewing a session or looking for a piece of important information later. In effect, this book has already been highlighted with a see-through marker.

Like anything else, HyperCard has a vocabulary that includes terms you may not recognize. When a new term is introduced in this book, it's printed in **boldface** so it's easy to spot. At the end of each session, you'll find all of the new terms collected in a list of key words. Exercises and projects at the end of each session will help you test your knowledge and understanding and further develop your HyperCard skills.

If you forget a detail and can't remember where you saw it, use the inside covers and the appendices at the end of the book. You'll find summaries of menu and keyboard commands, a short cookbook of essential HyperCard procedures, a troubleshooting guide to answer common questions, and an annotated list of references to help you find answers to questions that aren't covered in this book.

One final word: *HyperCard 2 in a Hurry* is intended to get you up and running with HyperCard quickly. But that doesn't mean you should rush through the material. You'll learn more and learn faster if you take your time and relax while working through these examples. HyperCard is fun—*enjoy it!*

HyperCard 2 in a Hurry

SESSION 1

Objectives

By the end of this session you should be able to

- Use menus to perform basic file and disk management operations on the Macintosh
- Begin a HyperCard session
- Open a HyperCard stack from the Home card
- Use HyperCard buttons, menu commands, keyboard shortcuts, and palettes to navigate a HyperCard stack and return to the Home card
- Terminate a HyperCard session

HYPERCARD FOR BROWSERS:

MAKING TRACKS THROUGH STACKS

The Problem

You've contracted a serious case of information anxiety. You're sitting in the middle of an information explosion, and the gap between what you know and what you think you *should* know is getting wider every day. Traditional information-gathering tools just don't seem to help anymore. Books take too long to read, and they're often obsolete by the time they become widely available. Magazines and newspapers are timely, but the information they contain is almost impossible to find when you need it. Radio provides no practical tool for sifting the relevant from the repetitive. And TV, which promises so much and delivers so little, is probably the worst time waster of all. Computers helped create this rapidly expanding sea of information. Can they help keep you from drowning? Perhaps HyperCard can help.

Introduction

This first session will introduce you to the Macintosh and HyperCard. Whether you're a newcomer to computers or an experienced Macintosh user, you'll learn in this session how to create your working disk and a backup disk. When you're ready, you'll learn the basics of navigating in HyperCard. Take your time, take notes on things that aren't clear, and take breaks when the spirit moves you. Have fun!

Customizing This Session

If You're New to the Macintosh . . .

Relax. Macintosh computing is easy, intuitive, and fun. You'll be up to speed soon if you take the time to learn a few Macintosh basics.

This book assumes that you know little or nothing about computers in general and the Macintosh in particular. But since HyperCard is our focus, you won't find detailed instructions on those aspects of the Macintosh that aren't directly related to HyperCard.

If you can, start your Macintosh journey with the disk-based **Guided Tour** that Apple provides with every Macintosh. If you take the time to explore the material in this self-paced tour, Macintosh mastery will come easier and faster.

If You're a Macintosh Veteran . . .

You can safely skip much of the material in this session. Follow the instructions at the beginning of the section called "Meet Mac." Proceed quickly through the remaining material. Focus on the check-box instructions and reminder boxes, consulting the between-step explanations only for unfamiliar material. But beware: Some aspects of Hyper-Card run counter to conventional Mac wisdom. Pay attention! If you miss something along the way, feel free to go back, or simply consult the reference sections in the appendices at the end of this book.

Which HyperCard?

Version 2.0 of HyperCard exists in two basic forms: Apple's "light" version that's included with every Macintosh, and Claris Corporation's complete HyperCard package that includes several disks of supplementary stacks and development tools along with hundreds of pages of documentation. Each session of *HyperCard 2 in a Hurry* can be completed with either version. (The bundled Apple version of HyperCard is patched so that it can't be used for authoring and scripting without modification; Session 2 includes instructions for turning it into a fully functional version.)

Which System?

HyperCard 2 in a Hurry is designed to work with any Macintosh running System 6.05 or later and HyperCard version 2.0 or later. There are a few differences in how things look and work for users of System 7; this book will note those differences when necessary. Some details of getting started will vary slightly depending on whether your system is built around a hard disk, a network file server, or 3.5-inch disks. (3.5-inch disks are sometimes called **diskettes**, **flexible disks,** or **floppy disks**, because the magnetic disk inside the hard plastic case is flexible.) This book will point out the most common variations. You might want to make a note of any local idiosyncrasies in the margins. Let's start with some general pointers for each class of users.

> Feel free to skip those tips that don't apply to the system you're using.

Hard Disk

Tips for Hard Disk Users

Although HyperCard doesn't specifically demand a hard disk, it expresses a clear preference for one. An **internal hard disk** (one that's inside the Mac) or an **external hard disk** (a separate box with its own on-off switch) will save you time and frustration by allowing you to store large quantities of information in a quickly accessible form. Here are a handful of hard disk tips:

- Your hard disk should contain the standard **system files,** Hyper-Card, and the stacks called Home, Appointments, and Addresses. If it doesn't, you'll need to have disks containing those files. (It's helpful if your hard disk also contains HyperCard Tour, HyperCard Help, Help Extras, HyperTalk Reference, and the other stacks that come in the Claris HyperCard package.)

- If the hard disk is shared, remember to leave it in the same condition you found it. Don't leave it littered with your personal files, and don't change or delete any files that aren't yours. Later in this session you'll create a working disk with copies of the stacks you'll be modifying, so you can use these without fear of damaging the originals.

- If you have a password-accessible partition on the disk, keep your password private.

Tips for File Server Users

Although all file servers don't work the same way, most commonly used file servers simply appear as another icon on the user's screen above or

File Server

below the system disk. That's appropriate, since a **file server** is little more than a giant, slow, shared disk. Like any shared property, the server probably has more restrictions than you'll find on your private property; you won't be able to erase it, for example. Most file servers require you to have a specially prepared **System Folder** on a disk in your disk drive (or on a hard disk). Here are some general tips:

- Make sure you have the right version of the network System software for your installation.

- If your file server doesn't contain HyperCard and the stacks called Home, Appointments, and Addresses, you'll need a disk containing those files. (If your file server also contains HyperCard Tour, Hyper-Card Help, Help Extras, HyperTalk Reference, and the other stacks that come in the Claris HyperCard package, all the better.)

- If you have a password-accessible storage area on the file server, keep your password private.

- Leave the server in the same condition you found it. Don't leave it littered with your personal files, and don't change or delete any files that aren't yours. Later in this session you'll create a work disk with copies of the stacks you'll be modifying, so you can use these without fear of damaging the originals.

Tips for Floppy-Disk-Based System Users

Diskette

Using HyperCard from a floppy-disk-based system can be challenging, but it's not impossible. Here are a few guidelines:

- You'll need a **system disk** containing the Macintosh system files, version 6.05 or later and a disk containing HyperCard. One of these disks should contain the stacks called Home, Appointments, and Addresses. (If you have disks containing HyperCard Tour, HyperCard Help, Help Extras, HyperTalk Reference, and the other stacks that come in the Claris HyperCard package, all the better.)

- Make sure your system disk isn't cluttered with unnecessary files, fonts, and desk accessories. If you aren't sure about what should be on the disk, check with your lab administrator or consult your Macintosh manual.

- If you're using high density Apple FDHD Superdrives (standard drives on all Macintoshes except the Plus since August 1989), invest in **high density (HD) disks** that can hold almost twice as much information. With these disks, you can put HyperCard and the System Folder on one disk, so that you have a drive free for data files. There's one disadvantage to this method: Your disks won't be readable on Macs that don't have the Superdrive.

Hard Disk   File Server

Diskette

Tips for Everybody

- Because HyperCard *automatically saves changes regularly throughout a session*, those changes are, effectively, permanent. If you're working in a public lab with shared copies of HyperCard and its stacks, remember that others will be following in your footsteps. In this session you'll create a personal disk that contains **working copies** of the stacks you'll need. Always work with your own personal copies of stacks rather than the public originals.

- Whether you're working with public files or not, it's important to know how to make **backup copies** of your files. Whenever you create something with a computer, there's a risk that you'll lose what you've done when your hard disk bites the dust or your floppy disk goes through the laundry in your shirt pocket. You can protect yourself from that kind of calamity by regularly backing up your stacks on different disks. For important projects, keep at least one backup in a safe place away from the working copy. Unless you're working with your own private hard disk system, you'll need at least two blank disks: one to store your stacks and one for backups. If you have a personal hard disk, you'll need only a disk for backups.

- If your Macintosh doesn't have Apple's FDHD Superdrive, it can't read HD disks. Be careful not to use HD disks in machines that don't have the Superdrive. (HD disks are easily identifiable; they have small square holes at two corners; standard disks have only one square hole.)

- Keep your disks away from dust, moisture, and magnetic fields. If your environment is particularly harsh, keep them in a plastic disk box, zippered plastic sandwich bags, or some other sealed container.

- Before you make major changes in a project, save a copy. Don't burn your bridges.

- Always leave some empty space on your working disk to allow room for your stacks to grow.

- In some situations HyperCard won't allow you to complete an operation because there's not enough internal memory (RAM) available. (Sometimes it will tell you explicitly; other times it simply won't let you perform the operation.) If you suspect a memory shortage, reset HyperCard's allocated memory to a higher amount or turn off Multifinder. Consult your Macintosh manual for details.

The next two sections have two goals: to familiarize you with Macintosh file operations, and to prepare a disk containing the files you'll use in the next session. If you're familiar with the Macintosh operations for copying, moving, and organizing files, you may want to skip these sections and simply prepare the disk on your own. On pages 18–19, under the heading "Customizing Your Work Space," you'll find a description of the finished disk, along with instructions for how to use it with your particular system. If you have trouble configuring the required disk, return to this point and let these sections guide you there.

Meet Mac

Booting the Mac

It's time to make things happen. We'll start by **booting** our machine. (Why booting? The machine pulls itself up by its own bootstraps.)

☐ **If you're using a compact Mac (Classic, Plus, or SE) or Mac LC, reach around the left side of the Mac and turn on the power switch. If you're using a Mac II, turn it on by pressing the key marked with a triangle in or above the top row of the keyboard.**

The Macintosh will awaken with a chime.

Once it's awake, the computer starts groping around for the **operating system** files that tell it how to go about its business.

If your Mac has a hard disk, it should find those files on that disk and boot as soon as the drive is up to speed.

 If it can't find a hard disk, it'll use the flashing disk to ask, "Where's the system disk?" The Mac needs a **startup disk**—one containing system files. We'll refer to this disk as the system disk, but the name doesn't matter.

☐ **If your machine doesn't boot by itself, insert your system disk, metal end first, label up. Gently push it all the way into the slot under the screen.**

The metal door on the disk protects it from dangerous dust, scratches, and fingerprints, so don't open it yourself; the machine will take care of that.

You'll soon see a little Mac on the screen smiling as if to say, "Thanks." (If you accidentally insert a disk that doesn't have the system files on it, the disk drive will spit out the disk: "No thanks." If that happens, turn the machine off for a second if necessary and try again, making sure you're using a disk with system files. If it happens again, try again with a different system disk.)

After the system has finished booting, you should see the electronic **desktop** on the screen. The scene should include at least two **icons**, one representing your system disk (or the hard disk) and one labeled **"Trash."**

If you're connected to a **network** with a file server, your specially configured system disk should alert the server to your presence. In some cases, you may have to formally sign on by typing your name and/or a password to access the server. If you need to do more than simply turn on the machine, check with the lab staff for details.

Mousing Around

You're staring at your electronic desktop (brought to you by an important system program called the **Finder**). This desktop is your work space when you're dealing with the Macintosh, and you can organize it or clutter it the way you would any desktop. But first you have to learn how to move things around. That's what the mouse is for.

☐ **Holding the mouse so its cable points away from you, move it around and watch the pointer move.**

You'll be rolling your mouse around whenever you use your Mac, so find a comfortable location for it and keep that area clear. If it bumps into something or reaches the edge of the desk or mouse pad, pick it up and move it to a roomier location; lifting the mouse doesn't move the pointer on the screen.

☐ **Move the pointer so that its tip touches the trash can icon; push and release the mouse button once.**

This is called **clicking** the mouse. Watch the trash can icon change from white to black.

☐ **Put the pointer on the disk icon and click the button once.**

The trash can is now back to normal, and the disk icon is now black. This inverted coloration (Apple calls it **highlighting**) indicates you have **selected** the icon by clicking on it.

☐ **Point to (put the pointer on) the trash can and press the mouse button. Move the mouse to the left with the button held down, and watch an outline of the can move with the pointer. Let go.**

This is called **dragging** an icon.

☐ **Drag the trash back where you found it.**

Opening Windows

A **window** is a tool for looking into something. Most of the icons on your desk have windows associated with them. Let's open one.

☐ **Click on the system disk (or hard disk) icon to select it.**

> When you use the Macintosh, you generally *select* something before you issue a command to do something.

Macintosh commands are hidden in the **menu bar** at the top of the screen.

File	
New Folder	⌘N
Open	⌘O
Print	
Close	⌘W
Get Info	⌘I
Duplicate	⌘D
Put Away	
Page Setup...	
Print Directory...	
Eject	⌘E

☐ **Point to the word File and press and hold the mouse button.**

The **File menu** that appears is called a **pull-down menu**, because you pull the pointer down to the item you want to select.

☐ **Without releasing the button, drag the arrow down the list. When you reach Open, release the button to select it.**

If you overshoot Open, just move the pointer back up to Open, or roll off the edge of the menu with the button down and try again.

Notice that some of the commands in the File menu are gray; those are commands that aren't appropriate for what you have selected; the Macintosh dims them to indicate that they're unavailable. When you select Open, the window that zooms out from the disk icon should display at least one icon: the System Folder, which contains the system files.

System Folder

☐ **Position the mouse pointer on the System Folder and click twice in rapid succession (double-click).**

Double-clicking is the shorthand way to open something—in this case, a window looking into the selected folder. (If nothing changed on the screen, try again, making sure that the two clicks are close together.) As you can see, there are many items in the System Folder, each representing one of the files used by the operating system to keep things running smoothly behind the scenes.

You can drag the System Folder window around on the screen.

☐ **Position the mouse pointer on the System Folder's window title bar (at the top, where the name is), press the button, and drag it to one side so that the system disk (or hard disk) window is visible.**

▤□▤▤▤▤▤▤▤▤▤ **System Folder** ▤▤▤▤▤▤▤□▤

Notice that the system disk (or hard disk) window's title bar is no longer striped; that's because it's not **active**. When you opened the System Folder, it became the active object on the screen.

Changing the View in a Window

☐ **Click on the System Folder window. If the window contains a list of file names rather than a collection of icons, select By Icon from the View menu.**

> The **View menu** allows you to look at the information in a disk or folder window in several different ways, depending on whether you want information about the size, most recent modification date, or type of the files. If you don't need this information, it's usually easier to work with files in the icon view.

Notice that there's an icon count below the title bar. If the count doesn't match what you see, it's because some of the icons are hidden outside the borders of the window. You can hide more by resizing the window.

☐ **Select the size box in the lower right corner of the window. Press the mouse button and drag the size box to a point about two inches below and to the right of the window's upper left corner.**

It's hard to see the big picture through this compact window, but it's possible to see everything by using the **scroll bars**—those arrow-ended bars on the right and bottom edges of the window.

☐ **Point to the up-arrow and press the mouse button. Then point to the down-arrow and press.**

Your view will scroll up and down through the window, with the white **scroll box** moving through the scroll bar like a tiny elevator to show you the position of your window relative to the overall listing.

☐ **Try dragging the scroll box to a different position on the scroll bar. Then try clicking in the gray area above and below the box.**

These kinds of scroll bars are common throughout all Macintosh applications, including HyperCard.

☐ **Click in the zoom box in the upper right corner of the window.**

This box toggles the window between its current size and a larger size that almost fills the screen.

☐ **Do it again.**

Knowing how to work with folders and windows is important when you're working with HyperCard. But you normally don't need to look in the System Folder, so let's close it up and create a working disk.

Closing Windows

☐ **Click on the system disk (or hard disk) window to make it active.**

The System Folder moves to the background, since you've selected the system disk (or hard disk) window.

☐ **Select (by dragging) Close from the File menu.**

Since the system disk (or hard disk) window is the selected object, you're commanding it to close. It should vanish from the desktop.

☐ **Close the System Folder by clicking in the close box in the upper left corner.**

This is the shortcut for selecting Close from the File menu.

Ejecting a Disk

If you've worked with other computers, you may be surprised to learn that you have to ask the Macintosh for your disk before you can take it out of the drive. This exercise in politeness prevents you from accidentally damaging your disk by removing it at an inappropriate time. The command for ejecting a disk may be in one of two menus, depending on which System you're using; look in both places if you aren't sure.

☐ **Click on the system disk icon and select Eject from the File menu or the Special menu (unless you're working from a hard disk).**

The disk should pop out like a piece of toast. (This won't work if you're using a hard disk.) The disk icon is still on the screen, but it's now shaded gray—gone but not forgotten.

☐ **If you have two drives, re-insert the disk.**

The computer will sometimes need to refer to this disk, so if you're using a one-drive system, you will be asked to swap this disk in occasionally.

Stacks, Macs, and Backups

This section will lead you through the process of organizing the stacks you'll need on a single working disk and backing up that disk. If you use this disk as your working disk throughout this and future sessions, you'll avoid the possibility of damaging shared public files. (If you're using a *personal* hard disk system with no shared files, you can use the floppy disk as a backup and put a working copy of your files on your hard disk.)

In the process of creating working and backup disks, you'll learn the basic Macintosh disk and file procedures so you can continue to keep your HyperCard stacks in well-organized folders on personal working and backup disks. You'll need two blank disks in addition to your system disk or hard disk to complete this section.

Initializing a Disk

Let's initialize one of your blank disks. Why? A new disk contains no information at all—just a magnetic surface waiting to be used. But your disk drive won't let you store any files on it until you **initialize** (or **format**) the disk. If you think of the disk as a freshly paved circular parking lot for files, initializing the disk is like painting stripes and stall numbers on the pavement so the attendant can easily park and unpark the files.

☐ **Locate one of your blank disks and make sure it's unlocked.**

Check the little square hole to the right of the label. If you can see through the hole, the disk is **locked** (**write-protected**) so the computer can't add to, change, or erase any of the information stored on it. You'll need to slide the plastic cover over the hole if it's not already there.

☐ **Insert the blank disk in the available disk drive.**

☐ **If you are recycling a disk that's been used before in a Macintosh, an icon representing that disk will appear on the desktop. If that's the case, click on the icon to select it and choose Erase Disk from the Special menu.**

The Erase Disk command tells the computer to reinitialize the disk. (Are you sure there's nothing of value on this disk? There's no turning back!)

You'll see a **dialog box** that looks something like this:

Dialog boxes are, as the name implies, used to establish two-way communication between you and the computer. Sometimes you respond to a dialog box by typing something, but more often you respond simply by clicking on-screen **buttons.**

If you're given a choice, you'll want to select two-sided so that you can store twice as much information (800K versus 400K) on the disk. (One **K** is approximately 1000 characters worth of storage space.) There's one disadvantage to two-sided (or double-sided) disks: They can't be used in a pre-1987 one-sided (or single-sided) Macintosh drive. If your lab has a mix of one- and two-sided drives, be careful: *It's easy to wipe out everything on a double-sided disk by putting it in a single-sided drive.*

If you're using a high density disk, the dialog box won't give you a choice of sizes; it just has buttons labeled Eject and Initialize. There's only one way to initialize a high density disk, and the end result is a disk with a capacity of 1440K.

☐ **Click on Two-Sided or Initialize.**

☐ **When you see a box asking you to name the disk, type a new name.**

We'll use the name *Working Disk* in this example. But if you're working in a public lab, you should use your name and other ID information (for example, *Benjamin CS101 disk 1*) so you and your disk can be reunited if you are accidentally separated.

You can always rename a disk icon (or any other icon on the Macintosh desktop) by clicking on the icon or its name and typing a new name.

Copying Files

☐ **Double-click on the new Working Disk icon.**

You should see an empty window, ready to fill with the stacks you'll be using in the next session. (If you're using your own personal hard disk, you'll probably want to use the files on the hard disk rather than the ones you put on this floppy disk. If that's the case, think of this as your backup disk.)

Home

☐ **Locate the Home stack on your hard disk, file server, or Hyper-Card disk.**

You may have to open one or more folders to find it, depending on how your system is organized.

☐ **If necessary, resize or move windows until you can see the Home icon and the Working Disk window.**

☐ **Drag the Home icon into the Working Disk window.**

You have just told the Macintosh to make a **copy** of Home on your disk.

Dragging an icon from one disk window to another copies that file onto the new disk *without disturbing the original*. If the icon is a folder, the folder and all of its contents are copied to the new disk. There are three situations in which this kind of copying won't work:

1. The destination disk is locked or write-protected. (Solution: Unlock it.)

2. There's not enough space on the destination disk. (Solution: Delete or move some files from the disk, or use another disk.)

3. A file already exists in the destination window with the same name as one you're copying. A dialog box will ask you if you want to "Replace items with the same names with the selected items?" (Solution: Change the name of one of the files before making the transfer, or else say goodbye to one. To change a file name, just click on the icon and type a new name.)

When the copying process is completed, you should see two Home stacks: the original and the new one on the working disk. You can make changes to the new one whenever you like without changing the original.

If you want to copy several files from one window to another without copying all of them, you can do some selective selecting. In the same folder you should find stacks called Addresses and Appointments; you can copy both onto the working disk at once.

☐ **Click on the icon called Addresses.**

You can **Shift-click** on another icon to select it without letting go of the currently selected icon.

☐ **Hold down the Shift key and click on the Appointments icon.**

Appointments is highlighted, and so is Addresses. Now you can move both of them at once.

☐ **Drag either one of the selected (highlighted) icons to the window of Working Disk.**

Since they're both selected, the other will follow.

Here's a selection summary:

Four Ways to Select Multiple Icons in an Active Window

- Choose **Select All** from the Edit menu (or press Command-A).

- Drag a selection rectangle around them.

- Shift-click on them in succession.

- Select a larger group and Shift-click on selected icons to deselect them.

Note: These Finder techniques for selecting multiple icons do *not* work in HyperCard because HyperCard icons represent buttons.

Organizing with Folders

Time to get organized.

☐ **Click on the Working Disk window or icon to make it active.**

☐ **Select New Folder from the File menu (or press Command-N).**

A new folder should appear in the disk window.

☐ **Type "Session 2 Stacks" to rename that folder.**

If the name doesn't change, click on the icon or the name under it and try again.

☐ **Drag the Addresses and Appointments stacks on your Working Disk into the Session 2 Stacks folder icon.**

The icons disappear, but they aren't really gone.

☐ **Double-click on the Session 2 Stacks folder icon.**

The window opens, revealing the icons that had disappeared.

When you drag an icon into the window or icon of a folder on the *same* disk, the original is **moved**—not copied—into that folder.

You can create folders and move your personal stacks into them to help prevent desktop clutter. If you use meaningful names and an intuitive organizational scheme, you'll have no trouble locating those stacks when you need them.

Backing Up a Disk

Before we get started with HyperCard, let's make a backup copy of the working disk, if for no other reason than to learn how.

☐ **Select Eject from the File menu (Command-E) and insert your second blank disk into the vacated drive.**

☐ **Initialize that disk and give it a different name.**

☐ **Drag the icon for your working disk onto the icon for this newly initialized disk.**

A dialog box will ask you if you want to completely replace the contents of your new disk with the contents of the original.

☐ **Click OK in the dialog box or press the Return key.**

A button in a dialog box surrounded by a thick dark line represents the **default option**; pressing Return on the keyboard has the same effect as clicking that button.

All of the files on your working disk will now be copied onto the backup disk, making an exact **copy** of your working disk.

> When one disk icon is dragged on top of a second icon of the same type, the contents of the second disk are replaced with the contents of the first. The first remains unchanged.

Using the Trash

☐ **Click on your working disk's window to activate it.**

☐ **Select New Folder from the File menu.**

Another new folder appears in the active window.

☐ **Drag the Empty Folder into the Trash icon.**

When your pointer reaches the trash can, the can will turn black, indicating that the selected item is now inside it. (Open the can to check if you like. If you're having second thoughts, you can drag the folder out of the Trash window and back onto the original disk window.) The folder is still on the disk, even though the icon has disappeared from the disk window. This feature can come in very handy—even the best of us occasionally have to dig through our own garbage. You can dispose of it when you're really sure.

☐ **Move the pointer up to the Special menu and drag it down to Empty Trash.**

There's another use for the Trash.

☐ **Drag the icon of your backup disk into the trash.**

You aren't trashing the disk; you're simply telling the computer that you don't want to use that disk right now. The disk pops out and its image disappears from the desktop.

Customizing Your Work Space

The disk that remains is your working disk. If you followed instructions correctly, it should contain Home and a folder called Session 2 Stacks; the folder should contain Addresses and Appointments stacks.

☐ **The last step depends on what kind of system you have. Choose one of the following:**

- If you're using your own personal hard disk system, all you need to do is make sure your hard disk contains Home, HyperCard, and the Session 2 Stacks folder.

- If you're using a HyperCard-equipped hard disk in a public lab, you're ready to go. (You'll keep your working disk in the disk drive).

- If you're using a HyperCard-equipped file server from a machine with two disk drives, you're ready to go. (You'll keep your system disk in one drive and your working disk in the other.)

- If you're using a HyperCard-equipped file server from a machine with one disk drive, you can avoid unnecessary disk swapping by copying Home and the Session 2 Stacks folder onto your system disk.

- If you're using a machine with two HD disk drives and no hard disk or file server, you'll need to copy HyperCard onto your working disk to avoid disk swapping.

- If you're using a machine with two 800K disk drives and no hard disk or file server, you probably won't have room on your working disk for HyperCard unless you copy the Session 2 stacks folder to your system disk and delete it from the working disk. Later in this session and the next, you'll need to remember to look for this folder on the system disk rather than the working disk.

Break Point

This is a good time to take a break if you need one. Simply select **Shut Down** from the Special menu and retrieve your disk. When you return, turn on the computer, insert your disk, and continue from here.

Hello, HyperCard

Ready to go? Let's start up **HyperCard**.

Launching HyperCard

☐ If HyperCard is not on a hard disk or file server, insert the working disk (or any disk containing HyperCard and the Home stack).

Home

☐ **Open the window for the disk or folder that contains Home by double-clicking (clicking twice in rapid succession) on the icon.**

☐ **Open your working disk window and locate the Home icon.**

Make sure you're looking at your own copy of the Home stack, not the original on a public disk or file server.

☐ **Double-click on the icon to open Home. (You could also select the Home icon and select Open from the File menu.)**

Opening a stack icon on the desktop tells the Macintosh to do three things:

■ Launch HyperCard.

■ Locate the Home stack (even if that's not the stack that was double-clicked).

■ Locate and open the stack that was double-clicked.

When you launch HyperCard, you're transported to the **Home** card—your HyperCard base of operations. Your Home card will probably look something like one of the following:

Home

Welcome to HyperCard

HyperCard is a unique software tool that allows you to do more with your computer.

With HyperCard, you can use "smart" documents called **stacks**. Stacks can help you do many different things—for example, you could use a stack to keep track of your appointments, manage your expenses, learn a new language, or play music from an audio compact disc. A few stacks are included here to get you started. The HyperCard Basics booklet explains how to use them. You can obtain additional stacks from Apple dealers and user groups.

©1990 Apple Computer, Inc.

More

Home

Appointments

Addresses

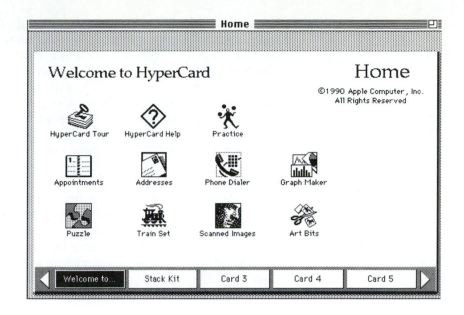

The card will fill the entire screen or just occupy a window on the screen, depending on the size of your screen.

Opening via the File Menu

HyperCard has pull-down menus just like the ones on the Finder's desktop. Let's take a minute to try one of the commands to see how it differs from its desktop cousin.

☐ Select **Open Stack...** from the File menu.

Hello, HyperCard   **21**

You'll see a dialog box with a list of HyperCard files and folders that are visible on the current disk—your working disk. (It won't show files that can't be opened by HyperCard, but other than that, it shows the same files and folders you'd see on the desktop.) The **Drive** and **Eject buttons** allow you to switch views to another disk drive and eject the currently selected disk, respectively. Using a combination of these two buttons, you can access any disk that's readable by your machine. (If you're using System 7, the Drive button is replaced with a **Desktop button** that allows you to perform the same operations in a slightly different way.)

☐ **Click the Drive button (if it's not dimmed) and watch the disk name in the dialog box change. Repeat until you're back to your working disk. (In System 7: If you have no Drive button, click on the Desktop button. You'll see all of the available disks in a list in the dialog box. Double-click on the name of your working disk.)**

Locating a File in a Folder

☐ **Open the Session 2 folder in the dialog box by double-clicking on it.**

That folder's icon replaces the disk in the dialog box, and the files stored in that folder are listed.

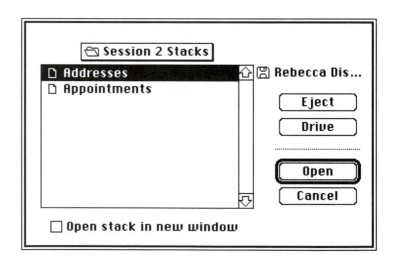

You really don't want to open anything in this folder; you're here to learn how to navigate your way out of a folder in a dialog box. So for the sake of learning, assume you want to open a file that's not in this folder.

☐ **Point to the Session 2 folder icon on the left side of the dialog box and press the mouse button.**

The folder turns into a **pop-up menu**, with each menu item representing one level of the folder hierarchy. In this case, there are no folders nested within folders, so the menu only has two items: the Session 2 folder and your working disk.

☐ **Drag down this menu to your working disk and release the button.**

You're looking once again at one folder and the home stack on the working disk.

☐ **Click on the Cancel button in the dialog box to retract the Open command and return Home.**

| Cancel |

> The **Cancel button** in a dialog box works like an emergency exit. When you click the Cancel button, you're essentially saying, "Never mind."

These are the kinds of dialog boxes you'll see repeatedly when you're working with the **Macintosh's Hierarchical File System (HFS).**

> ### Where is____?
>
> When you're working through this and future sessions, you may see a dialog box that asks you "Where is XYZ?" where XYZ is the name of a particular HyperCard stack. Except for that question, this dialog box looks and works like the Open Stack... dialog box. Respond by locating the missing file, remembering the HFS dialog box navigation rules.

Here is a summary of those rules:

HFS Dialog Box Navigation Rules

- Clicking the Drive button (System 6) switches to the next drive (or file server). Repeatedly clicking Drive cycles through all available drives.

- Clicking the Desktop button (System 7) takes you to the Desktop (highest) level of the hierarchy, allowing you to select from all available drives.

- Clicking the Eject button ejects the disk currently displayed in the box. (This button is dimmed if the current drive is a file server or hard disk, or if there is no disk in the other drive.) It's useful if you need to insert another disk.

- Double-clicking a folder opens that folder and takes you into that folder.

- Dragging down from the current folder icon reveals a pop-up menu that takes you out of that folder.

As you can see, it's not difficult to move in and out of folders when you're looking for a document. But folder hopping gets old in a hurry if documents aren't stored according to some kind of sensible organization scheme. Keep that in mind when you're creating and organizing stacks in later sessions.

It's comforting to know that HyperCard menus work like all Macintosh menus; that kind of consistency makes it easy for Macintosh veterans to quickly master new software packages. But buttons, rather than menus, are HyperCard's primary navigation tools.

Taking a Tour

The Claris version of HyperCard comes with a useful **HyperCard Tour** stack; Apple's bundled HyperCard contains no such stack. If your Home card has no HyperCard Tour icon, you won't be able to follow the instructions in this section. Nonetheless, it's important that you read this material since it introduces concepts that apply to all HyperCard stacks.

The Home card is populated with icons. Each of these icons is a HyperCard **button** waiting to perform some operation when you click it with the mouse.

> HyperCard buttons, like all Macintosh buttons, respond when clicked *once* with the mouse. This is always true—even when the buttons look like icons.

☐ **Click once on the icon/button labeled HyperCard Tour.**

This click transports you to another HyperCard stack that will introduce you quickly to the basics of HyperCard. (If you see a dialog box that says "Where is HyperCard Tour?" locate the HyperCard Tour stack using the folder icons and the Drive button. If you can't find the stack, click Cancel and simply read along for the remainder of this section.)

Notice that the menu bar has disappeared; many HyperCard stacks hide the menu bar. Buttons are also often hidden in HyperCard. A **hidden button** fills this entire card; clicking that button transports you to the next card.

☐ **Click anywhere on the card to proceed to the next card in the stack.**

This screen appears:

> **W**hat is HyperCard®? You could call it an "information organizer"—but it's a lot more than a set of file folders. HyperCard lets you put words, pictures, and sounds together in an infinite variety of ways. You can use it for something as ordinary as an address book; but you can also use it to teach your children, catalog your inventory, or control a mainframe computer—the possibilities are endless.
>
> In this tour, you'll find out how HyperCard works and get some ideas about how you might use it yourself.
>
> Click to continue.

☐ **Click anywhere on the screen to continue.**

A hidden button takes you to the next card.

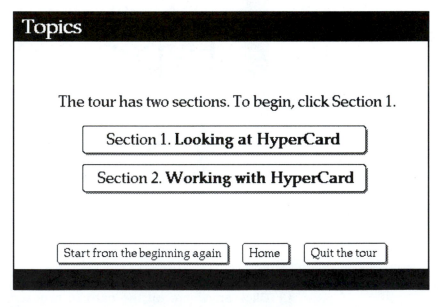

This screen contains several visible buttons for navigating.

☐ **Click on the first button: Section 1. Looking at HyperCard.**

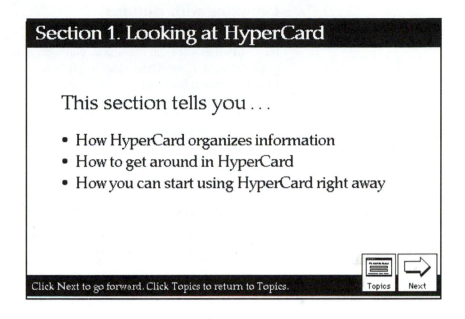

This card also contains several buttons, including one with a standard meaning in most HyperCard stacks.

☐ **Click on the right-arrow button to go to the next card in the stack.**

The next card has two arrow buttons: one for moving forward through the stack, and another for going back to the previous card.

☐ **Click on the left-arrow button to go back one card.**

☐ **Proceed through the tour by repeatedly clicking on the right-arrow button on each card.**

During this tour you'll see that buttons can take a variety of shapes and perform a variety of operations. The last card contains another "standard" HyperCard button: the **Home button**.

☐ **Click on the Home button to return to the Home stack.**

Browsing with Buttons

If your Home card has arrow buttons, you can use those buttons to move to other cards in the stack. Navigation buttons are all you need to explore most HyperCard stacks. Here's a summary of the most common navigation buttons:

Common HyperCard Navigation Buttons

Go to the Home card.

Go to the next card in the stack. If you're at the end of the stack, go to the first card.

Go to the previous card in the stack. If you're currently at the beginning of the stack, go to the end.

Go to the first card in the stack.

Go to the last card in the stack.

Return to a previously visited card. The **return-arrow button** always takes you back, but how far back depends on the stack. It might take you back to the stack from which you came; it might take you back to a title page; it might take you back to a higher level card containing a menu.

Tell me more. The **asterisk** is generally used in the same way it's used in books—to let the reader know that there's more to say on a subject.

Tell me about it. The **cartoon balloon** and the **light bulb** usually indicate sources of background information about the current stack or card.

Give me an overview of the stack. This button provides the big picture.

Help me. The **? button** usually provides **on-line help** for users who are having trouble navigating or using the stack.

Find a key word in the stack. Next session you'll see how to use the Find command; this icon is sometimes used as a shortcut to that command or a variation.

Navigating with the Go Menu

There are other ways to get around in HyperCard. The **Go menu** contains several commands for quickly moving within and between stacks.

```
Go
Back        ⌘~
Home        ⌘H
Help        ⌘?
Recent      ⌘R
First       ⌘1
Prev        ⌘2
Next        ⌘3
Last        ⌘4
Find...     ⌘F
Message     ⌘M
Scroll      ⌘E
Next Window ⌘L
```

☐ **Select the Next command from the Go menu.**

This command has the same effect as clicking on a right-arrow button, but it works even if the current card has no right-arrow button.

☐ **Select the Prev command from the Go menu.**

This is the command equivalent of the left-arrow button.

☐ **Select the Last command from the Go menu.**

This command takes you to the last card in the stack. We'll return to this card soon.

☐ **Select the First command from the Go menu.**

This command takes you back to card 1 from any point in the stack.

Navigating by Keyboard

Look at the Go menu, and notice the symbols to the right of each command. Those symbols represent **keyboard shortcuts** for those commands. The key with the cloverleaf symbol (⌘) is called the **Command key** because it allows the other keys to represent commands rather than characters. For example, Command-H is the keyboard shortcut for **Go Home**; pressing this keyboard combination will transport you to the Home stack from almost anywhere in HyperCard.

Let's browse through the Home stack using keyboard shortcuts.

☐ **Press Command-3 (Next) repeatedly to flip sequentially through all of the cards in the Home stack.**

When you reach the last card in the stack, Next takes you back around to the first card.

☐ **Press Command-2 (Prev) repeatedly until you return to the Home card.**

This has just the opposite effect; it goes backward through the stack, one card at a time, wrapping around to the back when it reaches the first card.

☐ **Press Command-4 (Last).**

This takes you to the last card in the stack.

☐ **Press Command-1 (First).**

An especially useful navigation key is the **Tilde** (~). (If you have an **Esc key,** it's functionally equivalent.) This key, with or without the Command key, takes you back one step in your HyperCard journey each time you press it.

☐ **Press the Tilde (~) or Esc key to go back one card. Press it several times, observing where it takes you.**

Pressing the **Go Back** key (~ or Esc) retraces your steps through the cards, reversing the order in which you viewed them. This is *not* the same as going backward through the stack.

Note: When you're working with HyperCard's paint tools, this key becomes an "undo" key when used by itself. When used with the command key, it *always* means go back.

If you have to retrace more than a few steps, there's an easier way.

☐ **Select Recent from the Go menu (or press Command-R).**

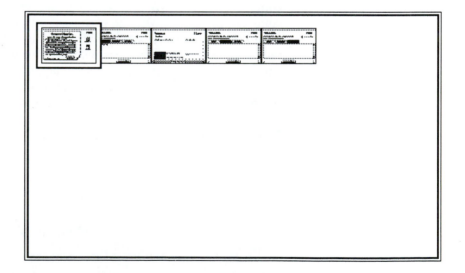

You're looking at tiny pictures of HyperCard screens that you've seen. It's as if you took one snapshot each time you visited a card for the first time. Those snapshots are arranged here in the order you took them. The number of screens you see depends on how many cards you've visited this session.

> Recent (Command-R) displays the last 42 cards of the session in the order they were visited, not necessarily in the order they appear in the stack(s).

☐ **Click on any of the small cards to go to that card; from that card, go Home.**

You can also use the **arrow keys** on your keyboard (if you have them) to navigate. The left- and right-arrow keys work the same as left- and right-arrow buttons on the screen; the down-arrow is another Go Back key (like ~), and the up-arrow retraces your steps forward through cards you've gone back through with the down-arrow.

☐ **Try navigating through this stack using the arrow keys. End your explorations on the Home card.**

Using the Navigator Palette

If you don't think you'll be able to memorize all of these commands and keyboard shortcuts, here's a way you can have instant access to almost all of the navigation tools you've seen so far. The catch is that you have to actually *type* a command to make it happen. Here's how.

☐ **Select Message from the Go menu (or press Command-M) to open the message box.**

The long window at the bottom of the screen, called the message box, allows you to send messages to HyperCard.

☐ **Type "nav".**

nav

When you press Return, you should see this tiny window floating above the stack. (If you don't, your Home stack has probably been modified so that it no longer recognizes the shorthand command. Try typing "palette navigator" followed by Return.)

The Navigator Palette

The **navigator palette** appears when you type "nav" or "palette navigator" in the message box. It provides one-touch access to HyperCard's most important controls in the same way a VCR's remote control device provides VCR controls. Here's a summary of the palette control buttons and their menu-bar command equivalents:

Button	Function	Go Menu Command
🏠	Go to the Home stack	Home
◇?	Go to the Help stack (if available)	Help
⊲⊲	Go to the first card in the stack	First
⊳⊳	Go to the last card in the stack	Last
⊲	Go to the card before the current card	Prev
⊳	Go to the card after the current card	Next
↩	Go back to the last card visited, wherever it is.	Back
▦	Show 42 most recently visited cards	Recent
▤	Go to the next HyperCard window if others are open	Next Window
▭	Show/Hide the message box	Message
🔍	Show/Hide the message box with the Find command (see Session 2)	Find…

Note: The navigator palette is an external window—that is, it's not one of the standard windows built into HyperCard; it's an add-on accessory that's provided with the software. The distinction, important to programmers, is generally of little consequence from the user's point of view.

☐ **Try navigating through the Home stack with the navigator palette controls.**

Using the Scroll Window

If you're working on a standard nine-inch Mac screen, you may not be aware that the Home stack is actually a window on your screen. The title bar is hidden behind your menu bar and the window has no scroll bars or size box. Nonetheless, it's a window that can be resized and moved so you can view other windows. Changing a HyperCard window's size is different than resizing a standard Macintosh window; it requires a special **scroll window**.

☐ **Select Scroll from the Go menu (or press Command-E) to open the scroll window.**

This window represents the shape of the currently visible stack.

☐ **Move the pointer to the bottom edge of the white box in the scroll window.**

It turns into a double-headed arrow, indicating that it can be moved up or down. Since you're at the bottom of the box, the only way to go is up.

☐ **Drag up to about the center of the scroll window.**

You'll see a horizontal line rising in the box like the bottom of a window shade. At the same time, a horizontal line rises in the Home stack window. When you release the mouse button, the part of the Home card below the line vanishes. The bottom half of the card is still there; you just have to scroll to see it.

☐ **Move the pointer over the top half of the white box (the part above the line).**

It turns into a hand, waiting to push the picture around.

☐ **Drag the hand pointer down, then up, watching the Home card as you do.**

You're controlling which part of the Home card is visible. You can reduce the horizontal size of the window by dragging the left or right edge of the box. By dragging a corner you can change both dimensions of the window at once.

☐ **Reduce the vertical and horizontal size of the Home window and try scrolling in all directions.**

> The scroll window makes it possible to work with a stack whose cards are bigger than your screen. It also makes it easy to view partial contents of several stacks at one time, memory permitting. Changing the size of a stack's window with the scroll window does not change the size of the cards in the stack. It's possible to resize the cards using the Stack Info dialog box, discussed later, but all cards in a given stack must be the same size.

☐ **Return the Home window to full size.**

You may do this by double-clicking in the scroll window, or you may use the zoom box on the right side of the Home window's title bar. If you can't see the title bar, that's because it's hidden behind the menu bar. Here's how to look behind the menu bar.

Hiding and Showing the Menu Bar

☐ **Press the Command key and the Space bar at the same time.**

Notice how the menu bar disappeared.

☐ **Press Command-Space again.**

The menu bar is back. When you're learning HyperCard, it's best to keep that bar visible. But because many stacks hide the menu bar without your permission, it's important to know how to get it back when you need it.

Finding Hidden Buttons

As you've seen, not every button has an icon. How can you know where buttons are hiding on a card? There's one almost sure-fire technique for exposing hidden buttons.

☐ **Hold down the Command and Option keys at the same time (Command-Option).**

Every button on the card is outlined as long as you hold those two keys down. (Exception: Buttons that have been specially programmed to remain hidden aren't revealed.) This is an important trick to remember when you're working with stacks that don't use icons for buttons.

Asking for Help

If you're wondering how you're going to remember all of this information, you'll be interested in learning about HyperCard's on-line help facility. By pressing **Command-?** or selecting **Help** from the Go menu, you can transport yourself to HyperCard's detailed **Help stack**—provided you have it. (Apple's bundled HyperCard has no Help stack; so if you're using that version you'll have to depend on this book for help.)

Main Topics for HyperCard Help

1. Click an item to get a list of topics:

HyperCard basics
Browsing and finding information
Typing and editing text
Printing

Working with stacks
Working with backgrounds
Working with cards
Working with buttons
Working with text fields
Working with graphics

HyperCard Help

🔍 Find Topic   ☀ Overview of Help

Besides providing its own menu and the interactive table of contents shown above, the three-stack HyperCard Help set includes options for navigating in a variety of ways, as outlined on this card. The Help stack is an excellent example of the kind of nonlinear reference document sometimes called hypertext or hypermedia. If you have access to it, take some time to explore it.

Overview of Help

| **Where am I?** |
| **What can I do?** |
| **Where can I go?** |

Besides using the Main Topics card to locate topics, you can:

• Click the **Find Topic** button at the bottom of every card to look for topics matching words that you enter.

• Click the **Tips** and **Troubleshooting** buttons at the bottom of a topic card to see tips or potential problems related to the topic. Click **Related Topics** to jump to other topics in this stack related to the one you're on.

• Click active text (text with a thick gray underline) to see a pop-up definition.

🔍 Find Topic   ↵ Go Back

When you're using the Help stack, or any other stack, remember that Command-H will take you back Home.

Ending a HyperCard Session

☐ **Press Command-Q (or Select Quit HyperCard from the File menu) to return to the desktop.**

There are many other keyboard commands in HyperCard. Here's a summary of the HyperCard keyboard commands you've seen so far, plus a couple of new ones in boldface type:

Keyboard Commands (and Their Menu Equivalents) for Browsers

Go to the last card visited.	(Command)- ~ or down-arrow	Go: Back
Go forward through retraced cards.	up-arrow	
Go to the previous card in the stack.	Command-2 or left-arrow	Go: Prev
Go to the next card in this stack.	Command-3 or right-arrow	Go: Next
Go to the first card in the stack.	Command-1 or up-arrow	Go: First
Go to the last card in this stack.	Command-4 or down-arrow	Go: Last
Go to the next open HyperCard window.	**Command-L**	Go: **Next Window**
Go to the Help stack (if available).	Command-?	Go: Help
Go to the Home stack.	Command-H	Go: Home
Open the scroll window	Command-E	Go: Scroll
Show most recent 42 cards visited.	Command-R	Go: Recent
Open a new stack.	Command-O	File: Open Stack...
Open a new stack in a new window.	**Command-Shift-O**	
Show (peek at) outlines of most buttons.	Command-Option	
Show or hide the menu bar.	Command-Space	
Cancel current action.	**Command-Period**	
Quit HyperCard, return to Finder.	Command-Q	Quit HyperCard

As you can see, there are many ways to accomplish the same task in HyperCard. It's not necessary to memorize all the different commands, shortcuts, and tricks to make the most of HyperCard as a tool. Use the ones that work best for you, adding new tricks to your repertoire as you need them.

Shutting Down

If you just turn off your machine when you're through, you won't be able to take your disk with you. What's worse, you won't give the machine a chance to take care of last minute disk-keeping details.

☐ **If someone is waiting to use your machine, select Restart from the Special menu and leave it on. Otherwise, select Shut Down and turn it off.**

Summary

After just one session, you're on your way to HyperCard literacy. If you're new to the Macintosh, you learned how to start your computer, move things around on the desktop, issue commands, work with windows, and end a Macintosh session. You created a personal working disk for your stacks, learning basic Macintosh disk and file operations in the process. You learned how to launch HyperCard and navigate through stacks using on-screen buttons, menu commands, and keyboard shortcuts.

Session 2 will show you how HyperCard stacks can be used to keep track of text and numerical information. You'll learn how to store, organize, and retrieve that information efficiently using a pair of linked personal information management stacks. Then the real fun begins: In Session 3, you'll learn how to build your own HyperCard stacks.

Key Words

? button

active (window or object)

arrow keys

asterisk

backup copy

booting

button (dialog box and HyperCard)

Cancel button (dialog box)

cartoon balloon

clicking

close box (window)

Close command

Command key

Command-? (help)

Command-Option (show buttons)

Command-Period (cancel current action)

Command-Space (show/hide menu bar)

copy (disk)

copy (file)

default option

desktop

Desktop button (System 7 dialog box)

dialog box

diskette

double-clicking

dragging

Drive button (System 6 dialog box)

Eject button (dialog box)

Eject command (Command-E, Finder)

Empty Trash command (Finder)

Esc key

File menu

file server

Finder

First command (Command-1, Go menu)

flexible disk
floppy disk (diskette)
format (a disk)
Go Back (~ or Command-~)
Go Home (Command-H)
Go menu
Guided Tour
hard disk (internal and external)
Help command (Command-?, Go menu)
Help stack
hidden button
Hierarchical File System (HFS)
high density (HD) disk
highlighting
Home
Home button
HyperCard
HyperCard Tour
icon
initialize (a disk)
K
keyboard shortcuts
Last command (Command-4, Go menu)
left-arrow button
light bulb
locked or write-protected (disk)
menu bar
message box
Message command (Command-M, Go menu)
moving a file
navigator palette
network
New Folder command (Command-N, Finder)
Next command (Command-3, Go menu)
Next Window command (Command-L, Go menu)

on-line help
Open command (Command-O, Finder)
Open Stack command (Command-O)
operating system
pointer
pop-up menu
Prev command (Command-2, Go menu)
pull-down menu
Quit HyperCard command (Command-Q)
Recent command (Command-R, Go menu)
Restart command (Finder)
return-arrow button
right-arrow button
scroll bar
scroll box
Scroll command (Command-E, Go menu)
scroll window
Select All command (Command-A, Finder)
select
Shift-clicking
Shut Down command (Finder)
size box (window)
Special menu (Finder)
startup disk
system disk
system files
System Folder
Tilde
title bar (window)
Trash
View menu (Finder)
window
working copy
zoom box (window)

Self-Testing Exercises

1. What is the difference between the Back command and the Prev command? Under what circumstances will they produce different results?

2. What is the difference between the Next command and the right-arrow button? Under what circumstances will they produce different results?

3. List several different things that can happen when you click a button in HyperCard.

4. What happens when you double-click a button in HyperCard?

5. List three ways to go to the next card in a stack.

6. What is the usual meaning for each of these icons in HyperCard?

a.　　　　　　　　　　　　　e.

b.　　　　　　　　　　　　　f.

c.　　　　　　　　　　　　　g.

d.

7. What is the keyboard shortcut for each of the following commands?

   a. Quit HyperCard

   b. Go to the First card in the stack

   c. Go Home

   d. Go Back

8. Consider this picture:

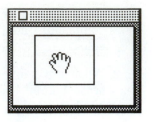

    a. Describe what's happening.

    b. What is this window called?

    c. How can you make it appear?

9. Consider this picture of the navigator palette:

    a. How can you make the navigator palette appear?

    b. Describe the functions of each of the buttons on the navigator palette.

10. You created a folder for Session 2 stacks. Where is the folder located? How is it useful to have the folder? In what ways is a Macintosh folder similar to and different from a paper folder in a file cabinet?

Projects

Note: These projects involve modifying standard HyperCard stacks that accompany Claris's version of HyperCard, but not Apple's bundled HyperCard.

1. Open the Puzzle stack. (If you're working in a public lab with shared files, open a copy of the file. In order to make sure you open *your*

copy, rather than the public copy, use the Open Stack... command.) Read the stack overview. Put the puzzle together. Take it apart. Go to the "Make your own" section, substitute a different picture in the puzzle, and play with that puzzle.

2. Open the Scanned Images stack. Examine the pictures, imagining how you might use them in your own stacks. Return Home.

SESSION 2

Objectives

By the end of this session you should be able to

- Use HyperCard to manage your personal information
- Enter text and numeric information into HyperCard fields
- Edit text in a field
- Use the Clipboard to copy and move text from one field to another
- Add a card to a stack
- Delete a card from a stack
- Sort cards into alphabetical order
- Use the Find command to locate a card with a specific piece of information
- Customize a stack by rearranging fields

THE DYNAMIC FILE CABINET:

INFORMATION STORAGE AND RETRIEVAL

The Problem

Your work space is a mess. You haven't paid your bills for two months because you can't find them on your desk. You need to call your brother, but you lost his new phone number. You have an appointment with the head of your department sometime next week, but you can't remember where you wrote down the time. You're within two days of the final deadline for an important project, and your notes are scattered everywhere. If only you could organize all these bits of information in your life. Perhaps HyperCard can help.

Introduction

In Session 1 you explored HyperCard as a window shopper, browsing but never touching or changing anything. Now it's time to learn how to personalize HyperCard stacks by adding new information, changing old information, and rearranging existing information. All versions of Hyper-Card 2 come with two practical stacks that work together to provide a personal information management system. We'll use those to put Hyper-Card through its paces as an information storage and retrieval system.

HyperCard as a Database

Many of the tasks we'll be asking HyperCard to do in this session would normally be done in the business world by a **database** program—a program designed for the organized storage and retrieval of information. In a typical database, a **data file** (like the library's card catalog) is made up of many identically structured **records** (the cards in that catalog), each of which is divided into **fields** of information (author's name, book title, and so on).

At first glance, HyperCard has a similar structure: Stacks are made up of cards, each of which can have fields. In fact, this similarity is no accident; HyperCard performs many common database functions with ease. But as you'll see, HyperCard's buttons allow it to be used in ways that you wouldn't think of using a conventional database.

Home Base

Starting at Home

When you open HyperCard by double-clicking on the HyperCard icon, the first thing it does is look for the Home stack. If it can't find Home in the immediate neighborhood, HyperCard will probably ask you in a dialog box, "Where is Home?" To avoid having to navigate this dialog box (and to make sure HyperCard uses your personal copy of Home) you can double-click on Home, rather than HyperCard, right from the start.

☐ **Double-click on the icon of *your* copy of Home in your disk window.**

You're looking at the Home card—the top card in the HyperCard Home stack. As you learned last session, there are several other cards hidden behind this one.

Changing the User Level and Name

It's time to reset the user level so we can do some typing.

☐ **Press Command-4 (or select Last from the Go menu) to go to the last card in the stack.**

In addition to having a space for your name, this card allows you to set the **user level**. (You may have two choices or five choices, depending on your version of HyperCard. If you have only two, you'll learn how to add three more later.)

☐ **Click on the Typing button.**

Typing user level allows you to type new information into HyperCard stacks and change existing information, while still maintaining your rights and privileges as a browser. It won't let you accidentally modify pictures or buttons. To test your new typing privileges, let's change the user name.

☐ **If there's no name entered in the "Your Name" blank, position the pointer over that blank and click. If there's already a name on the card, select it by dragging the mouse from the first character to the last character and press the Delete key.**

You should see a flashing vertical line at the beginning of the blank line.

☐ **Type your name.**

Your Name: Mark Twain

If you make any typing errors, use the Delete (Backspace) key to erase the offending characters.

☐ **Click on the button labeled "Return to First Card."**

Changing the Home Memory

If you'll be using the disk you created as a working disk, you need to take care of one more piece of business to make sure your Home stack doesn't outsmart you later.

> HyperCard uses the Home stack to keep track of where you store your other stacks. When you click on a button to open a stack, HyperCard looks for that stack in the folders where it has found other stacks in the past. If it can't find the stack in those places, HyperCard asks you to locate the stack. When you find the stack in a folder, HyperCard adds that folder to its list of stack storage places.

Here's the problem: The Home stack that you copied may remember where the *originals* of all your copied files are stored, so it will go to those originals, rather than your copies, when you click on their icons. You can prevent that by erasing that part of your Home stack's memory. Here's how.

☐ **Press Command-3 (or select Next from the Go menu) repeatedly until you reach a card that says "Search Paths... Stacks."**

Search paths   Home

HyperCard uses the information in the field   ☼ About Search Paths...
below to find your stacks.

| **Stacks** | **Applications** | **Documents** |

:HyperCard Stacks:

Return to First Card

☐ **Click on the light bulb icon.**

You'll see an explanation of search paths and their uses. Although it looks like a different card, this explanation is really a **pop-up field** that can be made visible—or invisible—at the click of a button.

☐ **When you've seen enough, click anywhere in the pop-up field to hide this explanation.**

Your card's list of search paths may not look like the one shown here, but it serves the same function. The next step is to delete the list.

☐ **Drag the mouse from the beginning of the first item in the search path list to the end of the last item in the list.**

All of the text you selected should be highlighted in black.

☐ **Press the Delete (Backspace) key.**

Everything that was highlighted in black should be gone, so HyperCard won't automatically look in those folders for stacks. You're about to teach it where to look for the files instead.

☐ **Press Command-1 (or select First from the Go menu) to go to the first card in the stack: the Home card.**

Locating a Stack

Each icon on the Home card is a button that will take you to a particular HyperCard stack when you click once on it. The Appointments and Addresses stacks turn HyperCard into a personal information management tool, combining the functions of a date book, an address book, a notepad, and a file cabinet.

Appointments

☐ **Click on the Appointments icon on the Home card.**

If you followed the instructions in the last section, you'll probably see a dialog box like this:

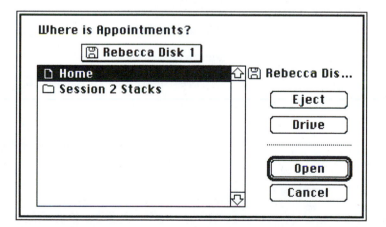

(If, instead of seeing this box, you're transported to the Appointments stack, then HyperCard managed to find the stack in spite of your efforts, probably because the HyperCard application and the Appointments stack are in the same folder. If you're working on a public machine, select Open Stack... from the File menu and use the Drive/Desktop button in the Open dialog box until your disk is showing. Then carry on.)

You put the Appointments stack, along with all the others, in the folder called Session 2 Stacks. So double-click on that folder icon in the dialog box, and you'll see this:

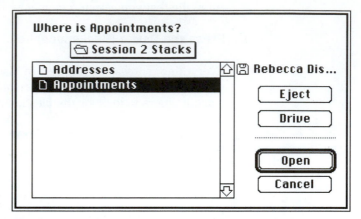

HyperCard needs you to show it the obvious. Double-click on Appointments. You won't need to repeat this every time you open a stack, because your Home stack will remember where it found this stack.

Browsing through the Appointments Stack

When HyperCard opens the Appointments stack, it checks to see whether there's a card for today's date. If there isn't, it asks you via a dialog box if you want to update the calendar.

☐ **Click the OK button in the dialog box.**

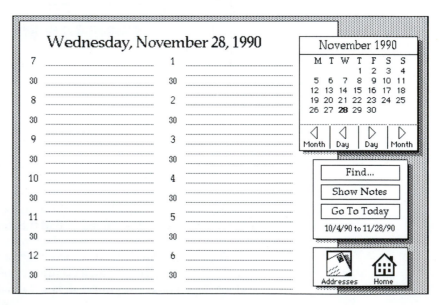

There are several navigation buttons on this card, including the familiar Home button. Of course, it's also possible to navigate with keyboard commands or the Go menu. But this stack has additional navigation commands hidden under the Utilities menu.

☐ **Select Stack Overview from the Utilities menu.**

> While most stacks use standard HyperCard menus (or no menus at all), some stacks change the menu bar by adding their own specialized menus.

You're transported to a card that provides instructions and help for using the stack. In spite of its different look, the Stack Overview card is still part of the Appointments stack.

> When you're working with HyperCard, the name and boundaries of the current stack aren't always apparent. Going to a card with a different background doesn't necessarily mean that you've gone to a new stack.

☐ **Click on the light bulb icon.**

The pop-up field explains how to **import** and **export** text between this stack and other Macintosh applications. It's a **scrolling field**, equipped with standard Macintosh scroll bars.

☐ **Try scrolling through the text.**

☐ **Click on the button that says "Return to Appointments."**

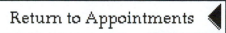

The calendar buttons have obvious functions.

☐ **Use the arrow buttons below the calendar to move backward and forward through the dates.**

Although they're not technically buttons, the calendar dates are also "hot."

☐ **Click on any date in the calendar.**

There's still another navigation button below the calendar.

☐ **Click on the button that says "Go To Today."**

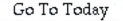

HyperCard's Text Fields

Entering Text into a Field

Entering information in this digital date book is straightforward; it involves the same kind of text-editing techniques that you use in Macintosh word processors, outliners, and databases.

☐ **Move the pointer over the lined daily appointment calendar.**

Notice how the pointer turns from a hand into an **I-beam** as you move it over a lined field.

☐ **Position the I-beam at the beginning of the first line of the appointment calendar and click once.**

As you move the I-beam away, you leave behind a flashing **insertion bar** (sometimes called a **cursor**, for CURrent poSition indicatOR). That's the spot where you'll type your first note.

☐ **Type "Wake up!"**

You can fill the page with appointments like this.

☐ **Move the I-beam to the 12:00 field, click to reposition the insertion bar, and type "Lunch".**

> Don't confuse the I-beam with the insertion bar. The I-beam is for
> positioning the insertion bar. But until you click, the insertion bar
> remains where you left it.

There's another, much larger, pop-up field for entering longer notes
into the Appointments stack.

☐ **Click on the Show Notes button.**

Show Notes

The flashing insertion bar marks the spot where you'll type your first
note, complete with a few errors to correct:

☐ **Type:**

Set aside some time today to do session 2 of
HyperCard inn Hurry!!!

Don't press the Return key when you reach the end of a line.

> Like most word processors, HyperCard fields automatically wrap
> text around to the next line when you reach the end. The only
> time you need to press Return is when you want to force some-
> thing to go to the next line before the current line is full.

Editing Text

> If you're familiar with Macintosh-style text **editing** (insert-
> ing, deleting, and changing), you may want to skip to "Using
> the Clipboard."

The three exclamation points are a bit much.

☐ **Use the Delete (Backspace) key to delete two exclamation points.**

You can backspace as far back as you like to correct errors, but it's usually faster and easier to reposition the insertion bar.

☐ **Place the I-beam immediately to the right of "inn" and click to reposition the insertion bar.**

☐ **Press Delete (Backspace) to turn "inn" into "in".**

When you **delete text**, everything to the right shifts left to fill the void. **Inserting text** is just as easy.

☐ **Type a space followed by "a".**

By first deleting text and then typing something new, you can **replace** any text in the field. But it's often easier to **select** the offending text first and then type the replacement.

☐ **Drag the pointer through the first "s" in "session".**

The *s* is highlighted, indicating that it is selected. Anything you type now will replace it.

☐ **Type "S".**

Selecting a whole word is easy; you don't need to drag exactly from the beginning to the end of the word.

☐ **Double-click on "do" to select it.**

☐ **Type "complete".**

You can combine the double-click and the drag to select multiple words.

☐ **Double-click on "some", holding the button down on the second click, and drag through "time". Then type "two hours".**

Using the Clipboard

You can do more than delete or change selected text; you can copy it or move it using the Macintosh **Clipboard**. The Clipboard is an invisible portion of the Macintosh memory that can be used to store text, pictures, buttons, fields, and other forms of information so that they can be easily moved, duplicated, or reused. Macintosh veterans should be familiar with the basic Clipboard commands:

Let's use the Clipboard to clone today's reminder.

☐ **Select the entire sentence by dragging straight from the beginning of the first word to the end of the last word. (You do *not* need to drag though every word.)**

☐ **Select Copy Text from the Edit menu.**

Your screen doesn't change, but a copy of the selected text is hiding in the Clipboard. To retrieve something from the Clipboard, use the Paste command.

☐ **Click on the right-arrow button labeled "Day" to move to the next day in the calendar. (You may be prompted that HyperCard is creating a new date card; click OK again.)**

☐ **Click in the note field to position the insertion bar and select Paste Text from the Edit menu.**

A copy of the reminder appears.

☐ **Change the 2 in this message to 3, so it reads "Session 3".**

Since the Clipboard still has the message, we can fill in the next day, too.

☐ **Move to the next day and press Command-V, the keyboard shortcut for Paste.**

Think of the *V* as an insertion caret to remember this shortcut.

☐ **Change the 2 in this message to 4, so it reads "Session 4".**

If you decide that you want to go to the beach the day after tomorrow, you can easily move your Session 4 commitment to another day.

☐ **Select the complete message.**

☐ **Press Delete (Backspace).**

Wait! If you clear the message that way, you'll have to retype it again on the other day. But we can get it back.

☐ **Select Undo from the Edit menu to bring back the deleted text.**

The **Undo** command (**Command-Z**) will *usually* restore your work as it was before you executed your last command or did your last round of typing. If you're human, you should probably memorize the keyboard shortcut, Command-Z, right away, so you have it at your fingertips.

But Undo can't solve all your problems; it can only take you back one step, so it won't help if you've done anything since your last error. And it's not always clear what "back one step" means. For example, HyperCard doesn't always recognize that you've completed a step when you're typing information in a field until you start working outside of that field.

☐ **Select the complete message again and press Command-X (Cut Text).**

☐ **Move to another date and press Command-V (Paste Text).**

If you've ever lost work when something went wrong in the middle of a computing session, you may be thinking that it's time to save what we've done so far. If you were working with a typical Macintosh application, your instincts would be right. But HyperCard is different.

HyperCard regularly saves changes to a stack *automatically*, but it doesn't automatically save backups. If you're about to do something that you think might cause irreparable damage, or if you want to make a backup of the current stack on another disk, you can use the **Save a Copy...** command.

Break Point

Basic Database Operations with HyperCard

If you have no interest in using HyperCard as a database, feel free to skim this section without performing all of the operations. Don't skip the section on adding and deleting cards, though, if you plan to do any of the later operations.

HyperCard can be used for keeping track of people, too.

Browsing through the Addresses Stack

Addresses

☐ **Click on the icon labeled Addresses.**

The Addresses stack opens in a new window.

> HyperCard 2 does not always close the window for one stack when you open another stack. If you are working on a machine with limited memory, it's a good idea to close windows of stacks you aren't using.

```
═══════════════════ Addresses ═══════════════════

     Name    A. Royce Walthrop
   Company   Acme Sprockets

     Street   1234 Main Street            ⇦  ⇨
City & State  Some Town, California        Find...
  Zip Code    95014                      Show Notes
                                          New Card
                                         Delete Card
  Telephone   ☎ (415) 555-1234 (work)
              ☎
              ☎                          Appointments  Home
              ☎
```

Utilities

Sort by Name
Sort by Company
Sort by City
Sort by State
Sort by Zip Code

Print Addresses
Import Text...
Export Text...

✓Addresses
Stack Overview
Sort Preferences
Mark Cards

☐ **Select Stack Overview from the Utilities menu.**

☐ **Read the Stack Overview card; return to the first address card by pressing Command-1.**

Each address card has nine editable fields: one each for name, company, street address, city and state, and zip code, and four for phone numbers.

☐ **Try changing one of the addresses in the stack. When you're done, click outside the field somewhere.**

Adding and Deleting Cards

For an address book to be useful, you must be able to add and remove pages. There's a New Card button on this card, but let's use the standard HyperCard command for doing the same thing.

☐ **Select New Card from the Edit menu (or press Command-N).**

> **New Card (Command-N)** creates a copy of the current card and locates it immediately after that card. If the current card contains text in fields, the text is *not* copied onto the new card.

The insertion point is automatically positioned at the beginning of the name field.

☐ **Position the insertion point at the beginning of the name field and type "Roger Rabbit".**

> In name-and-address stacks like this one, it's important that the names be entered in the same order (for example, Firstname Lastname) on every card if you want to be able to alphabetize them later.

☐ **Press Tab twice to skip past the company field. Type "123 Toon Terrace" in the street field, press Tab, type "Toontown, California", press Tab, and type 987/555-4321.**

> The **Tab key** generally advances the insertion bar automatically to the next editable field in the card. If the field contains text, the text is highlighted, so anything you type will replace it. Tabbing from the last field takes you to the first field. **Shift-Tab** moves you *backward* through the fields of a card.

You'll need to create several more cards before you can use this stack as a database.

☐ **Add cards to the address stack for each of the following names. For our purposes, it's only necessary to fill in the name and city/ state fields. Use the New Card button on the card, the New Card** command, or the keyboard shortcut for that command (Command-N) to create new cards. Remember to use the Tab key for moving between fields.

NAME	CITY/STATE
Donald Duck	Eugene, Oregon
Daisy Duck	Columbia, Missouri
Huey Duck	Tampa, Florida
Dewey Duck	Berkeley, California
Louie Duck	St. Paul, Minnesota
Scrooge McDuck	New York, New York
Benny Beaver	Corvallis, Oregon
Mickey Mouse	Bend, Oregon
Minnie Mouse	Ashland, Oregon
Porky Pig	Washington, D.C.
Daffy Duck	Boston, Massachusetts
Homer Simpson	Springfield, USA

The last one really doesn't belong, so let's delete it.

☐ **Press Command-Delete (Command-Backspace).**

This is the keyboard shortcut for the **Delete Card** command in the Edit menu. There's also a Delete Card button on this card.

Using the Clipboard with Cards

If a card is out of order in a stack, you don't have to delete it and recreate it in a new location. It's possible to cut, copy, and paste cards, using the Macintosh Clipboard. The commands Copy Card and Cut Card allow you to place a card in the Clipboard. (As usual, Cut removes the original whereas Copy leaves the original in place.) When there is a card in the Clipboard, the Paste command in the Edit menu becomes Paste Card. Selecting Paste Card places the contents of the Clipboard after the current card in the stack.

You can't try these commands at this point, though, because your user level is set to typing. HyperCard doesn't allow you to use the Clipboard for cards unless the user level is set to authoring or scripting.

Utilities

Sort by Name
Sort by Company
Sort by City
Sort by State
Sort by Zip Code

Print Addresses
Import Text...
Export Text...

✓Addresses
Stack Overview
Sort Preferences
Mark Cards

Sorting a Stack

Using Cut Card and Paste Card might be a good way to rearrange the cards in alphabetical order. It might be, but it isn't, because there's a much more convenient way: The **Sort commands** in the Utilities menu allow you to arrange the cards in order using any of five different fields as a key.

☐ **Select Sort Preferences from the Utilities menu.**

☐ **Click on the buttons labeled "First name first," "Sort by last name," and "Return to Addresses."**

These preferences apply to all future sorts until you change them.

☐ **Select Sort by Name from the Utilities menu.**

Almost instantly, the stack of names is rearranged in order by last name. Flip through them to check, if you like.

☐ **Select Sort by State.**

☐ **Flip through the cards to check the order.**

The cards should be grouped by state. Within each state, they should be in alphabetical order by name.

Sorting Hierarchy

For multiple-level sorts, perform the sorts in reverse order of importance: the last sort performed takes precedence over the others.

Now that the cards are in order, it should be easy to find any card in the stack by flipping through the cards. But there's a better way.

Using the Find Command

☐ **Click the Find button.**

A dialog box appears:

What text do you want to find?

[OK] [Cancel]

☐ **Type "Benny Beaver" and press Return.**

Faster than you could type it, HyperCard will find the first card in the stack with that name. If it finds a card for somebody else with the same name, just press Return again to restart the search.

This dialog box is not unique to the Addresses stack; you'll see it if you use the Find button in the Appointments stack too. But there's another tool for finding text that works in almost any HyperCard stack.

☐ **Select Find from the Go menu (or press Command-F).**

```
 ▫
 find "｜"
```

The message box appears with an incomplete message: the **Find command,** waiting for you to tell it what to find. Later you'll learn how to type other messages to HyperCard in this box, but for now all you need to do is fill in the space between the quotation marks.

☐ **Type "Minn" and press Return.**

You don't need to type a complete word into the Find command; you just need to type enough characters so that the term you're searching for can be identified uniquely. In this case "Minn" wasn't quite enough to uniquely identify *Minnie;* it's also part of *Minnesota*.

☐ **Press Return again**.

Find Tips

When you use the Find command (Command-F), each time you press Return you're taken to the next word in a searchable field that begins with the characters you have typed. If you type more than one word, you're taken to the next card that contains both those words in searchable fields. (Some text fields, cards, and backgrounds are defined in such a way that they can't be searched. Paint text, introduced in the next session, also can't be searched.)

Two cautionary notes:
- You get what you asked for, even if it's not what you wanted.
- Conversely, you don't get what you don't ask for, so make sure you ask for exactly what you want. (The one exception: Case is irrelevant, so you might find "BASIC" if you look for "basic".)

Examples: If you type "cath", you might find "Cathy" or "cathedral" or "cathode" but not "Kathy".

The moral: Choose your search patterns carefully!

Using the Phone Dialer

Once you locate the card you're looking for, what can you do with it?

☐ **Click on the phone icon.**

If your disk contains the Phone stack (not included with Apple's bundled HyperCard), you'll see a dialog box asking if you want to dial the number. Click OK to hear a series of beeps. If you happen to have your phone properly connected to the computer's sound jack, or if you hold the phone's handset close to the computer's speaker, those beeps will dial the selected number for you. The dialing is done by the Phone stack; you're temporarily transported there when you push the phone button, but you're automatically returned to where you started when the dialing is done. You can customize the dialer by going back to the phone dialer card.

Marking Cards

The more names you add to your database, the more useful it can be as a quick reference tool. You can add the names and addresses of frequently called businesses, community organizations, long-distance correspondents, government agencies, and so on. But a large, diverse database presents new challenges for organizing information so that it can be easily retrieved. HyperCard 2 allows you to **mark cards** in large databases so they can be quickly accessed or grouped for printing.

☐ **Click on the upper right corner of the white part of one of the address cards.**

There's a hidden button there that marks the card, at the same time changing its appearance so that it looks like the corner of the card is folded over.

☐ **Click once again on the folded-over corner.**

The card is no longer marked. For larger databases it's much more efficient to mark and unmark cards in groups.

☐ **Select Mark Cards from the Utilities menu.**

You'll see the dialog box shown at the top of the next page.

☐ **Click on the "Name contains:" check box.**

☐ **Type "duck".**

☐ **Click on the Mark The Cards button.**

```
┌─────────────────────────────────────────────────────────┐
│ Mark Cards                                  Addresses     │
├───────────────────────────────────────────────────────────┤
│ Mark cards on which:              ┌──────────────────┐   │
│  ☐ Name contains:                 │  Mark The Cards  │   │
│                            ·············┘──────────────────┘   │
│  ☐ Company contains:      ·····························  │
│  ☐ Street contains:       ·····························  │
│  ☐ City/State contains:   ·····························  │
│  ☐ Zip Code contains:     ·····························  │
│  ☐ Telephone contains:    ·····························  │
│  ☐ Notes contains:        ·····························  │
├───────────────────────────────────┬───────────────────────┤
│  ·Ö·   Using Marked Cards          │ Return to Addresses ◀ │
└───────────────────────────────────┴───────────────────────┘
```

You'll be asked whether you want to unmark all currently marked cards before proceeding.

☐ **Click Yes**.

Another dialog box asks if you want to go to the first marked card.

☐ **Click OK**.

☐ **Flip through the cards, watching the upper right corner of each card.**

Those cards that contain ducks have turned-down corners, indicating that they've been marked. (Notice that McDuck is marked, too. If we didn't want this one included, we should have typed a space before "duck" when we indicated the cards to be marked.)

☐ **Hold down the Shift key and click the right-arrow button. Try it several times.**

> The **Shift key** generally acts as a constraint key in HyperCard and other Macintosh applications. When used with a tool or command, it constrains that tool or command so it has a more specific meaning.

In this case, the Shift key is telling HyperCard *not* to go to the next card, but to the next *marked* card.

☐ **Hold down the Shift key and click the left-arrow button.**

As you've probably guessed, this takes you *backward* through the stack to the previous marked card.

Suppose you want to mark every card satisfying one of two criteria. To be marked, a card should have (1) "duck" in the name field *or* (2) "Oregon" in the city/state field.We already have all the duck names marked, so we just need to add the Oregon cards to the list.

☐ **Select Mark Cards.**

☐ **Click on the "City/State contains:" check box and type "Oregon".**

☐ **Click on the "Name contains:" check box to unselect it (remove the X).**

☐ **Click on the Mark The Cards button.**

☐ **When you're asked whether you want to unmark already marked cards, click No.**

Remember, we want to retain the marks on the duck cards.

☐ **Flip through the marked cards to see if they're marked correctly.**

Now suppose you decide that what you really want is to select only ducks from Oregon; that is, cards that contain (1) "duck" in the name field *and* (2) "Oregon" in the city/state field.

☐ **Select Mark Cards.**

☐ **Click on the check box for "Name contains" to put the X back in it.**

There should already be an X in the "City/State contains" check box. We're narrowing the selection criteria by adding a second check.

☐ **Click on Mark The Cards.**

☐ **When you're asked whether you want to unmark already marked cards, click Yes.**

☐ **Click OK to go to the first marked card.**

☐ **Check the results.**

You've just extracted three different subsets of cards from the set of cards known as the Addresses stack. In the process, you've put to work the basics of **boolean algebra**. Here's a summary of those basic principles:

Boolean Algebra and Marked Addresses

When you select multiple criteria for marking cards in the address stack, you're applying the principles of boolean algebra. Here are the specific selection rules:

- To select the **union** of two subsets (Group A *and* Group B; for example, name contains "Beaver" and ZIP contains "97331"), mark one set first, then mark the second set without unmarking the first.

- To select the **intersection** of two subsets (Group A *or* Group B; for example, state contains "New York" or state contains "Massachusetts"), mark both criteria in the same pass.

Note: Not all HyperCard stacks have automated card-marking capability. If you don't know HyperTalk, you may need to mark individual cards in other stacks by clicking Card Marked in the Card Info dialog box or by typing "Mark Card" in the message box.

The tools for selecting marked cards in the Addresses stack, while useful, are fairly primitive when compared with the selection tools in more powerful database programs. For instance, most database programs allow you to use relational operators for selecting cards. (Example: Select all records with income less than $10,000). If you need this kind of capability in a HyperCard stack, you'll need to build it yourself using HyperTalk.

Printing Card Images

HyperCard is handy for recording appointments and looking up addresses . . . as long as you're sitting in front of the computer. But if you use HyperCard to store names, phone numbers, appointments, and other essential information, you need to have a way of making a **hard copy** so you can take the information with you when your computer stays home.

The **Print Card** command (Command-P) prints an image of the current card—nothing more, nothing less. The **Print Stack...** command allows you to print images of every card in the stack (or, if you prefer, every *marked* card in the stack).

☐ **Select Print Stack... from the File menu.**

The dialog box that appears allows you to customize your printout in a number of ways.

In the interest of saving paper, we'll print just the marked cards.

☐ **Click on the Marked cards button.**

We'll also save paper by reducing the size of the printed images so that more can be printed on each page.

☐ **Hold the mouse button down while pointing to the Printed card size (probably Full). A pop-up menu reveals several other card size choices; select Half.**

We don't need split page format (a format designed for printouts that will be folded in half) or high-quality (slow) printing.

☐ **If there is an X in either check box, click to remove it.**

You can control the size of the card images, the spaces between images, and the page margins by dragging on corners and handles in the picture on the left side of the dialog box. For more exact adjustments, you can monitor the numbers in the Dimensions box while you drag.

☐ **Drag the margin handle in the lower right corner of the page image to change the margins to .750 on all sides.**

☐ **Click on the Spacing button in the Dimensions box so you can view changes in the spacing between images.**

☐ **Drag the lower right card image so that its edges come close to the new margins.**

The bottom of the dialog box allows you to create a customized **header** that appears at the top of each page of the printout. The icons allow you to insert page number, date, and time into the header; the arrow allows you to tab to the center and again to the right of the header between items. You'll use some of them now to create a header that contains the date on the left, the page number in the center, and your name on the right.

☐ **Click on the calendar icon, the arrow (tab) icon, the page number (#) icon, and the arrow icon again. Type your last name.**

☐ **If you don't want to print the report, click Cancel. Otherwise click Print... and respond to the next dialog box by clicking OK.**

If nothing happens, your computer may not be properly connected to a working printer.

Before printing anything, you might need to use the **Chooser** in the Apple menu and the **Page Setup** command in the File menu to select a printer and control the layout of the page.

Printing a Report

In many situations it's useful to print part of the information from your stack without reproducing complete card images.

The **Print Report...** command can be used to print database-style **reports**, mailing labels, address book pages, or other custom printouts. This command allows you to control which fields will be printed, how they will be arranged, and what information will appear in the header at the top of each page.

☐ **Select Print Report... from the File menu.**

The Addresses stack allows you to create several different reports using prefabricated **report templates**—one for mailing labels, one for address book pages, and one for creating a name and address list. The **Reports menu** allows you to choose a report template.

☐ **Select Address Book from the Reports menu.**

The picture in the dialog box shows you the page layout for the report and allows you to adjust it if necessary.

☐ **If you don't want to print the report, click Cancel. Otherwise click Print... and respond to the next dialog box by clicking OK.**

Creating a Report Template

If none of the existing templates meets your needs, you can easily create your own. Let's create a simple phone list.

☐ **Select Print Report... from the File menu.**

☐ **Select New Report from the Reports menu.**

☐ **Type "Phone List" to name the report.**

```
┌─────────────────────────────────────────────┐
│  ┌─────────────────────────────────────────┐ │
│  │ Report Name:                            │ │
│  │ ┌─────────────────────────────────────┐ │ │
│  │ │ Phone List                          │ │ │
│  │ └─────────────────────────────────────┘ │ │
│  │              ┌────────┐  ┌──────────┐   │ │
│  │              │   OK   │  │  Cancel  │   │ │
│  │              └────────┘  └──────────┘   │ │
│  └─────────────────────────────────────────┘ │
└─────────────────────────────────────────────┘
```

First you'll need to change the layout of the report so that the cells aren't shaped like mailing labels.

☐ **Point the handle on the lower right corner of the upper left cell and drag it up and to the right, as shown here:**

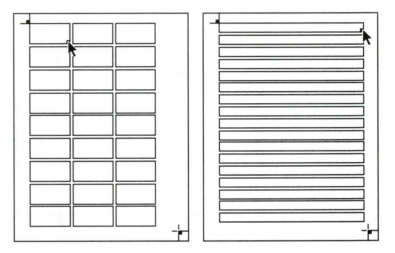

These cells don't contain anything yet; it's time to specify which fields will appear in each of them.

☐ **Double-click on one of the cells (or select Report Items... from the Edit menu, or press Command-E.)**

The next dialog box shows a closeup of one cell.

☐ **Select New Item from the Items menu.**

☐ **Double-click on the dotted box that appears in the cell (or select Item Info... from the Items menu, or press Command-I.)**

The dialog box allows you to specify what, exactly, will appear in each cell. You could type the item in the dialog box, but it's easier to just select the items you want from the scrolling list of available fields.

☐ **Scroll through the list of background fields; select Name and click OK.**

Item Info

Contents of item:

field "Name"

OK

Cancel

Background fields:

Name
Company
Street
CityState
Zip

☐ Font
Geneva

☐ Size
9

☐ Style
☒ Plain
☐ Bold
☐ Italic
☐ Underline
☐ Outline
☐ Shadow
☐ Condense
☐ Extend

☐ Line height

Align:
◉ Left
○ Center
○ Right

Columns: 1

(This dialog box also allows you to control font, style, and other aspects of the printed field; you'll learn about these topics in later sessions.)

☐ **Drag the corner of the new report item so that it's big enough to show a long name.**

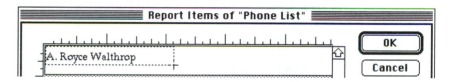

Now we need to add the phone number to the cell.

☐ **Select New Item again; choose Phone 1 from the scrolling list of fields, and click OK.**

The new field image should appear right on top of the old one.

☐ **Point to the center of the new report item and drag it to the right. Drag its corner to enlarge it so it can show a whole phone number.**

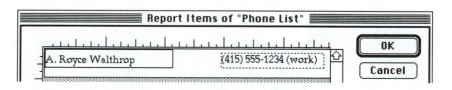

☐ **Click OK to return to the Print Report dialog box.**

□ **Refine your layout if you aren't happy with it; then click Print... or Cancel.**

You'll be asked whether you want to save changes to the new report. If you decide to save, remember to choose your own disk in the Save dialog box.

> Report templates are saved with stacks, so it's not necessary to create templates each time you print a report. A stack can have up to 16 associated templates. Once you've created a report template for one stack, it's possible to copy the template and paste it into another stack.

Break Point

Customizing Cards

> If you're content using HyperCard stacks just they way they come out of the box, you can stop here. But if you want to learn how to modify those stacks so they more closely meet your personal needs, this section is essential. The techniques you'll see here will be covered in more detail in future sessions, so don't worry if some of the concepts seem foreign now.

The Addresses and Appointments stacks are good examples of the kinds of stacks that are available to make HyperCard a useful office tool. If we think of computer software as an extension of the human mind, then canned stacks such as these are designed to extend the *average* computer user's mind. But the concept of "average" often has little to do with reality; a person with one foot in ice and the other in fire is not, on the average, comfortable. Programs written for average people aren't written for real people. Fortunately, HyperCard makes it easy to customize existing stacks or create brand new stacks that can meet the exact needs of individual users.

Suppose, for example, you want to modify the Addresses stack by deleting two of the four phone buttons and replacing the corresponding phone number fields with a field for recording the person's birthday (or electronic mail address, or whatever). The procedure is straightforward if you understand the basics of HyperCard. These buttons and fields are stored in the **background** shared by all cards in the stack. When you add, delete, or change a field in the background, you're affecting every card in the stack. So to delete or modify the buttons and fields, it's necessary to go into the background layer.

Card layer   **Background layer**

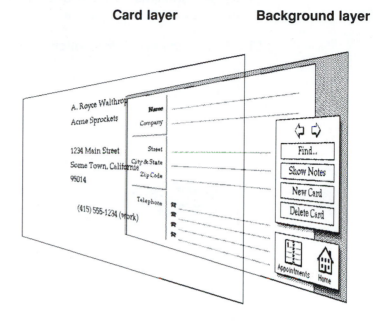

There are two kinds of fields in the background of the Addresses stack's cards: editable fields that contain different information on each card, and locked fields that share the same text on all cards. Hyper-Card's **Field tool** is used for working with both kinds of fields. We'll use the Field tool to delete one of the phone number fields and reposition another so it's appropriate for birthdays. Then we'll duplicate one of the locked labels, unlock the duplicate, type a new name in it, relock it, and position it. In addition, we'll remove the two extra phone buttons with the **Button tool**. Ready?

Resetting the User Level (with Magic)

At the beginning of this session, you reset the user level to level 2, typing, so that you could modify stacks by adding cards, deleting cards, and editing text in fields—things you couldn't do at the **browsing** level. HyperCard's browsing and typing user levels are designed to protect your stacks from being accidentally modified by untrained users. It's time to set your user level to level 4, authoring. (Level 3 is painting; we're skipping that level because it doesn't allow us to create new buttons, cards, or stacks.) The **authoring** user level gives you access to all of HyperCard's tools except scripts, which will be introduced in Session 5.

☐ **Press Command-H (or select Home from the Go menu) to go Home.**

☐ **Press Command-4 (or select Last from the Go menu) to go to the last card of the Home stack.**

☐ **Click on the Authoring option.**

Preferences   Home

    Your Name: <u>Mark Twain</u>

    Click the user level you want: Other settings:

5 Scripting	Edit scripts of buttons, fields, cards, backgrounds, and stacks.	
▷ **4** Authoring	Create buttons and fields. Link buttons to cards and stacks.	
3 Painting	Use the Paint tools to change the appearance of cards and backgrounds.	☐ Power Keys
2 Typing	Enter and edit text in fields.	☐ Arrow Keys in Text
1 Browsing	Explore stacks but make no changes.	

◀   [Return to First Card]   ▶

 If you were able to successfully follow the instructions to this point, proceed to the next section, "Saving a Copy."

If you see only two choices, Browsing and Typing, then you'll need to remove a barrier that was included in Apple's bundled HyperCard to keep beginners from exploring HyperCard's higher levels without adequate documentation. Armed with this book, you're ready to remove the protective patch.

☐ **Press Command-M to bring up the message box.**

☐ **Type "magic" in the message box and press Return.**

---

magic

Three more user level buttons should appear. It's not really magic; you just sent a message to the card to hide two large white button patches that covered these three buttons. (This command works because this card's script is specially programmed to understand the command "magic". You'll learn more about how this works in later sessions.)

☐ **Click on the Authoring option.**

Your Home stack is now fully functional. (If you ever want to put it back the way you found it, "magic" works both ways.)

Saving a Copy

☐ **Press Command-R (or select Recent from the Go menu).**

☐ **Click on the image of any card from the Addresses stack to go to that card.**

☐ **Select Save a Copy... from the File menu.**

You're preserving a duplicate before you make any changes.

☐ **When the dialog box appears, check the destination disk to make sure the copy is going where you want it and press Return.**

The saved copy will remain unchanged regardless of what you do to the original.

Going into the Background

Now you're ready to modify the Addresses stack. Because you want the changes to affect every card, the first step is to go to their shared background.

☐ **Select Background from the Edit menu (or press Command-B).**

You're now looking at the background that's shared by every address card in the stack. (The **striped menu bar** always indicates that you're in the background. So does the striped margin bar in this text.)

Deleting Buttons and Fields

☐ **Select the Button tool from the top row in the center of the Tools menu.**

All the buttons on the card should be clearly outlined, including the four phone buttons.

☐ **Click on the third phone button from the top of the card.**

Since the Button tool is selected, clicking on the button selects it without activating it.

☐ **Press the Delete (Backspace) key to delete the selected button.**

☐ **Select and delete the bottom phone button.**

Now it's time to work with fields.

☐ **Select the Field tool from the upper right of the Tools menu.**

Every field in the background should be outlined with solid lines, including the four phone number fields.

☐ **Click on the third phone field to select it and press the Delete (Backspace) key.**

A dialog box will ask if you want to delete the field, warning that if you do you'll wipe out everything that's stored in that field for every card in your stack.

☐ **Click Delete.**

Copying a Field

We could delete the fourth field, too, but then we'd have to create a new birthday field. It's simpler just to give this field a new label and function. We'll need to create a label field like the ones for name, company, and the rest. We could use the New Field command, but then we'd have to tweak the field quite a bit to make it match the other labels. It makes more sense to make a copy of one of those fields, position the copy where we want it, and put "Birthday" in it.

☐ **Hold down the Option key and drag the field with "telephone" in it down toward the bottom of the card.**

This is a labor-saving shortcut for copying the field.

> **Option-drag** creates a *copy* of the field (or button), leaving the original behind while the copy is moved.

☐ **Position the new field so that it's below the original field and next to the lowest field on the card.**

Labeling the Field

Now we just need to put "Birthday" in the new field. But we can't do that until we unlock the field so we can type in it.

☐ **Double-click on the new field.**

The dialog box that appears provides a complete profile of the field. We can ignore most of the options for now; they'll be covered in later sessions as we need them. Here are the two that concern us here:

> If the **Shared Text** option is checked, text in a background field is shared by every card with that background.
> The contents of a field cannot be changed as long as the **Lock Text** option is checked.

☐ **Type "Birthday Label" to rename the field.**

☐ **Click on the Lock Text check box to unlock the text and click OK.**

☐ **Select the Browse tool (the pointing hand) from the Tools menu.**

The pointer should turn back into a hand.

☐ **Position the pointer over the new field and click.**

The pointing hand becomes an I-beam, which places an insertion bar in the field.

☐ **Type "Birthday".**

Now we need to lock the field again so we don't inadvertently change our label later.

☐ **Select the Field tool from the Tools menu.**

☐ **Double-click on the Birthday Label field.**

☐ **Click on the Lock Text check box to lock the text; then click OK.**

☐ **Select the Browse tool from the Tools menu.**

If your card looks like this one, you're ready to leave the background and try it out.

☐ **Press Command-B or select Background from the Edit menu.**

The stripes should vanish from the menu bar as you return to the card layer.

As you flip through the cards, they'll all reflect the changes you made in the background. You may want to test the modified field by typing in birthdays on some of the cards.

Shutting Down

We could spend more time exploring HyperCard's information management tools. But you've seen the basics now, and the exercises and projects will give you a chance to apply the principles you've learned in a variety of interesting ways.

☐ **Select Quit HyperCard from the File menu.**

☐ **Select Shut Down (or Restart) from the Special menu.**

Summary

You've accomplished quite a bit in this session. You learned how to enter and edit text in HyperCard fields. You learned how to add cards, delete cards, sort cards, and find particular items on those cards using character string pattern matches. Finally, you got a feel for what's involved in customizing stacks by working with the Field and Button tools.

You're a certified HyperCard user now, prepared to browse and type your way through all kinds of HyperCard stacks. If you have no intention of creating your own stacks, you can quit now. But be forewarned: The best is yet to come.

Key Words

authoring user level
background
boolean algebra
Browse tool
browsing (user level)
Button tool
Chooser
Clipboard
Copy command (Command-C)
cursor
Cut command (Command-X)
data file

database
Delete Card command
   (Command-Delete, Command-
   Backspace)
deleting text
double-click-drag
editing text
export (text)
field (database and HyperCard)
Field tool
Find command (Command-F)
hard copy

header
I-beam
import (text)
inserting text
insertion bar
intersection
locked text (field)
Mark Cards command
marking cards
New Card button
New Card command
  (Command-N)
Option-drag
Page Setup command
Paste command (Command-V)
Phone icon
pop-up field
Print Card command
  (Command-P)
Print Report... command

Print Stack... command
record (database)
replacing text
report
Reports menu
report template
Save a Copy... command
scrolling field
selecting text
shared text (field)
Shift key
Shift-Tab
Sort commands
striped menu bar
Tab key
typing (user level)
Undo command (Command-Z)
union
user level

Self-Testing Exercises

1. There's no Save command in HyperCard. Is it necessary to use the Save a Copy... command to save your work? Explain.

2. Give three examples illustrating *different* reasons why the Find command might not take you to the sought-after card.

3. Why is it important to make sure all of the names in an address book stack are listed with the first and last names arranged in the same order?

4. Explain the difference between deleting and cutting a card.

5. What is the difference between printing a stack and printing a report? Describe situations when each is appropriate.

6. What are the advantages of using HyperCard as a personal information manager rather than using a conventional paper address book/ appointment calendar system? What are the disadvantages?

Projects

Note: Some of these projects involve modifying standard HyperCard stacks that accompany the Claris version of HyperCard. If you're working in a public lab with shared files, use copies of these files. In order to make sure you open *your* copy, rather than the public copy, use the Open Stack... command to locate each file on your disk. Many of the stacks used in these projects are not included with the Apple version of HyperCard.

1. Open the Addresses stack and save a copy. Delete all the cards from your copy and build a new Addresses stack that includes the addresses of your friends and relatives. Sort the stack in alphabetical order by last name. Mark the cards that contain names of people you call frequently. Print an address book of all of the names in the stack and a phone list containing only names and phone numbers from marked cards.

2. Try using the Appointments stack to keep track of your schedule. What are the advantages and disadvantages of this system when compared to one you normally use?

3 Use the Find command in the Art Bits stack to answer the following questions:

   a. Which page contains pictures of the planets?

   b. How many pages include the word *sun* in the index?

   c. How many pages include the word *drum* in the index?

4. Use the Graph Maker stack to create the following charts:

   a. A column chart illustrating the median income for men by level of education using the figures shown here (from 1986):
Men with four or more years of college	$33,304
Men with one to three years of college	23,738
Men with high school diplomas	9,772
Men with less than four years of high school	13,401

   b. A bar chart comparing the median income of men and women with four or more years of college education, using these figures:
Men with four or more years of college	$33,304
Women with four or more years of college	18,065

   c. A pie chart showing the occupational breakdown of the population completing four years or more of college, using the following figures:
Professional and managerial	68%
Technical, sales, and administrative	24%
Service	3%
Blue collar	5%

5. Open the Stack Templates stack (probably accessible from a button on the Stack Kit card of your Home stack). Following the instructions in the stack overview, create and customize a stack from one or more of the templates.

6. There are thousands of HyperCard stacks in existence. If you have access to a library of HyperCard stacks (there may be one on your lab file server), locate and explore several stacks in your area of interest. Pay attention to how these stacks work; compare their similarities and their differences.

SESSION 3

Objectives

By the end of this session you should be able to

- Create and name a new HyperCard stack and save a copy of that stack

- Use the Rectangle tool, the Oval tool, the Straight Line tool, the Pencil tool, the Paint Bucket, and the Patterns palette to create a drawing

- Use the Paint Text tool to add different styles of text to a stack

- Use the Eraser, the Undo command, and other editing tools to edit the graphics in the stack

- Create a button with a labeled icon and link it to a new card in the stack

- Copy a portion of a picture and paste it on another card

- Copy a button and paste it on another card

STACKS FROM SCRATCH:

BUILDING WITH BUTTONS

The Problem

Your local museum is preparing an exhibit on the seven wonders of the ancient world. They've asked you to prepare an interactive display on Egypt's Great Pyramid that will (1) show a cross section of the pyramid revealing passages and rooms; (2) provide close-up views of the King's Chamber and other rooms; and (3) be interactive and self-explanatory, so anyone can explore it. You don't have the time or money to create physical models, and you don't have the wall space to hang drawings or photos. Perhaps HyperCard can help.

Introduction

So far we've focused on using HyperCard as a tool for storing and accessing information. We've explored some professionally designed HyperCard stacks, modifying one so that it can be used in a slightly different way than the designer envisioned. As you'll see in this session, it's almost as easy to create your own stacks as it is to browse through or modify stacks created by others. HyperCard does such a good job of breaking down the distinction between computer *user* and computer *programmer* that you might not even notice when you cross that line in this session. Programming has never been easier.

Stack Construction Toolbox

Creating a New Stack

☐ **Start HyperCard by double-clicking on the Home Stack.**

☐ **Select New Stack... from the File menu.**

(If the New Stack... command is dimmed in the menu, double-check to make sure your user level has been set to authoring, as explained in the "Customizing Cards" section of Session 2.)
You'll see this:

```
┌─────────────────────────────────────────────────────────────┐
│  ┌──────────────────────────┐      Card size: ┌─────────────┐ │
│  │    🖫 Johann...   │       🖫 Johanna'...  │ Standard 9" │ │
│  │ 🗋 Home          ⇧│                   ↔512   ↕342     │
│  │ 🗁 Session 2 Stacks │     ┌────────┐                    │
│  │                     │     │ Eject  │    ▒▒▒▒▒▒▒▒▒▒      │
│  │                     │     └────────┘    ▒ ▒ ▒          │
│  │                     │     ┌────────┐    ▒ ▒ ▒          │
│  │                   ⇩│     │ Drive  │    ▒▒▒▒▒▒▒▒▒▒      │
│  New stack name:            └────────┘                    │
│  ┌─────────────────────┐    ┌────────┐                    │
│  │                     │    │  New   │                    │
│  └─────────────────────┘    └────────┘                    │
│  ☐ Copy current background   ┌────────┐                    │
│  ☐ Open stack in new window  │ Cancel │                    │
│                              └────────┘                    │
└─────────────────────────────────────────────────────────────┘
```

New Stack Dialog Box Options

In addition to the usual disk and folder selection options, the New Stack dialog box offers several choices:

- Copy current background: Check this box if you want your new stack to use the current stack's background. Backgrounds are discussed in more detail in the next session.

- Open stack in new window: Check this box if you want to keep the current stack open when the new stack is created. This is a good choice if you'll be switching back and forth between stacks, but it requires more memory.

- Card sizes: This pop-up menu allows you to choose between several common sizes or create your own. Here's what the Help stack says about it:

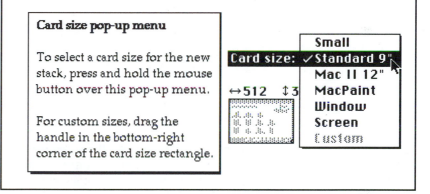

Card size pop-up menu

To select a card size for the new stack, press and hold the mouse button over this pop-up menu.

For custom sizes, drag the handle in the bottom-right corner of the card size rectangle.

In this book we'll consistently choose the standard 9-inch size because that size is completely visible on every Mac screen.

☐ **Make sure that both check boxes are turned off and that Standard 9" is the selected screen size.**

☐ **Make sure the disk shown above the Eject button is the appropriate disk for saving the stack (probably your working disk or a blank disk). If it's not, use the Drive and/or Desktop and/or Eject buttons to locate the appropriate disk.**

(If you're working on a file server and your system disk is in the only available drive, you can save your stack on that disk to avoid swapping.

Later, you can copy the stack to another disk to make room for your next stack.)

☐ **Type "Pyramid".**

This is the name you're assigning to your about-to-be-created stack.

Naming a Stack

You can choose any name you like for a stack, as long as

- It is less than 32 characters long and contains no colons (:)

- It is not the same as the names of any other files in the same folder on the disk

It's usually a good idea to choose a name that describes the stack contents, so you don't need to actually open the stack to remember what it does.

We're starting with a plain white background with no buttons, which is what you get if you don't copy the background from the current stack. You'll learn more about how backgrounds work in the next session.

☐ **Click New.**

Except for the menu bar, the screen (or HyperCard window on a large-screen machine) will turn white. You're looking at the first (and only) card in your new stack. It's totally empty now, but it's still saved on disk. HyperCard will automatically save this stack on this disk regularly as you work on your stack.

Tearing Off the Tools Menu

You'll be heavily using the **Tools menu** for a while, so let's put it where it's more accessible.

☐ **Drag your mouse (with the button held down) from the title of the Tools menu down past the bottom of that menu. Drag the dotted outline of that menu to the right side of the screen near the top.**

As you can see, Tools is a **tear-off menu**. You can now select tools from the Tools menu (it's still there) or from the **Tools palette** that you just created. The top three tools in the Tools menu/palette are **general tools** that allow you to choose between browsing, working with buttons, and working with fields; all of the remaining tools are **paint tools** specifically designed for painting. Notice that the Browse tool—the pointing hand—is highlighted. That means that it's the selected tool—the one that's currently being controlled by the mouse. When you select any of the paint tools, you tell the computer you want to paint on the screen or you want to modify something that's already painted on the screen.

> Painting in HyperCard is really just the process of telling the computer which **pixels** (picture elements or dots) in the card should be black and which should be white. Those are the only two choices; shades of gray are made of different black and white patterns. Technically, this is called **bit-mapped graphics**, because each pixel on the screen is controlled by one **bit**, or binary digit of the computer's memory. HyperCard has many sophisticated tools to make it easy to paint complex shapes, lines, words, and patterns, but all of these tools are doing the same thing: telling HyperCard to display some card pixels white and others black.

Drawing Lines

☐ **Click on the Pencil tool to select it.**

The Objects menu disappears, only to be replaced by three other menus. These menus are used for painting, so they aren't visible when you aren't using paint tools.

☐ **Move the pointer over the HyperCard card—the white screen below the menu bar (inside the window if you're using a large screen).**

Notice how the pointer turns into a pencil.

☐ **Hold down the mouse button and drag the Pencil tool around on the screen.**

☐ **Try signing your name, remembering that you can pick up the mouse and move it if you run out of desk space. Then underline your signature.**

As you can see, it's easy to draw with the mouse, but not particularly easy to draw *well*. Straight lines are particularly difficult. Fortunately, there's another tool designed to make that easier.

☐ Select the **Straight Line tool**.

The pointer turns into cross hairs, ready to draw.

☐ **Drag the mouse with the button held down between any two points in the window.**

Notice how a straight line stretches like a rubber band between those two points. Wherever you let go, that's where the line stays. Draw a few more lines if you like. When your screen becomes hopelessly cluttered, you can erase anything you don't like.

Using the Eraser

 ☐ **Select the Eraser tool from the palette by clicking on it. (If you prefer, you can select the Eraser in the Tools *menu*.)**

Notice how the pointer turns into a square when you move it over the white card.

☐ **Drag the Eraser through part of your scribbles with the mouse button held down.**

The parts you erase disappear without a trace. But erasing like this can be tedious if you want to clear the entire screen. Fortunately, there's a shortcut.

☐ **Double-click on the Eraser tool.**

> Double-clicking on the Eraser clears everything that's painted on the card. This is a handy—and potentially costly—trick. If you ever do it by mistake, remember Command-Z, the Undo command.

By this time, you're anxious to do some serious doodling. If so, take a few minutes to experiment. When you're done playing, double-click on the Eraser to clear the screen and we'll build a pyramid.

Drawing Polygons

☐ Select the **Polygon tool**.

This tool works like the Straight Line tool, except that it draws a series of connected lines. Each successive mouse click forms another angle and another new line; the lines stop forming when you click on the starting point or somewhere outside the window or when you double-click.

☐ **Draw a triangle with the Polygon tool by clicking on three different points on the screen. Complete the triangle by clicking once more on the starting point.**

If your triangle doesn't look like a pyramid, never mind. You already know one way to remove it: You can double-click on the Eraser to clear the window. But Undo will work here, too:

☐ **Press Command-Z (or select Undo from the Edit menu).**

If you haven't clicked the mouse button anywhere else since you drew the last triangle, the triangle will vanish.

☐ **Draw two more overlapping triangles. Press Command-Z *three times* after you draw the second one. Watch how the picture changes each time you select Undo.**

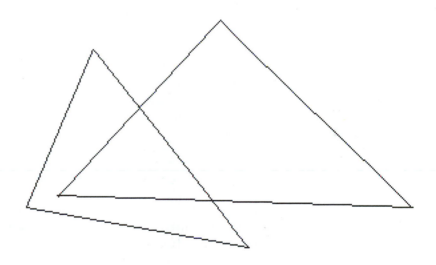

Since Undo can't take you back more than one step, you'll never be able to remove that first triangle with it. That's why it's important to check your work after each step before doing any more typing, clicking, or dragging.

Graphics Insurance

When you're working with paint tools, it's easy to spoil a work in progress with an accidental slip of the mouse. You can avoid serious, irreversible damage by remembering and using these insurance commands:

- The Go Back key (~ or Esc) backtracks one step when you have a paint tool selected. (To go back to the last card when you have a paint tool selected, press Command-~ or Command-Esc.)
- Undo (Command-Z) backtracks exactly one step.
- **Keep** (in the Paint menu, or **Command-K**) tells HyperCard to save the current picture.
- **Revert** (in the Paint menu) tells HyperCard to go back to the last saved version of the picture.

When you're painting in HyperCard, your picture is saved to disk when you do any of the following:

- Switch to another card.
- Switch to or from the background layer (You'll learn about backgrounds in Session 4).
- Select any of the three general tools at the top of the Tools palette.
- Select Keep (Command-K).

When you're painting, make a habit of selecting Keep (or pressing Command-K) every few minutes. If you make an error, try to erase it using Undo, ~, or Esc. If that doesn't take you back far enough, use Revert.

☐ **Double-click on the Eraser to clear the window.**

If you've been trying to make your triangles look like pyramids, you've probably noticed that it's not easy to make the two sides exactly the same length. Here's a trick that might help.

☐ **Hold down the Shift key while drawing the triangle with the Polygon tool.**

When you're using many of the paint tools, the Shift key serves as a **constraint key**, temporarily constraining the tool in some helpful way.

In this case, it constrains the Polygon tool so that every line is either horizontal or a multiple of 15 degrees from horizontal. It's much easier to draw true horizontal lines and equal angles when the tool is constrained this way; you can be sure you will hit the horizontal or the vertical right on the mark. Even with this constraint, you'll probably have to try a few times to get the pyramid to come out right. If it doesn't work, just erase and try again. Your goal is to produce a triangle with two equal sides that fills about the top three-fourths of the window, like this:

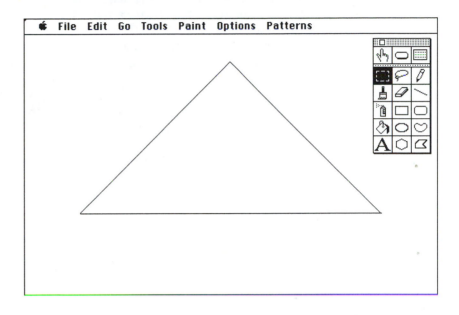

(Your local Egyptologist might tell you that this pyramid doesn't exactly match the geometry of the Great Pyramid. Never mind; he just lacks perspective.)

Pouring Paint Patterns

Shape notwithstanding, the pyramid doesn't look authentic because it lacks texture. The Great Pyramid was built with gigantic granite blocks (enough blocks to stretch three-fourths of the way around the planet if laid end to end). We can simulate the granite blocks by painting our pyramid. Unlike real-world paint, HyperCard paint comes in patterns rather than colors. A selection of these patterns is available in the **Patterns menu,** which can be torn off and made into a portable **Patterns palette**.

☐ **Drag the Patterns menu down from the menu bar and over to the right side of the screen so it's below the Tools palette.**

Notice that black paint is selected when you first open the palette.

☐ **Click to select the pattern that looks like bricks.**

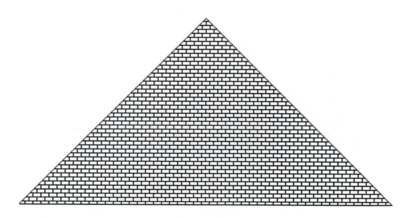

This is the paint we'll use on the pyramid.

☐ **Select the Paint Bucket tool from the Tools palette. The pointer should turn into a paint bucket.**

The Paint Bucket tool allows you to pour paint into any white area that's completely enclosed by black (or into a black area that's enclosed by white).

☐ **Position the Paint Bucket so that the dripping paint is some-where inside the triangle and press the button to pour the paint.**

Your triangle should fill with bricks. If the whole screen fills with bricks, your triangle has a leak.

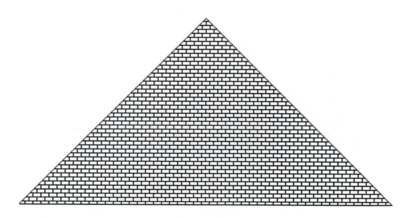

> The area to be filled with poured paint must be completely sur-rounded by black (or by white if you're pouring into a black area). Even the tiniest pinhole in the boundary will allow paint to leak out to fill a larger area. If your paint ever leaks unexpectedly, select Undo *immediately*, locate and correct the leak with the Pencil (or redraw the shape), and pour the paint again.

We have a pyramid; let's add the desert.

☐ **Use the Pencil tool to draw a line from the left edge of the bottom of the pyramid to the left edge of the screen. Make sure that there are no gaps at either end of the line. Repeat on the right side of the pyramid. (If necessary, drag the Patterns palette out of the way using the bar at the top of the palette.)**

These lines represent the desert's horizon in our landscape. For instant desert, just add sand.

☐ **Select the Paint Bucket tool and the pattern that looks like irregular grains of sand. Position the paint drip on the lower half of the screen to fill the desert with sand.**

Once again, if there's even the slightest pinhole in the horizon, you'll get more sand than you bargained for. If necessary, choose Undo, fill the leaks, and try again.

☐ **When you picture looks OK, select Keep from the Paint menu (or press Command-K), just in case you need to revert to this picture later.**

Using Paint Text

Even though you may have no trouble identifying the Great Pyramid in your picture, others might need a hint. So let's add a title. You worked with text fields in Session 2, but for this job there's another kind of text that's more appropriate.

Two Kinds of Text in HyperCard

■ **Paint text**, after it's typed, blends into the whole painting, becoming just another pattern of black and white dots on the screen. Consequently, it can't be edited later using the standard editing techniques. (Nor can it be found with the Find command.)

■ **Field text** remains text forever. Unless a field is locked (see Session 5), you—or any user—can always edit it using the usual editing techniques.

Since we don't want casual users of our stack to mess with the title, we're better off using paint text.

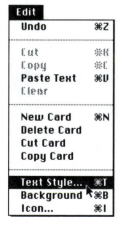

☐ **Select the Paint Text tool (the letter _A_).**

The pointer turns into an I-beam. As you saw in the last session, the I-beam is used to position the cursor for typing.

☐ **Position the I-beam just below the bottom of the pyramid in the center and click.**

A flashing cursor appears, beckoning you to type.

☐ **Type "The Great Pyramid".**

The words are there, all right, but they lack style. We can fix that.

☐ **Double-click on the Paint Text tool.**

This is a shortcut to save time. The alternative is to select **Text Style...** from the Edit menu (or press **Command-T**).

You'll see a dialog box that looks something like this one:

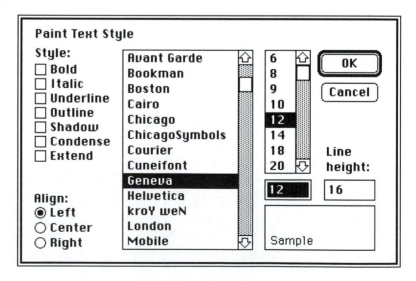

This crowded dialog box gives you control over the way the text looks, rather than what it says. If you haven't clicked anywhere since you typed your title, you can change the style of the title text by simply clicking on different options. But first, a brief explanation of the available options is in order.

The Text Styles Dialog Box

The text **styles** listed on the left side of the dialog box—bold, underline, and the rest—can be used to draw attention to text and add visual pizzazz to a screen. But beware: It's easy to overuse these styles and make your stack look like a reject from a supermarket tabloid.

The names in the center of the box represent **fonts**—basic typefaces—that are stored in your System. Different fonts have different looks; compare this text with the text of the instruction below this box. The font names that you see on your screen probably don't match those shown here; you have different fonts stored in your System file. There are hundreds of fonts available for Macintosh users: Some come free with the System; others must be purchased; still others are available free in the public domain. Consequently, it's rare for two computer systems to have the same set of fonts.

You can also control the **size** of the text by clicking on different sizes. (Sizes are measured in **points**; a point is a typographer's unit of measure.) Once again, the sizes that are available are determined by the fonts that are stored in your System. What's more, different fonts may have different available sizes. You can type in sizes that aren't stored with the system for a particular font, but, depending on how your System is configured, you may end up with lumpy, hard-to-read letters on the screen. The sample text shown in the lower right corner of the dialog box can be used to preview the options.

Finally, the dialog box lets you control **alignment** of the text. Typically, text is aligned to the left, but you can also specify right alignment or automatic centering around the insertion point.

□ **Experiment with the sample text in the lower right corner of the dialog box by choosing different combinations of fonts, styles, and sizes. When you're done experimenting, click on styles Bold, Shadow, and Extend, on font Geneva, on size 24 point (if it's visible; otherwise click on the largest available number), and on align Center. Then click on the OK button to apply all these changes to your title.**

The Great Pyramid

If the title didn't change, it's probably because you clicked somewhere else on the window before choosing Text Style.... Remember, paint text "dries" as soon as you let go of it.

From an aesthetic point of view, these letters leave something to be desired. (Outline and shadow characters generally do.) But they'll serve our purposes because they stand out even when surrounded by sand.

Since the text cleared a path in the sand, we need to do some touch-up work with the Paint Bucket.

☐ **With the Paint Bucket and the sand pattern selected, position the paint drip over part of the area whited out by the text and click to pour.**

☐ *Carefully* **position the end of the paint drip inside the opening in the *P* and pour; fill the *d* the same way.**

If you make any mistakes, remember to select Undo before you click anywhere else.

If your screen looks like this, you've completed the artwork on your first card:

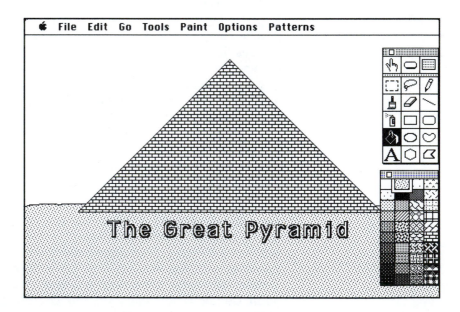

Creating a Button

☐ **Click on the Button tool in the top row of the Tools palette.**

The Paint, Options, and Patterns menus are replaced by the **Objects menu,** and the pointer turns into the familiar arrow.

Objects
Button Info...
Field Info...
Card Info...
Bkgnd Info...
Stack Info...
Bring Closer ⌘+
Send Farther ⌘-
New Button
New Field
New Background

☐ **Select New Button from the Objects menu.**

This is the generic HyperCard button. It's up to us to make it look and act the way we want it to. Let's start by making the button bigger.

☐ **Place the pointer at the corner of the button and drag it away from the button's center.**

If you found the right spot, the button should stretch as you drag. If it doesn't, reposition the mouse and try again.

☐ **Drag the corner until the button is about twice its original length.**

```
┌ ─ ─ ─ ─ ─ ─ ─ ─ ─ ─ ─ ─ ─ ─ ─ ─ ─ ─ ┐
│            New Button              │
└ ─ ─ ─ ─ ─ ─ ─ ─ ─ ─ ─ ─ ─ ─ ─ ─ ─ ─ ┘
```

This button is inconveniently located right on top of our pyramid, but it's easy enough to move.

☐ **Place the pointer in the middle of the button and drag it down between the bottom of the card and the title.**

What does this button do?

☐ **Try clicking once on this button to see what it does.**

Nothing happens.

> HyperCard buttons work only when clicked by the Browse hand tool; the Button tool is used to create and change buttons, not to click them.

But in this case, switching to the Browse tool wouldn't help, because we haven't told the button what to do when it's clicked. We're ready to do that now.

☐ **Double-click on the New Button button.**

```
┌──────────────────────────────────────────────┐
│  Button Name: │New Button              │      │
│  Card button number: 1                         │
│  Card button ID: 1                             │
│  ⊠ Show Name              Style:               │
│  ☐ Auto Hilite            ○ Transparent        │
│                           ○ Opaque             │
│                           ○ Rectangle          │
│  ┌─────────┐              ○ Shadow             │
│  │ Icon... │              ● Round Rect         │
│  ├─────────┤              ○ Check Box          │
│  │ Effect..│              ○ Radio Button       │
│  ├─────────┤                                   │
│  │ LinkTo..│                                   │
│  ├─────────┤      ┌──────────┐  ┌──────────┐   │
│  │ Script..│      │    OK    │  │  Cancel  │   │
│  └─────────┘      └──────────┘  └──────────┘   │
└──────────────────────────────────────────────┘
```

This dialog box is what you'll use to "program" the new button. It allows you to name the button something besides New Button, change what the button looks like, and establish what the button will do when clicked.

Let's start by changing the name of the button.

☐ **Type "Click here to see inside".**

Since the original name of the button, New Button, was highlighted, that name is replaced by your typing.

We have several choices of button styles; for this button, the already-selected round rectangle is just fine. But it might be nice if we could have the button flash black when clicked, like official Macintosh dialog box buttons do.

☐ **Click on Auto Hilite.**

Linking the Button

Now you're going to **link** this button to a new card showing a cross section of the pyramid, so that a click on that button transports the viewer to that cross-section card.

☐ **Click on LinkTo...**

A new window appears in the center of the screen:

```
┌──────────────────────────────────────────┐
│ ▓□▓▓▓▓▓▓▓▓▓▓▓▓▓▓▓▓▓▓▓▓▓▓▓▓▓▓▓▓▓▓▓▓▓▓▓▓▓▓▓ │
│  Link to:                                  │
│   ┌─────────────┐ ┌─────────────┐ ┌─────────────┐ │
│   │  This Card  │ │ This Stack  │ │   Cancel    │ │
│   └─────────────┘ └─────────────┘ └─────────────┘ │
└──────────────────────────────────────────┘
```

This window is asking you to locate the card (or stack) that's to be linked to this button. In this case, that card doesn't yet exist, so we'll have to create it.

☐ **Select New Card from the Edit menu (or press Command-N, the keyboard equivalent).**

You're looking at a brand-new, all-white card, located right behind the first card in your stack. It's partially obscured by the small window, still waiting for you to tell it if we've reached the destination yet.

☐ **Click on the button labeled This Card.**

The window and the new card disappear, and you're back at the first card again, with a new name on the button.

```
┌────────────────────────────────────────┐
│     Click here to see inside             │
└────────────────────────────────────────┘
```

Adding a Visual Effect

Well-chosen **visual effects** can enhance the look and feel of your stack as it moves from card to card. To add an effect we need to return once more to the Button Info dialog box.

☐ **Double-click on the button once again.**

☐ **Click on the Effect... button.**

```
┌──────────────────────────────────────────────────┐
│  Effect for card button id 1:                      │
│  ┌──────────────────────────────────────────────┐ │
│  │                                                │ │
│  └──────────────────────────────────────────────┘ │
│  ┌────────────────────────┬─┐   Speed:             │
│  │ barn door open         │⬆│   ○ Fast             │
│  │ barn door close        │▓│   ◉ Normal           │
│  │ checkerboard           │▓│   ○ Slow             │
│  │ dissolve               │▓│   ○ Very Slow        │
│  │ iris open              │▓│                       │
│  │ iris close             │▓│   ┌──────────────┐   │
│  │ scroll left            │▓│   │      OK       │   │
│  │ scroll right           │▓│   └──────────────┘   │
│  │ scroll up              │ │                       │
│  │ scroll down            │⬇│   ┌──────────────┐   │
│  └────────────────────────┴─┘   │    Cancel     │   │
│                                  └──────────────┘   │
└──────────────────────────────────────────────────┘
```

The Edit menu:

```
┌─────────────────────┐
│ Edit                │
├─────────────────────┤
│ Undo          ⌘Z    │
├─────────────────────┤
│ Cut           ⌘X    │
│ Copy          ⌘C    │
│ Paste Picture ⌘V    │
│ Clear               │
├─────────────────────┤
│ New Card      ⌘N    │
│ Delete Card         │
│ Cut Card            │
│ Copy Card           │
├─────────────────────┤
│ Text Style... ⌘T    │
│ Background    ⌘B    │
│ Icon...       ⌘I    │
└─────────────────────┘
```

☐ **Scroll through the list of visual effects until you see "shrink to top". Click on that one, then click OK.**

It's time to test the button.

☐ **Press Command-Tab.**

This is the keyboard equivalent of selecting the Browse tool (the hand) from the Tools palette.

☐ **Click on the button you created.**

If it worked properly, the button flashed black and the entire scene shriveled up until it vanished at the top of the window. You've been transported to your new, all-white card. The Tools palette is still visible; it travels with you until you put it away. (If you're not there, you didn't link the button properly. You can remedy the situation by choosing the Button tool, double-clicking on the button, clicking on LinkTo..., pressing Command-4 to go to the last card in the stack—the new one—and clicking on This Card.)

Using the Clipboard

Now return to the first card so we can borrow from our previous artwork to decorate this card.

☐ **Press Command-1 (or select First from the Go menu).**

We'll copy this picture to the Clipboard so we can use it as raw material for our next card. But before a graphic can be copied to the Clipboard, it must be selected. There are many ways to select a graphic in Hyper-Card.

HyperCard Graphic Selection Techniques

- To select the entire card's graphics including the white spaces between them, double-click on the **Selection rectangle** *or* use the **Select All command (Command-A).**

┌ ┐
└ ┘

- To select all of the graphic objects on the card without selecting surrounding white spaces, double-click on the **Lasso** *or* use the **Select command (Command-S).**

- To select the most recently painted object (before you click anywhere else), do nothing (it's automatically selected) unless you want to move it; in that case, use the Select command (Command-S).

- To select a rectangular area, use the Selection rectangle.

- To select an irregularly shaped area, use the Selection rectangle with the Option key held down, *or* use the Lasso, *or* use the Select command after selecting an object with the rectangle.

Note: We'll modify this list next session when we work with backgrounds.

We'll use the Selection rectangle momentarily and the Lasso in the next session. For our current job, the most appropriate tool is the Select All command.

☐ **Choose Select All from the Paint menu (or press Command-A).**

A dotted line should be moving around the edge of the screen, indicating that the whole picture is selected.

☐ **Press Command-C (or select Copy Picture from the Edit menu).**

You can't see it, but you just placed a copy of the entire drawing in the Clipboard.

☐ **Press Command-~ (Go Back) to return to the blank card.**

When you're using the paint tools, the ~ (Tilde) key means Undo the last step when typed by itself. To use it to go back one card, press the Command key with it. (This combination always takes you back, whether you're painting or not.)

☐ **Press Command-V (Paste Picture).**

The entire pyramid portrait should appear on the card, ready to be revised into a cross-section view. (Notice that the button did not copy with the artwork.)

The first thing we want to do is eliminate the title from this page so we have room for our subterranean passages.

☐ **Choose the Selection rectangle (the dashed rectangle) from the Tools palette.**

When you drag a diagonal with the Selection rectangle, you're selecting the rectangular area determined by that diagonal.

☐ **Drag a diagonal from the top right corner of the title to the bottom left corner, making sure to include the whole title in the rectangle. If you miss, click outside the selected area and try again.**

You should see a moving dashed line around the area you've selected. (Because of these moving dashes, the Selection rectangle has been nicknamed the marquee, or more informally, marching ants.)

☐ **Press the Delete (Backspace) key to delete the selected portion of the picture.**

That leaves a white space, because you deleted some sand, too.

☐ **With the sand pattern selected, select the Paint Bucket and click once in the white rectangle to fill it with sand paint.**

Painting Passages

☐ **Double-click on the Straight Line tool.**

This is the shortcut equivalent of selecting **Line Size...** from the Options menu. You're going to be drawing some underground passages, and you'll need a line that's thicker than the one you've been using.

☐ **Click on the fourth line in the dialog box:**

☐ **Select the Straight Line Tool and drag a line that looks like this:**

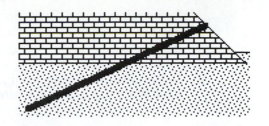

☐ **Now add another:**

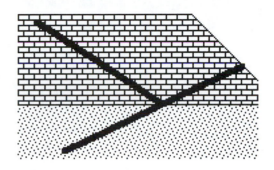

☐ **Hold down the Shift key to constrain the Straight Line tool and draw two horizontal lines:**

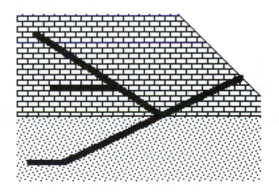

With the straight passages drawn, you're ready to draw the crooked escape passage.

☐ **Select the Paintbrush tool.**

☐ **Select black paint from the Patterns palette.**

Double-click on the Paintbrush tool. Another keyboard shortcut, this one has the same effect as choosing **Brush Shape...** from the Options menu.

☐ **Select a brush shape from the dialog box (you *must* select one, even if it's the one that's already selected).**

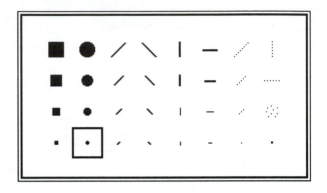

☐ **Use the Paintbrush to draw the curved passage. If you make a mistake, press Command-Z (Undo) and try again.**

Now we can add the chambers.

Drawing Rooms

☐ **Select the Rectangle tool from the palette.**

When you drag between two points with this tool, you create a rectangle with those two points as opposite vertices.

☐ **Draw a rectangular-shaped chamber under the pyramid like this:**

Notice that the sides of the rectangle are the line thickness that we selected earlier; that thickness applies to all shape tools until we specify otherwise.

To be consistent with the black passages, we should paint the subterranean chambers black, too.

☐ **Select the Paint Bucket and the black paint.**

☐ **Place the paint drip *inside* the rectangle and click to pour.**

You can combine those two steps—creating a shape and filling it—by telling HyperCard that you want to draw filled shapes.

☐ **Double-click on the Rectangle tool.**

This is the same as selecting **Draw Filled** from the Options menu. Notice how the shape tools in the palette are now filled.

☐ **Select the Rectangle tool and draw two rectangles inside the pyramid, like this:**

The Polygon tool also draws filled.

☐ **Double-click on the Straight Line tool and select the thinnest line width.**

☐ **Select the Polygon tool.**

☐ **Draw a parallelogram like the one shown here by clicking around its vertices in order, starting and ending at the same corner.**

Notice how the shape fills with the selected paint when you complete it.

☐ **Add triangular peaks to the two internal chambers by clicking around the triangles with the Polygon tool.**

This is a good time to save your work, just in case.

☐ **Press Command-K (or select Keep from the Paint menu).**

This picture clearly needs some labels.

Drawing Labels

☐ **Select the Rounded Rectangle tool.**

This tool works like the Rectangle tool except that the corners of the drawn shapes are rounded. We'll use it to create labels. The labels should be filled with paint to obscure the pyramid bricks, but black paint would not be appropriate.

☐ **Select white paint from the Patterns palette.**

Even with the benefit of the HyperCard shape tools, it's difficult to make two shapes the same height. We can ensure that all of our labels are the same height, though, by forcing their edges to fall into some invisible grooves on the screen.

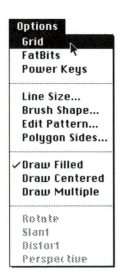

☐ **Select Grid from the Options menu.**

You'll notice the effect of the invisible grid as soon as you move the mouse around the card. Notice how the cross hairs jump from point to point rather than gliding smoothly across the screen.

> The grid is more effective than the human eyeball for aligning objects on the screen. When you turn on the grid with the Grid command, it stays on until you turn it off by selecting Grid again.

☐ **Draw four rounded rectangles like these:**

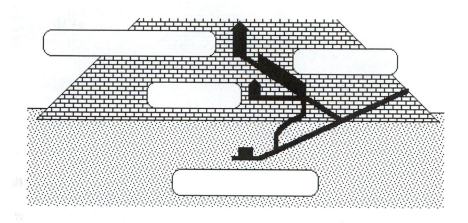

In addition to noticing the effect of the grid, note how the white paint fill obscures the pyramid bricks and the sand.

> There's a critical difference between white paint and no paint when it comes to filling a shape: A shape filled with white paint hides what it covers; an unfilled shape is transparent.

Now we can fill those shapes with text.

☐ **Double-click on the Paint Text tool (the letter *A*) to bring up the Text Styles dialog box.**

☐ **Select centered, 9-point, Geneva with all other styles turned off. Click OK.**

This combination will apply to all of the text you type until you change it.

☐ **Select the Paint Text tool, move the I-beam to the center of one of the rounded rectangles, click to position the pointer, and type. Repeat for the other labels in the following picture:**

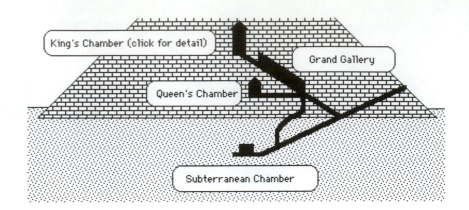

Creating an Invisible Button

Now let's provide our audience with a closer view of the King's Chamber.

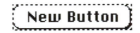 ☐ **Click on the Button tool in the Tools palette.**

☐ **Select New Button from the Objects menu.**

New Button

☐ **Drag this button so that it sits right on top of the King's Chamber.**

☐ **Stretch the corner so that it covers the chamber and the corresponding label completely.**

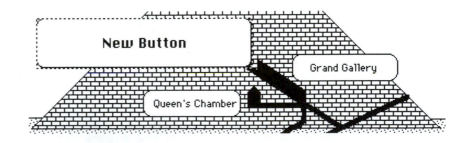

☐ **Double click on the button to bring up the Button Info dialog box.**

We want the button and its name to be invisible.

☐ Click on **Transparent** button style.

☐ Click to turn *off* **Show Name** option.

Since the name won't show up on the screen, it's not strictly necessary to change its name. Do it anyway.

> It's a good idea to name buttons and other objects, even if those names won't be visible to the user. Those names just might make it easier for you to figure out what's going on if you decide to change something later.

☐ Type "King's Chamber".

Before we link this button to another card let's specify a visual effect.

☐ Click on the Effect... button.

☐ Scroll to "zoom open" and click on it.

☐ Click on Very Slow.

☐ Click on OK.

Now it's time to link the button.

☐ Double-click on the button to bring up the Button Info dialog box.

☐ Click on LinkTo....

Link to:

[This Card]   [This Stack]   [Cancel]

As before, we'll create a new card.

☐ Select New Card from the Edit menu.

Another white card will appear.

☐ Click on the button labeled This Card.

When you return to the cross-section card, your button is visible only in outline form.

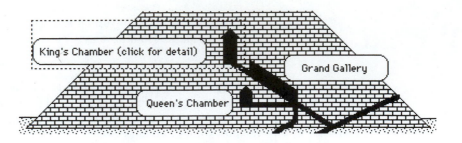

When you choose the Browse tool, the button will disappear altogether, but you'll know it's there because it will transport you to the new card when you click on it.

☐ **Press Command-Tab (or click on the Browse tool) and click on the King's Chamber.**

Drawing One Last Card

Now you need to fulfill the promise of the previous card by drawing a close-up view of the King's Chamber. Here's a sketch of what it might look like.

☐ **Use the Rectangle tool, the Polygon tool, the Straight Line tool, and the Eraser to draw a rough facsimile of this sketch on the blank card.**

Software Engineering Simplified

Software engineering is a branch of computer science that concerns itself with applying the design principles of engineering to the art and science of computer programming. When an engineer designs a bridge, we can generally assume that it won't fall down if we walk across it; when an engineer designs a TV set, it's probably going to be easy enough to operate that we won't need to read a 300-page manual to use it. Similarly, if a computer program is well engineered, we should be able to assume that it works reliably and that it has a **user interface** that's easy to understand.

Unfortunately, much software isn't well designed when measured against these criteria. But there's no reason we can't apply some basic software engineering principles to the stacks we create to make them reliable and easy to understand.

The surest way to determine the reliability of the stack's performance is to test it thoroughly while you're building it and after it's completed. We've been testing as we go, but you should still go back and try all the buttons in different orders when the project is completed. This kind of exhaustive testing isn't always possible with large, complex stacks, so we'll look later at other ways to ensure stack reliability.

Designing an intuitive and functional user interface is a process that generally begins long before you sit down in front of the computer. But for this stack we'll simply look at the existing design and ask ourselves the question, "If I were a naive user with little or no HyperCard experience, what problems would I encounter with this stack?"

Adding Emergency Exits

Of course, we'll want to look at the screens as we answer this question. But it's also helpful to examine a flowchart or **map** of the stack:

This diagram reveals a major design flaw: The stack is like a one-way street with a dead end; buttons lead you into the King's Chamber, but there's no button to take you out.

Always give the user at least one exit from each card.

Let's add a button to return to the first card in the stack.

☐ **Select the Button tool.**

☐ **Select New Button from the Objects menu.**

☐ **Double-click on the button.**

☐ **Type "Click here to return".**

☐ **Click on the LinkTo... button.**

☐ **Press Command-1 to go to the first card in the stack.**

☐ **Click on the This Card button to complete the link.**

☐ **Change the shape and location of the button so it looks like this:**

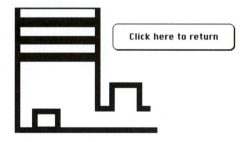

Finally, add a visual effect.

☐ **Click on the Effect... button.**

☐ **Select "zoom open" and click on Very Slow.**

☐ **Click on OK.**

Now let's test the button.

☐ **Select the Browse tool (Command-Tab).**

☐ **Click on the new button.**

You should be back outside the pyramid on card 1.

You've used two different visual effects so far. Here's a complete list of the available effects:

HyperCard Visual Effects

Effect	*Suggested Use*
dissolve	for gradual transitions
iris open	go to a card providing more detail
iris close	return after an iris open
zoom open (or zoom out)	go to a card providing more detail
zoom close (or zoom in)	return after zoom open
wipe left	go to next card
wipe right	go to previous card
wipe up	go to next card
wipe down	go to previous card
scroll left	go to next card
scroll right	go to previous card
scroll up	go to next card
scroll down	go to previous card
barn door open	introduce a topic
barn door close	end a topic
checkerboard	use between cards with high contrast
venetian blinds	use between cards with high contrast
shrink to top	flip to next card
shrink to center	flip to next card
shrink to bottom	flip to next card
stretch from top	flip to previous card
stretch from center	flip to previous card
stretch from top	flip to previous card

Of course, these effects can be used in other ways; it pays to experiment. Changing the speed can change the impact of an effect, too.

Borrowing a Button

We're almost through; all that remains is to provide the naive user with a graceful way to exit the stack and go Home. We need another button, but we won't create this one from scratch.

☐ **Press Command-H (Go Home).**

☐ **Click on the Addresses icon to open the Addresses stack.**

Addresses

Home

☐ **Select the Button tool from the Tools palette.**

☐ **Click on the Home button to select it.**

☐ **Press Command-C (or select Copy Button from the Edit menu).**

Because the Button tool is selected, the Copy command now says Copy Button instead of Copy Picture. You now have a copy of the Home button on the Clipboard.

☐ **Press Command-~ twice to go back two cards, so you're looking at the pyramid again.**

☐ **Press Command-V (or select Paste Button).**

A shimmering copy of the Home button, complete with icon, should appear.

☐ **Drag this button to the lower right corner of the window.**

This is not just a lookalike button; it comes complete with instructions to make it do exactly what the original did: Take you home. Let's test it.

☐ **Select the Browse tool (Command-Tab).**

☐ **Click the new Home button.**

You're home! Now let's go back and install similar buttons on the other cards in the stack so our users have a convenient exit at any level.

☐ **Press Command-~ to return to your stack.**

☐ **Select the Button tool.**

☐ **Select the Home button you just added and press Command-C to copy it to the Clipboard.**

Actually, we already had a copy of the button in the Clipboard, but not in the right position.

> When a button is copied from a card to the Clipboard and pasted on another card, it appears in the same relative location on both cards (until you move it).

- ☐ **Press Command-3 to go to the next card in the stack.**

- ☐ **Press Command-V to paste another copy of the Home button onto this card.**

    It should appear in just the right spot. You still have one card in your stack without a Home button.

- ☐ **Press Command-3 to go to the next (and last) card in the stack.**

- ☐ **Paste another Home button here.**

    Here's a map of the stack as it now stands:

There's plenty more we could do to this stack: We could use the Eraser, the Paint Bucket, and the Pencil to soften the lines at the base of the pyramid; we could use the Spray Can with a sand-patterned paint to give the pyramid a weathered look; we could add buttons to the first card to reveal interesting facts, theories, and mysteries concerning the pyramid; we could add buttons to the cross section to zoom in on the other chambers of the pyramid—the possibilities are limited only by our creativity and time.

But that's enough for now. Take a couple of minutes to try out the stack, making sure that you understand what it's doing each time you click a button.

We've covered a lot of ground in this session. The tools and procedures you've used to build this stack can be used to build dynamic business charts, educational presentations, interactive tutorials, multi-level maps, and all kinds of other stacks. The exercises at the end of this session will suggest several projects that you might want to try on your own to practice your new skills. In the next session you'll learn more HyperCard tricks that will make it even easier to build your own stacks.

Summary

In this session we've focused on the fundamentals of stack construction. You learned how to create new stacks and new cards. You used the Pencil tool, the Straight Line tool, various shape tools, the Paint Bucket, the Paintbrush, and the Patterns palette to draw pictures on cards. You used the Clipboard, the Undo command, and the Eraser to edit those pictures. You practiced using paint text in a variety of styles, sizes, and alignments. You learned how to create buttons, label them, size them, position them, add visual effects, and link them to other cards. Finally, you learned how to copy buttons from other stacks into your own stack. Nice work!

Key Words

alignment (text)
Auto Hilite (button)
bit
bit-mapped graphics
Brush Shape... command
constraint (Shift) key
Copy Button command
  (Command-C)
Copy Picture command
  (Command-C)
Draw Filled command
Effect... button
Eraser tool
field text
font
general tools
Grid command
Keep command
  (Command-K)
Lasso

Line Size... command
link
LinkTo... (button)
map
New Button command
New Stack... command
Objects menu
Paintbrush tool
Paint Bucket tool
paint text
Paint Text tool
paint tools
Paste Button command
  (Command-V)
Paste Picture command
  (Command-V)
Patterns menu
Patterns palette
Pencil tool
pixel

point (size)
Polygon tool
Rectangle tool
Revert command
Rounded Rectangle tool
Select All command
  (Command-A)
Select command
  (Command-S)
Selection rectangle
Show name (button)
size (text)

software engineering
Straight Line tool
style (text)
tear-off menu
Text Style... command
  (Command-T)
Tools menu
Tools palette
transparent (button style)
user interface
visual effect

Self-Testing Exercises

1. Under what conditions are the Paint and Objects menus visible?

2. What's the best way to draw a perfect square in HyperCard?

3. While putting the finishing touches on your drawing of Mom, you sneeze and make her ear way too big. Name two ways you can erase the offending line.

4. What's the fastest way to erase everything you've painted on the current card?

5. Describe how you can use the Clipboard to duplicate a button on a different card and to duplicate a portion of a picture on a different card.

6. List three visual effects, what they do, and suggested uses for each one.

7. What do each of these standard HyperCard tool icons represent?

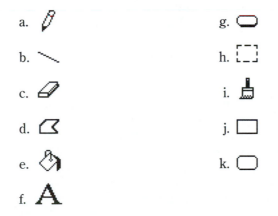

a.

b.

c.

d.

e.

f. A

g.

h.

i.

j.

k.

8. Many of the tools shown in question 7 have a special meaning when double-clicked. Which special meanings can you remember?

Projects

1. Draw a tree chart showing the organization of the top levels of government. Your chart should contain a box labeled U.S. Constitution with three subordinate boxes representing the three government branches (executive, legislative, judicial). Create buttons for each of these subordinate boxes and link those buttons to cards that illustrate, describe, or subdivide those branches. Add a return button to each new card and a Home button to the main chart card.

2. Draw a map of a baseball field with buttons on each fielder's position linked to "baseball cards" for each of these fielders on your favorite team. Include return buttons on each card and a Home button on the baseball field card.

3. Draw a chart representing at least three generations of your family tree. Add a button to each node and link each button to a card containing a description of that family member. Include a return button on each card and a Home button on the main tree card.

4. Draw a flowchart representing the major components of a computer (input, CPU, output, storage device). Add buttons to each of the boxes and link those buttons to cards describing and illustrating those components. Include return buttons on each card and a Home button on the main card.

5. Draw a hyper-greeting card. On the first card of the stack, draw the outside of the card, complete with graphics and the first part of the message. Add a button with a "click here" message and link it to the inside of the card containing the punch line and signature. Now go back and modify the original button's message and add a second button to the outside of the card offering the recipient an alternative message ("click here if you're male" on one, "click here if you're female" on the other; "click here if you're over/under 40"; click here if you want a plausible excuse/the truth," etc.) The two buttons should link to different inside cards with different messages; both of these cards should have Home buttons on them.

6. Draw a map of your house, school, or dorm. Place a transparent button on your room that will reveal a close-up view of your room. Add a return button to the close-up and a Home button to the original map. Variations: Draw expandable maps of your city, your state, your country, the world, the solar system, or the galaxy.

SESSION 4

Objectives

By the end of this session you should be able to

- Use all of the HyperCard paint tools and understand how the effects of many of these tools can be modified using menu commands and various keystroke combinations
- Use HyperCard's background layer to give cards in your stack a consistent look
- Create a stack with multiple backgrounds
- Design and build a complex network of cards to simulate a real-world environment

HYPERCARD'S HIDDEN LAYERS:

BACKGROUNDS AND BACKTRACKING

The Problem

Your cousin Andy—the smart one—is spending tomorrow afternoon at your house. You have no time for playing games with him; you're busy learning HyperCard. But you expect he'll leave you little choice unless you provide him with something interesting to do. What you'd like to do is throw Andy in a dungeon that's full of so many rooms and passages that it would take him all afternoon to find his way back to you. Perhaps HyperCard can help.

Introduction

You know how to build stacks now, but you still haven't learned about some of HyperCard's most impressive and useful stack-building tools. The paint box is full of surprises, both fun and practical. And all of the paint tools become doubly useful once you learn how to take advantage of HyperCard's multiple layers.

Every card has two layers—a transparent **card layer** and a **background layer**—and you can put text, graphics, and buttons on either layer. This simple idea is one of HyperCard's most powerful concepts. Unfortunately, many beginners also find it to be among HyperCard's most puzzling concepts. But as you work through this session's project, you'll find that those layers are crystal clear—and convenient, too.

This session's project is more complex than the last one. Consequently, there are more ways things can go wrong. So we'll spend some time looking at ways we can design the stack that will minimize the chances of errors.

Some Background on Backgrounds

Let's start by looking behind the scenes at Home to see how backgrounds work in a familiar environment.

Examining Home's Backgrounds

☐ **Turn on your computer. If you're using a hard disk, boot from the hard disk before inserting your Home disk. Otherwise, insert your system/Home disk(s) to boot the computer.**

☐ **Double-click on the Home stack icon.**

☐ **Choose Background from the Edit menu.**

(If your Edit menu doesn't have a Background command, your user level is probably not set at authoring; change that on the last card of the Home stack as before.)

You should see two changes:

1. The text and icons have vanished from the Home card, leaving some buttons at the bottom of the window and the word Home at the top.

2. The menu bar has grown candy **stripes**.

The stripes are there to remind you that you're looking, not at a card, but at a background.

☐ **Use the right-arrow key to browse through the stack while in background mode.**

You'll see the background for each card in the stack. In this stack each card has a unique background, but all the backgrounds have common design elements. Contrast this with the Addresses stack used in Session 2, in which almost all the cards share a common fill-in-the-blanks background.

☐ **Select Background from the Edit menu again, or use the keyboard shortcut, Command-B, to return to the card (foreground) layer.**

The Benefits of Backgrounds

In most stacks, the same background is shared by several, sometimes all, of the cards. There are practical and aesthetic advantages to designing a stack this way:

- It saves stack creation time, because you don't need to create or copy common elements on many different cards; you can build them once in the common background.

- It saves space on disk and in memory, because the stack isn't filled with redundant elements.

- It usually results in a more consistent user interface, which helps the user to find her way around.

- It gives the stack a more consistent, appealing look.

When we built the Pyramid stack, we left the background plain white and focused on the card layer. In this session we'll create a stack with several different backgrounds to maximize efficiency.

A HyperCard Adventure

Let's build a HyperCard dungeon to occupy cousin Andy. The dungeon will have all kinds of rooms linked together by doors, windows, and secret passages . . . and only one way out.

This is one variation on a popular kind of computer game known as the **adventure game.** Some adventure games are text-based **interactive fiction** in which the reader types commands to tell the main character what to do. Others, like the one we'll create, use graphics instead of text to show the setting and develop the plot of the game. Whatever its form, an adventure game can be thought of as a computer **simulation** of a real or not-so-real environment and situation.

A graphic adventure game is a perfect project for HyperCard; each room can be represented on one or more cards in a stack; hidden buttons can transport the player to other rooms. To save time and minimize duplication, we can create generic rooms in the background layer and fill in the details on the card layer.

Starting a Stack

Before we get started, it's only fair to warn you: Creating a maze can be as confusing as navigating a maze. If you don't pay attention and carefully follow every step of this process, you may become as lost as your intended audience. Check each step with a pencil as you complete it so you can be sure that you don't skip any steps. Focus on understanding the structure of the stack more than on making the graphics perfect. If you're working on a complex graphic, use the Keep command (Command-K) regularly to save your work in progress, so you don't risk losing your train of thought while you reconstruct a spoiled picture. Pay attention to whether you're in the card layer or the background layer throughout the session (the striped bar in the margin of this text indicates work in the background). If you don't understand why you're doing something, read ahead to find out. If you lose your bearings, backtrack through the steps until you find the point where you wandered off the path. If, in spite of everything, your stack becomes hopelessly botched, don't despair. If you don't have time to start fresh, simply read through the rest of the session, focusing on understanding the underlying concepts.

☐ **Select New Stack... from the File menu.**

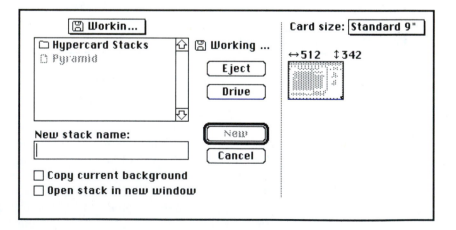

Make sure the disk shown in the window is your disk. Also, make sure neither of the check boxes are marked—you don't want your new stack to use the Home card's background, and you don't need to keep Home open in a separate window.

☐ **Type "Dungeon" and press Return.**

We now have the simplest stack of all: one card with a transparent card layer and an all-white background. Let's gather our tools and go to work on the background.

☐ **Tear off the Tools menu and place it in the upper right corner of the screen.**

☐ **Click on any paint tool to make the paint menus (Paint, Options, Patterns) appear.**

☐ **Drag the Patterns menu to the left side of the screen directly opposite the Tools palette.**

Drawing in the Background

☐ **Press Command-B (or select Background from the Edit menu).**

Every good adventure game needs an enticing introduction, preferably scrawled on a tattered scroll. So let's create a scroll in the background.

> It's easy to forget to change to the background layer, so always check the menu for stripes to make sure you are working in the background.

All of the paint tools work in the background just as they do in the card layer. Let's start by drawing one edge of our scrolled message:

☐ **Select the Pencil and draw a three-inch squiggly line something like the one shown at the left.**

If you don't get it right the first time, remember Command-Z, the Undo command.

☐ **Use the Selection rectangle to select the line and drag it until it's close to the Patterns palette but not hidden by it.**

That's the left side of the scroll; we need another line just like this one for the other side. We *could* copy and paste one, but we'll use the Option key to clone it instead.

☐ **Hold down the Shift and Option keys and drag the selected line until it's near, but not touching, the Tools palette.**

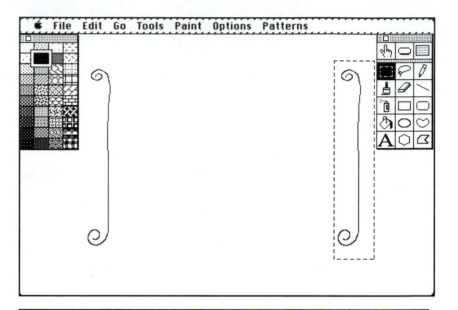

When Dragging a Selected Graphic Object

- The Shift key constrains the movement to horizontal or vertical only.

- The Option key leaves a copy behind.

- If you hold down the Command key and drag the *edge* of the object, the object doesn't move; it stretches or shrinks.

- If you hold down the Command and Shift keys and drag the *corner* of the object, the object stretches or shrinks while maintaining its original proportions.

Note: **Stretching** or **shrinking** bit-mapped graphics usually results in distortion, especially if you don't maintain proportions.

We have the sides; now let's draw the top and bottom of the scroll.

☐ **Use the Straight Line tool to connect the tops of the two lines.**

Remember the trick from the last session: If you hold down the Shift key when you drag between two points, you'll find that it's a cinch to draw perfectly horizontal (or vertical) lines.

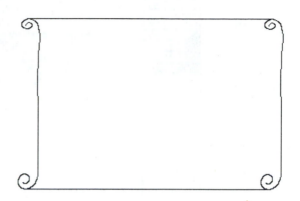

It's a start, but it's still not a scroll.

☐ **Add straight lines to the two left scroll corners, like this:**

Now we need to eliminate the curls from the right side of the scroll using the Eraser and the Pencil. The Eraser's large, square shape makes it awkward for that kind of fine detail work. We can't make the Eraser smaller, but we can make the details of the picture bigger.

☐ **Click once on the upper right corner of your scroll.**

You're telling HyperCard what part of the picture you want to focus on. Don't worry if you leave a mark there; you can erase it soon enough.

☐ **Double-click on the Pencil tool to zoom in for an extreme close-up.**

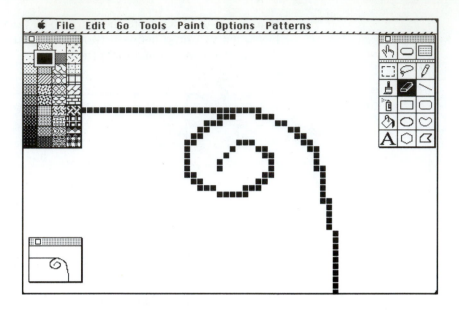

The Options menu command for doing the same thing is called **FatBits**. It's easy to see why, if you remember that each pixel (dot) on HyperCard's bit-mapped screen is represented by a bit in the computer's memory. In FatBits each of these bits is exactly eight times fatter than normal. The small window in the corner of the screen displays a normal magnification view of the same portion of your picture.

☐ **Use the Pencil and/or the Eraser to remove the unwanted curl from the picture.**

☐ **Hold down the Option key and use the Hand tool to drag the magnified picture up so that you can follow the scroll edge down to the curl in the lower right corner.**

☐ **Remove the unwanted curl in the lower right corner of the scroll.**

☐ **If necessary, use FatBits to touch up the other two corners of your scroll, making sure that all of the lines connect.**

☐ **Exit FatBits by clicking in the small normal view window (or select FatBits from the Options menu).**

FatBits Tips

- The Pencil is probably the most useful FatBits tool, because it allows you to turn each pixel on or off with just a touch. As usual, the Pencil draws black if you start on a white pixel and white if you start on black.

- The Eraser is also helpful because in FatBits it is much smaller relative to a pixel than it is in normal magnification.

- The other paint tools work in FatBits, but some may seem unwieldy at that magnification level.

- If you hold down the Option key while in FatBits, the pointer turns into a hand that you can use to drag the magnified picture so the FatBits window reveals a different part of the picture.

- The picture is shown actual size in the small window.

- You can return to normal magnification by clicking on the small normal view window or by selecting FatBits again.

Let's add a background pattern to this background layer.

☐ **Select a medium gray pattern.**

☐ **Use the Paint Bucket tool to paint the area surrounding the scroll.**

Before you do anything else, check to make sure that only the area around the scroll was painted. If part of the scroll changed, you'll need to select Undo, fix the leak, and repaint the areas.

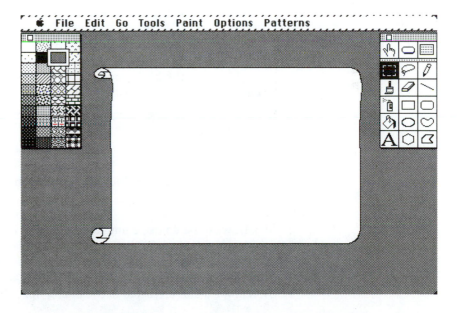

If you like, you can return to this background layer later to add some weathering and shading around the edges with the Spray Can and other tools. For now, let's leave the background and add words and a button to the card layer.

☐ **Press Command-B (or select Background from Edit).**

The only change you should notice is that the candy stripes vanished in the menu bar. We're now working in the card layer, but everything looks the same because *the card layer is transparent until you put something on it.*

If you missed the warnings at the beginning of this section, you might have just realized that you were drawing in the wrong layer. Don't worry; it happens to everybody, and it's easy to fix.

Oops! Wrong Layer!

If you create a drawing on the card layer that should have been in the background, you can move it like this:

1. In the card layer double-click on the lasso to select everything that's drawn in that layer.

2. Press Command-X (Cut Picture).

3. Press Command-B (Background).

4. Press Command-V (Paste Picture).

In general, any graphic, button, or field can be moved from the card layer to the background (or vice versa) by selecting, cutting, changing layers, and pasting.

Creating Titles

A   ☐ **Double-click on the Paint Text tool to bring up the Text Styles dialog box.**

Ideally, we'd like to use a font that looks like it was drawn by a medieval scribe. Such fonts exist, but not in the standard Apple system package. We'll use London here, but you can choose any font that you have in your System in a large size. (Remember that the sizes stored in your System for a font are listed in the dialog box when you select that font.)

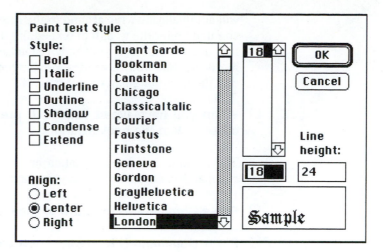

☐ **Select a font; then select the largest available size for your chosen font.**

☐ **Select Center alignment and click OK.**

When you put away this dialog box, you'll find that the Paint Text tool is automatically selected; HyperCard is anticipating your needs.

☐ **Click about a half-inch from the top of your scroll near the center.**

☐ **Type something like this, pressing Return at the end of each line:**

Since you're working with paint text, you don't have access to all of the conveniences of field text. Specifically, you can't assume that the text will automatically wrap around to the next line when one line is full, and you don't have the wealth of text-editing tools that we used in Session 2. If you make an error, your only recourse is to backspace to the offending characters and retype the remainder of the text. Once you reposition the insertion point or select another tool, your text is dried paint.

☐ **When you have typed your text, press Command-B to take another look at the background.**

The background doesn't contain any of the words you typed; it's still clean and available for use on your next card.

☐ **Press Command-B to return to the card layer.**

☐ **Press Command-N to create a new card.**

You're whisked out of the background layer and onto a new card that looks just like the old one, except that this one contains no text.

> When you create a new card with the New Card command (Command-N), the new card shares a background with the current card and is positioned directly after it in the stack.

Let's add some text to this card.

☐ **Double-click on the Paint Text tool, select Left alignment, and click OK.**

☐ **Position the insertion bar near the upper left corner of the scroll and type the following, pressing Return after each line:**

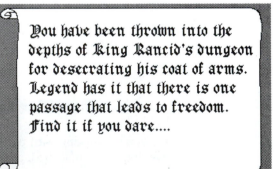

Borrowing a Background Button

We have two introductory cards, but no buttons to link the cards to each other and to the game. We *could* put a button on each card specifically linked to the following card, just as we did in the last session. But since these two cards share a background, we could install one "Go to the next card" button in the background layer that will service both cards. We can borrow just such a button from the Home stack.

☐ **Press Command-H to go Home.**

☐ **Press Command-4 to go to the last card.**

☐ **Select the Button tool.**

☐ **Click on the right-arrow button.**

This button takes you to the next card in the stack no matter where you are. That's exactly what we want our button to do.

☐ **Press Command-C to copy the button to the Clipboard.**

☐ **Press Command-~ twice to go back to your Dungeon stack.**

☐ **Press Command-B to go to the background.**

☐ **Press Command-V to paste the button.**

☐ **Drag the button to a position near the bottom of the scroll.**

All we need to do now is change the look of the button so that it fits in with the medieval decor.

☐ **Double-click on the button to open the Button Info dialog box.**

☐ **Double-click on the Icon... button in the dialog box.**

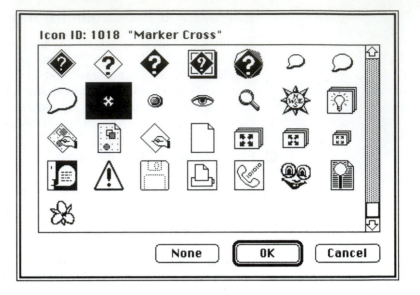

Icon ID: 1018 "Marker Cross"

☐ **Scroll through the icons, select an appropriate icon for the period, and click OK.**

Now let's change the visual effect.

☐ **Double-click on the button to bring up the Button Info dialog box.**

☐ **Click on the Effect... button.**

☐ **Click on stretch from center, Slow, and OK.**

☐ **Press Command-B to leave the background.**

☐ **Press Command-Tab to select the Browse tool (the pointing hand).**

☐ **Click on the button to try it.**

We've changed the look, but not the function, of the button. It takes us to the next card in the stack, whatever that might be.

A button created with the LinkTo... procedure is hard-wired to a particular card by an **absolute reference**. A button that says "Go to next card" uses a **logical reference** to link to the next card, whatever it might be. Computer spreadsheet users deal with a similar distinction every day when working with formulas in cells. So do you, unconsciously, when a stranger asks you, "Where is the office for the local newspaper?" The absolute answer, "435 Madison Street," is helpful if your questioner wants to send letters that will reach the editor from any mailbox in town. The logical answer, "six blocks south" or "the end of the street" is more helpful if the questioner has an appointment to meet with the editor today.

Each of these reference types has advantages and disadvantages. Absolute links (Go to this card; Go Home) take you to the specified destination card no matter how many or which cards are in between. Logical links (Go Next, Go Last) allow you to add cards to or remove cards from a sequence without having to relink the cards on either side. A logical "Go Next" button installed in the background can replace many absolute "Go to this card" buttons installed on the card layer. You'll see how each of these link types can be used in other situations as you progress through this book

Break Point

Creating a New Background

Our next card will be the first room of the dungeon. If we simply select New Card, the card we create will have the scroll background. We need to tell HyperCard to create a new card with a new background.

☐ **Go to the last card in the stack by pressing Command-4.**

☐ **Select New Background from the Objects menu.**

The menu bar is striped to indicate that we're working in the background—a new background that we'll use for the next few cards. We want to create a sort of generic dungeon room that can be customized in the card layer for different rooms in the dungeon.

> The **New Background** command creates a new card with a new background directly after the current card.

☐ **Select the Rectangle tool.**

☐ **Double-check the menu bar to make sure you're in the background. Then draw a rectangle like this in the center of the screen:**

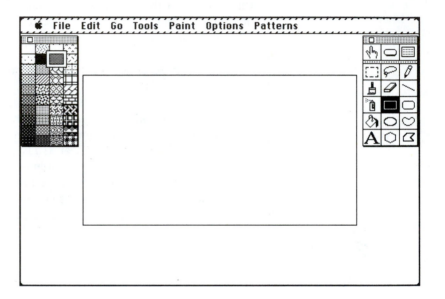

Use the Patterns palette and the Tools palette as guides when you're creating your rectangle. The exact size isn't important, as long as you do your best to center it.

☐ **Use the Straight Line tool to draw lines from each corner of the rectangle to the corresponding corner of the screen.**

For the top two corners, you'll need to drag the line behind the menu bar to the absolute corner of the screen.

> The top of a card may be obscured by the menu bar, but it's still there. You can press Command-Space to temporarily hide the menu bar so you can see what you're painting.

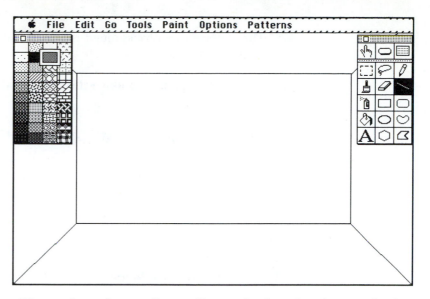

We now have three walls, a ceiling, and a floor, but they need paint.

☐ **Select the Paint Bucket tool and medium gray paint pattern.**

☐ **Pour that paint into the bottom (floor) and top (ceiling) sections of your picture.**

☐ **Select an irregular dot pattern or a light gray pattern and paint the three remaining sections with the Paint Bucket.**

It's tempting to use the brick paint for the walls, but if we use that or any other regular pattern on the side walls, the illusion of perspective we've created will be shattered.

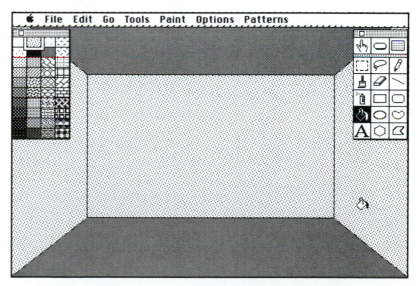

The generic room background is finished and ready to be customized on the card layer.

☐ **Press Command-B to leave the background.**

Shaping Doors and Windows

Let's start with a door.

☐ **Double-click on the Rectangle tool (or choose Draw Filled from the Options menu).**

☐ **Select a likely-looking pattern for the door.**

☐ **Select the Rectangle tool.**

☐ **Draw a door in the far wall of the room, like this:**

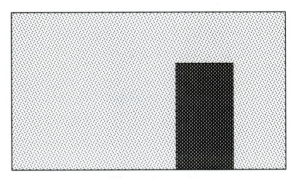

Notice how the door obscures the background.

> Objects drawn on the card layer hide anything behind them in the background layer (unless you specify that the object is transparent).

If this is truly a dungeon, it should have a barred window on the door. We could draw a window and then draw bars, but we can do a better job faster by creating a bar pattern.

☐ **Double-click on the black pattern in the Patterns palette (or choose Edit Pattern... from the Options menu).**

The box on the left shows you the currently selected pattern close-up; the one on the right shows it at normal size.

You can edit this pattern by clicking or dragging on the pixels in the left box; the results are immediately reflected on the right.

☐ **Draw the pattern shown here and then click OK:**

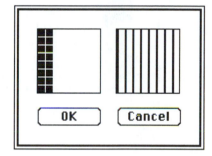

Notice how the original pattern has been replaced in the palette.

☐ **Select the new pattern and draw a rectangle in the center of the door like this:**

Now, in the spirit of covering our tracks, we should put that pattern back the way we found it.

☐ **Double-click on the bar pattern and edit it so it's all black again. Click OK.**

Let's add one more door to the side wall.

☐ **Drag the Patterns palette below the Tools palette.**

☐ **On the left wall draw a black rectangle that's taller and thinner than the first door.**

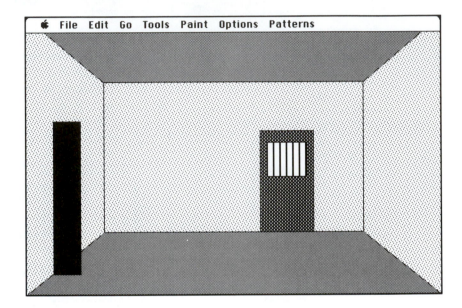

☐ **Use the Selection tool (the dashed rectangle) to select the black rectangle. (Make the marquee as close to the actual size and door as you can make it without leaving any part of the door out of the selection.**

Now we can apply a special paint effect to the selected area.

☐ **Select Perspective from the Options menu.**

The corners of the selected rectangle should have handles.

☐ **Drag the upper right corner of the rectangle down and the lower right corner up, changing the shape of the rectangle into a parallelogram, like this:**

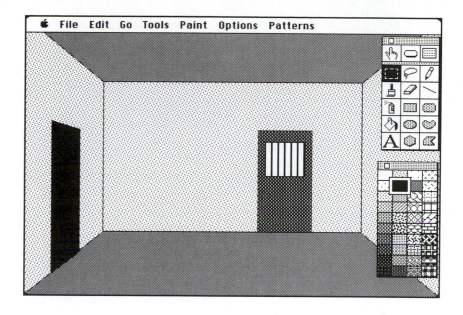

Rotate   Slant   Distort   Perspective

The **Rotate, Slant, Distort,** and **Perspective** commands in the Options menu can be applied to any area of a picture selected with the Selection tool. Each command produces handles on the selected rectangle; the handles can be dragged to produce the desired effect. Because HyperCard graphics are bit-mapped, the effect may take considerable time to appear and any text or fine graphics in the area may be distorted. **Rotate Right** and **Rotate Left** (Paint menu) quickly rotate any selected graphic, rectangular or not, 90 degrees.

Note: To simulate three-dimensional space in two-dimensional drawings, artists must follow certain rules of perspective. The Perspective command will not produce realistic three-dimensional perspective unless you also follow those rules.

This will be the door into the other chamber of our luxury dwelling. We need a button to take us there.

Creating a Two-Way Link

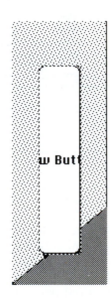

☐ **Select the Button tool.**

☐ **Select New Button from the Objects menu.**

Objects
Button Info...
Field Info...
Card Info...
Bkgnd Info...
Stack Info...

Bring Closer   ⌘·
Send Farther   ⌘·

New Button
New Field
New Background

> ⌐ **New Button** ⌐

☐ **Drag and reshape the button so that it covers the door on the left wall:**

☐ **Double-click on the button.**

Follow these familiar steps to fill in the dialog box:

☐ **Click on Show Name check box to turn it off.**

☐ **Click on Transparent.**

☐ **Type "room 1 door" (this step is optional).**

☐ **Click on Effect....**

☐ **Click on scroll right and OK.**

```
Button Name: room 1 door
Bkgnd button number: 1
Bkgnd button ID: 1
☐ Show Name          Style:
☐ Auto Hilite        ⦿ Transparent
☒ Shared Hilite      ○ Opaque
                     ○ Rectangle
   Icon...           ○ Shadow
                     ○ Round Rect
   Effect...         ○ Check Box
   LinkTo...         ○ Radio Button
   Script...      [   OK   ] [ Cancel ]
```

All that remains is to link the button.

☐ **Double-click on the button to bring back the Button Info dialog box.**

☐ **Click on LinkTo...**

```
Link to:
[ This Card ]  [ This Stack ]  [ Cancel ]
```

☐ **Press Command-N (or select New Card from Edit).**

The new card has the generic room background and is located after the starting room card in the stack.

☐ **Click on the This Card button.**

You're back in the starting room. As long as we're back in this room, let's borrow the black door so we can make it visible in the new room.

☐ **Hold down the Command key while dragging the selection rectangle around the black door.**

Holding down the Command Key forces the Selection rectangle to select only the door.

☐ **Press Command-C (Copy Picture).**

☐ **Press Command-3 (Next).**

☐ **Press Command-V (Paste Picture).**

We've put the door into the next room, but it's backward.

☐ **Choose Flip Horizontal from the Paint menu.**

☐ **Move the Tools and Patterns palettes out of the way and drag the door until it's positioned in the center of the right wall.**

The white areas are there because the selected picture is opaque; you can't see the background through it.

☐ **Select Transparent from the Paint menu.**

> The **Transparent** command allows the background to show through the nonblack portions of the selected graphic; **Opaque** turns those portions white so they hide the background. Neither command has any effect on buttons or fields.

Now the door is visible from both sides of the wall. But as it stands now, it's a one-way trip. We need to place an invisible button on the backside of the door that links back to the first room.

☐ **Click on the Button tool.**

☐ **Select New Button from the Objects menu.**

☐ **Drag and reshape the new button so that it covers the door.**

☐ **Double-click on the button to bring up the Button Info dialog box.**

☐ **Click on Show Name in the dialog box to turn it off.**

☐ **Click on Transparent.**

☐ **Type "room 2 door" (this step is optional).**

☐ **Click on Effect....**

☐ **Click on scroll left and OK.**

☐ **Double-click on the button to bring back the Button Info dialog box.**

☐ **Click on LinkTo....**

You'll see this familiar window, but you won't create a new card. This button should take you back.

```
┌─────────────────────────────────────┐
│ ☐                                    │
│  Link to:                            │
│  ( This Card )  ( This Stack )  ( Cancel )│
│                                      │
└─────────────────────────────────────┘
```

☐ **Press Command-2 (Go Back).**

☐ **Click on the This Card button.**

☐ **Press Command-Tab (Browse tool) and test the door both ways.**

Break Point

Building Portable Furniture

No good dungeon is complete without a secret passage. Let's build a bed and hide our passage underneath. We'll start by drawing a pillow.

☐ **Go to the last card in the stack (the room with only one door)**

☐ **Choose a pattern for the pillow.**

☐ **Select the Curve tool.**

The Curve tool works pretty much like the Pencil, except that the drawn shape fills automatically if Draw Filled is selected.

☐ **Draw a pillow anywhere, as long as it doesn't touch the door.**

(We're in the card layer, and the door is the only other painted object on this layer. As long as we don't put the pillow on the door, we can move it where we want later.)

If you can see the background pattern through your pillow, Hyper-Card thinks you want everything on this card layer to be transparent. Here's how to fix that.

☐ **Double-click on the Lasso to select all graphics in this layer.**

☐ **Select Opaque from the Paint menu.**

(If you had double-clicked on the Selection rectangle instead of the Lasso, the entire area inside the rectangle, including the area between graphic objects, would become opaque, hiding the background com-pletely.)

Now let's draw the bed.

☐ **Choose a pattern for the ends of the bed.**

☐ **Use the (filled) Rectangle tool to create a rectangle in the corner of the room, like the top one in this picture.**

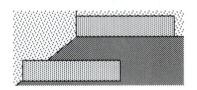

☐ **Choose Select from the Paint menu to select the new rectangle.**

☐ **Option-drag the rectangle to create the other end of the bed.**

☐ **Select the Polygon tool.**

☐ **Choose a pattern for the bedspread.**

☐ **Click around the corners of the top of the bed ends to create the shape for the top of the bed.**

When you click on the first point a second time, the shape should fill.

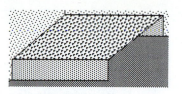

☐ **Click on the corners of the side of the bed to define its shape.**

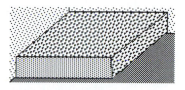

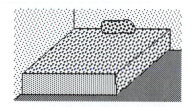 ☐ **Select the Lasso tool.**

☐ **Drag a line around the outside of the pillow without actually touching the edge of it.**

You don't need to drag all the way around the pillow; if you go most of the way and let go, the two ends of your curve will be connected automatically. When you let go, every painted object that's within the Lasso line in the card layer is selected, but none of the empty space between the objects or around the pillow is selected. The Lasso is a shrink-to-fit tool.

☐ **Drag the selected pillow onto the bed.**

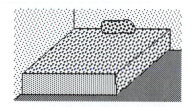

The Lasso is a particularly useful tool for selecting irregularly shaped objects, but it's not the only way. Let's revise the list of selection techniques we started in the last session:

Moving Furniture

If the secret passage is under the bed, we want to be able to move the bed with a click. We'll do that by linking a bed-sized button to a new card just like the current card, but with the bed in a different location. Repeat the now familiar steps for creating a linked button.

☐ **Select the Button tool.**

☐ **Select New Button from Objects.**

☐ **Drag and stretch the new button so it covers the bed, more or less.**

☐ **Double-click on the button to open the Button Info dialog box.**

☐ **Click on Transparent.**

- [ ] **Click on Show Name to turn off that option.**

- [ ] **Type "bed" (optional).**

- [ ] **Click on Effect....**

- [ ] **Click on wipe right and OK.**

- [ ] **Double-click on the button to bring back the Button Info dialog box.**

- [ ] **Click on LinkTo....**

- [ ] **Press Command-N (New Card).**

- [ ] **Click on the This Card button.**

- [ ] **Double-click on the Lasso to select all of the objects in this layer.**

  You can easily copy them all to the new card.

- [ ] **Press Command-C (Copy Picture).**

- [ ] **Press Command-3 (Next).**

- [ ] **Press Command-V (Paste Picture).**

  This card now looks just like the other one. It should, except that the bed must be moved to reveal the secret passage.

- [ ] **Lasso the bed and drag it to the right a couple of inches.**

  Where's the secret passage?

- [ ] **Select black paint and the Oval tool.**

- [ ] **Draw a black oval where the bed was originally.**

There's the secret opening, waiting for a button to link it to a new room or passage. Until that button is installed, the door is the only exit.

☐ **Press Command-Tab (Browse) and click on the door.**

That won't take us out because we haven't installed a button *on this card*. We can fix that.

☐ **Press Command-2 (Back).**

☐ **Select the Button tool.**

☐ **Click on the Door button.**

☐ **Press Command-C (Copy Button).**

☐ **Press Command-3 (Next).**

☐ **Press Command-V (Paste Button).**

This button is an identical copy of the button from the previous card, so it should do just what the other was trained to do: Take us back to room 1. Try it.

☐ **Press Command-Tab (Browse).**

☐ **Click on the door.**

You're back in the first room.

☐ **Try clicking on the black door to reenter room 2.**

Stackware Engineering Revisited

Uncovering a Bug

At this point you might notice a minor flaw, or **bug**, in our simulated dungeon: The bed has moved back to its original position. Of course, that's because the Door button was linked to the card with the bed in the corner. If we had anticipated this problem, we could have set it up so that moving the bed blocked the door; then the bed would have to be moved back (via another button) before we could go through the door again.

Since this is only a game, we'll sidestep the problem by assuming that either the bed is an enchanted homing bed or this dungeon has incredible room service. And we'll make a note of one of the most important principles of stack design:

Time spent planning a stack is almost always less than the time wasted repairing an unplanned stack.

Planning a Network

A late plan is better than no plan at all, so let's diagram what we've done so far and figure out where we're going from here. Here's our basic map:

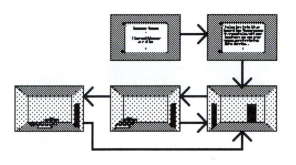

Map Tips

- When you're creating a complex stack, minimize errors by mapping the stack first.

- Show all possible links between cards on the map with arrows.

- Label the arrows with button names so the connections are obvious.

- Number the cards on the map to represent the order in which they'll be arranged in the stack.

- When you're constructing the stack, use the map as a visual checklist, checking off cards, links, and sections as you complete them.

One thing is clear from our map: This game, so far, isn't very interesting. We need more passages and pathways. We can start by adding a room with several exits: a couple of doors, a hidden passage, and a pit. Each of these exits will lead to other cards.

In the spirit of a good maze, some of these paths should be dead ends. We can, for example, have the Pit button link to a "Sorry, but you just fell into a pit of starving alligators" card. Other paths should wind back into rooms we've already seen. The two doors in the current room might connect to each other via a secret passage. Still other buttons will branch into multiple paths, only one of which ultimately leads to freedom.

We don't have time to develop a complete, lose-yourself-for-an-afternoon maze in this session, but our next diagram might look like this:

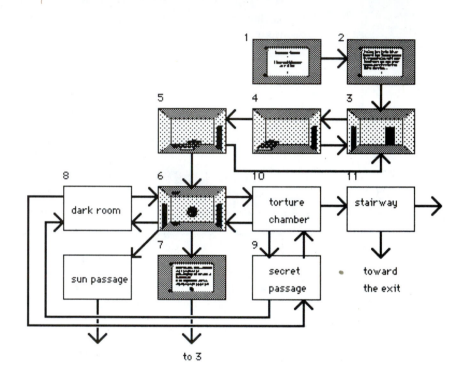

This kind of free-form structure is called a **network**. Network structures tend to be more error-prone than the sequences and loops we've worked with so far, because there are no real rules about the way they should be put together, and because there are so many loose ends to take care of. It's easy to leave things unconnected or to accidentally connect them incorrectly. That's why a map is so important.

Remembering the User

When we discussed software engineering in the last session, we focused on the user interface, developing guidelines to help users find their way around in a stack. Have we applied those guidelines this time around? We've provided the user with no Home or Quit buttons on any of the maze cards, and we've hidden all of the buttons; this stack is almost user-hostile by our earlier standards.

Of course, that's the point. If the buttons were all labeled "this way out" and "dead end" it wouldn't be much of a game. Still, a large, well-designed adventure game allows the player to quit before finishing, often allowing the player to save the current position so he or she can return at a later time. We're not equipped to do that in this session, but we can generalize the idea to an important principle that will make all of our stacks better:

> Always look at your stack design from the user's point of view.

Break Point

Secondhand Art

Since we're using the same backgrounds for so many rooms, it's important to add embellishments to each room so that it doesn't look like the last one. Embellishing dungeons can be time consuming, especially for nonartists. But we can always borrow.

Copying a Card

Let's start by borrowing a whole card, the one we just created.

☐ **If you aren't already there, go to the last card in the stack. Then select Copy Card from the Edit menu.**

A copy of this card—graphics, buttons, and all—is in the Clipboard, waiting to be pasted. We'll paste it as soon as we create a new button for the secret passage, using *almost* the same procedure we've done many times.

☐ **Select the Button tool.**

☐ **Select New Button from the Objects menu.**

☐ **Drag and stretch the new button so it covers the hole.**

☐ **Double-click on the button to open the Button Info dialog box.**

☐ **Click on Transparent.**

☐ **Click on Show Name to turn off that option.**

☐ **Type "hole under bed" (optional).**

☐ **Click on Effect....**

☐ **Click on scroll up and OK.**

☐ **Double-click on the button to bring back the Button Info dialog box.**

☐ **Click on LinkTo....**

Here's the new twist. Instead of using the New Card command, we'll paste a new card from the Clipboard.

☐ **Press Command-V (Paste Card).**

☐ **Click on the This Card button.**

As usual, you're carried back where you came from, but this time it's hard to tell, because the two cards look identical—for now.

☐ **Press Command-3 (Next).**

Deleting and Rearranging Graphics

It's easy to forget where we are—these two cards look so much alike. Let's change that.

☐ **Use the Lasso to select the bed.**

☐ **Press the Delete (Backspace) key to delete the selected bed.**

☐ **Select the black hole and Shift-Option-drag it straight up to the ceiling, leaving a copy behind.**

The top hole is the bottom of our secret passage; the bottom hole is a pit.

☐ **With the Option key held down, select the door with the Selection rectangle.**

This causes the Selection rectangle to shrink around the door like the Lasso.

☐ **Option-drag it to make a copy while leaving the original.**

☐ **Select Flip Horizontal and position the new door on the left wall.**

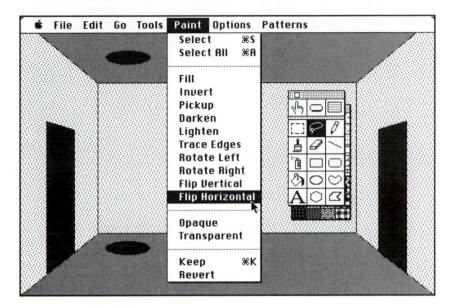

Borrowing Clip Art

 If you're using the Apple HyperCard package, you probably don't have the Art Bits stack. If you don't have that stack, read through the next few steps to the "Using Clip Art" box. At that point, use the paint tools to paint your own version of this sun on the wall of this card (in the card layer).

If you have the complete Claris HyperCard package, you can easily add some professionally drawn **clip art.**

Art Bits

☐ **Press Command-H to go Home.**

☐ **Click on the Art Bits icon.**

☐ **Read the Stack Overview and return to the Categories index.**

☐ **Click on Nature and Science and flip forward to the fourth of the five cards in this category by clicking on the arrows on the floating palette.**

☐ **Lasso (or Option-select with the Selection rectangle) the sun carving.**

☐ **Press Command-C (Copy Picture) (*not* Cut Picture!).**

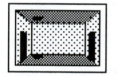

☐ **Press Command-R (Recent) and click on the miniature version of the unfinished dungeon room.**

☐ **Press Command-V (Paste Picture).**

☐ **Position the carving in the center of the wall.**

Here's the decorated room:

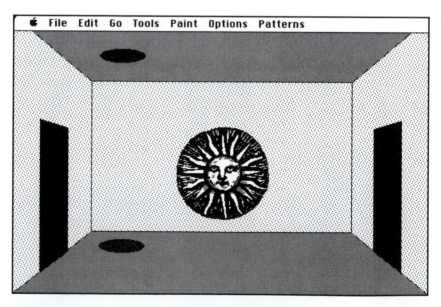

Using Clip Art

Clip art is available in a variety of formats. The Claris HyperCard package includes the Art Bits and Background Art stacks, but there's a much wider variety of HyperCard-appropriate clip art stored in **MacPaint** files. The **Import Paint...** command allows you to import MacPaint pictures directly into HyperCard, but this command gives you no control over what part of the 8 x 10 inch MacPaint image you'll use.

It's often more effective to open the clip art document with MacPaint, Studio 1, DeskPaint, SuperPaint, or some other paint application, copy to the Clipboard the portion of the picture you want, return to your HyperCard stack, and paste. (If you have several images to import, you can paste them all into the **Scrapbook** to minimize trips between your paint program and Hyper-Card.)

Appendix A describes paint applications, clip art sources, and **scanners** that allow you to turn drawings and photographs into HyperCard art.

Borrowing an Old Background

It's traditional in this kind of adventure game to display a message of condolences if the player blunders into an untimely death. We need to display just such a message if our unsuspecting player clicks on the pit. We should display the message on the scroll background that we used for our opening cards. How can we do that, though? If we create a new card here, the card will have the room background. If we go back to card 1 and create a new card, the background will be correct but the card will be in the wrong place. The solution is simple: Go to card 1, create a new card, and move that card to the end of the stack where it belongs.

☐ **Press Command-1 (First).**

☐ **Select New Card from the Edit menu.**

You're looking at a new card with a scroll background. It's located right after the first card in the stack.

☐ **Select Cut Card from the Edit menu.**

The new card is now in the Clipboard.

☐ **Press Command-4 (Last).**

☐ **Press Command-V (Paste Card).**

The card is now at the end of the stack.

☐ **Press Command-2 to go to the previous card in the stack.**

☐ **Select the Button tool.**

☐ **Select New Button from the Objects menu.**

☐ **Drag and stretch the new button so it covers the hole in the floor.**

☐ **Double-click on the button to open the Button Info dialog box.**

☐ **Click on Transparent.**

☐ **Click on Show Name to turn off that option.**

☐ **Type "pit" (optional).**

☐ **Click on Effect....**

☐ **Click on shrink to top and OK.**

☐ **Double-click on the Pit button.**

☐ **Click on LinkTo....**

☐ **Press Command-4 (Last).**

You're looking at your empty scroll card, right?

☐ **Click on This Card.**

☐ **Use the Browse tool to test the button.**

You've now linked the pit to the scroll card. It's time to fill in the scroll.

☐ **Double-click on the Paint Text tool, select your traditional font and size, and click OK.**

☐ **Type a message on your scroll like this:**

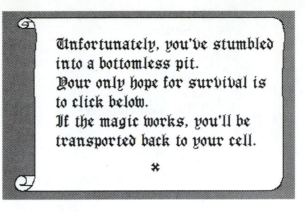

Unfortunately, you've stumbled into a bottomless pit.
Your only hope for survival is to click below.
If the magic works, you'll be transported back to your cell.

✻

There's only one problem. To find out what it is,

☐ **Press Command-Tab (Browse) and click on the button.**

This button, installed in the background, always goes to the next card, which in this case means wrapping around to Card 1. We want a different kind of button on this particular card. If we change the background button's link, that will change the link for all cards with this background. We can get around this problem by taking advantage of basic layering principles.

Buttons on Buttons

Buttons in the card layer can cover background buttons in the same way that card layer graphics cover background graphics. If a card layer button covers a background button, the card layer button takes precedence. It's also possible to cover one button with another button in the same layer. In general, the button on top takes precedence. **Bring Closer** and **Send Farther** commands (objects menu) can be used to rearrange objects so the one on top is the one you want to be on top.

☐ **Press Command-4 (Last).**

☐ **Select the Button tool.**

☐ **Select New Button.**

☐ Position and shape the new button so it covers the background button.

☐ Double-click on the new button to open the Button Info dialog box.

☐ Click on Opaque.

☐ Turn off Show Name.

☐ Click on Icon....

☐ Select a magical icon and double-click.

☐ Double-click on the icon to bring back the Button Info box.

☐ Click on Effect....

☐ Click on stretch from center, Slow, and OK.

☐ Double-click on the new button again.

☐ Click on LinkTo....

☐ Press Command-3 repeatedly until you see the first room card.

☐ Click on This Card.

☐ Use the Browse tool (Command-Tab) to try the new button.

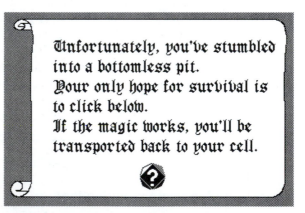

Unfortunately, you've stumbled into a bottomless pit.
Your only hope for survival is to click below.
If the magic works, you'll be transported back to your cell.

As your maze expands, you'll probably have lots of dead ends. Each time you need one, you can copy this card, complete with text, buttons, and background. When you paste the copy where it goes, all you need to change is the message. (In the interest of user friendliness, it might be a good idea to add a Home button to this card before you copy it.)

Loose Ends

Changing Links

Let's finish by illustrating another important design principle:

> Don't just tell the user; *show* the user.

Just for fun, let's add a graphic representation of the bottomless pit before the closing message. That means we'll have to insert a card between the pit room card and the final scroll, reconnecting the links as we do. The process is simple, provided you pay careful attention to what you're doing so you don't forget to tie everything up properly.

☐ **Press Command-4 (Last) and Command-2 (Previous).**

☐ **You should be looking at the room with the entrance to the pit.**

☐ **Select the Button tool and double-click on the Pit button.**

☐ **Click on LinkTo....**

☐ **Select New Background.**

☐ **Click on This Card.**

☐ **Press Command-3 to go to the new white card.**

☐ **Double-click on the Regular Polygon tool to choose a shape.**

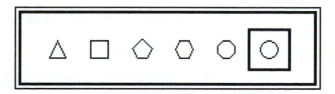

☐ **Click on the circle.**

Options
Grid
FatBits
Power Keys
———————
Line Size...
Brush Shape...
Edit Pattern...
Polygon Sides...
———————
Draw Filled
✓ Draw Centered
✓ Draw Multiple
———————
Rotate
Slant
Distort
Perspective

☐ Select **Draw Centered** and **Draw Multiple** from the Options menu. (If there's a check mark in front of Draw Filled in the menu, select Draw Filled to turn it off.)

☐ Drag from the center of the screen outward with an even motion, creating a series of concentric circles. Without lifting your finger from the mouse button, drag back toward the center if you need to fill gaps.

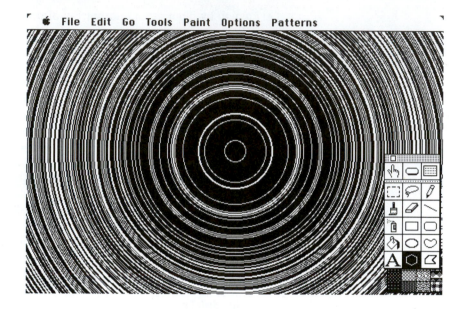

If necessary, double-click on the Eraser and repeat until you get the endless tunnel effect you like. (If you prefer, try one of the other shapes.)

We need a button to make this into a click-anywhere-to-continue screen.

☐ **Select the Button tool.**

☐ **Create a screen-sized new button.**

☐ **Double-click on the button to open the Button Info dialog box.**

☐ **Make it transparent.**

☐ **Turn on Auto Hilite and turn off Show Name.**

☐ **Click on Effect....**

☐ **Click checkerboard, Slow, and OK.**

☐ **Click on LinkTo....**

☐ **Press Command-3 (Next).**

You should be looking at the "sorry" scroll.

☐ **Click on the This Card button.**

☐ **Use the Browse tool to test the new button.**

Finishing the Game

There's still much to do before this game is finished, but you have the tools and techniques you need to carry it through on your own. If you want to continue, add buttons to the two doors and the sun picture in the last room, and link those buttons to new rooms. (You already have one button installed on the right-hand door, but it links to the wrong card. Why?) Don't be afraid to be creative, but keep in mind a few tips as you create:

Keeping Your Stack Orderly

- As you add cards, try to keep the overall stack in some kind of logical order.

- Remember that whenever you create a new card, that card is inserted immediately after the current card. If that's not where you want it, use Cut Card and Paste Card to move it.

- A nonlinear structure has to have some buttons that jump to other parts of the stack, but it's best to keep cards in logical groups as much as possible.

- Flip through all the cards in your stack with Command-3. It's easy to leave unfinished, unwanted cards embedded in a stack, and this is a good way to find them.

- If you find several cards that look alike, use temporary marks to flag them so you can tell them apart while you're troubleshooting; you can remove the extra cards and the marks when the job is done.

- Use Option-Command to reveal hidden buttons on each card; try each of these buttons. When you copy cards, you often end up with buttons that you didn't want linked to places you don't want to go.

As you expand this stack, practice borrowing cards, art, and buttons from other stacks until you're comfortable with the process. Try the paint tools and menu options that we haven't covered here, referring to the HyperCard Help stack, if available, for information and inspiration. Have fun!

Summary

In the process of building a game, you've learned a number of Hyper-Card concepts that you can apply directly to all kinds of serious and not-so-serious projects. You've used new paint tools and techniques to create complex graphic scenes. You've put buttons and graphics in backgrounds that were shared by several cards. You've seen the possible interaction between card and background objects, and you've learned how to take advantage of HyperCard layers to minimize your work and maximize your stack's efficiency and effectiveness. You've also discovered some of the pitfalls of designing and building a complex stack, and learned some principles that can help you avoid those pitfalls.

Next session you'll begin a journey underneath HyperCard's slick user interface into the fascinating world of HyperTalk. You'll see how this simple but powerful language can be used to add animation and sound effects to your presentations. You'll be amazed at the doors that a few well-chosen HyperTalk words can open for you!

Key Words

absolute reference (link)
adventure game
Background command
  (Command-B)
background layer
Bring Closer command
bug
card layer
clip art
Curve tool
Distort command
Draw Centered command
Draw Multiple command
Edit Pattern... command
FatBits
Hand tool (Option-FatBits)
Import Paint... command
interactive fiction
logical reference (link)

MacPaint
network
New Background command
Opaque command
Oval tool
Perspective command
Regular Polygon tool
Rotate command
Rotate Left command
Rotate Right command
scanner
Scrapbook (desk accessory)
Send Farther command
simulation
Slant command
stretching/shrinking graphics
  (Command-drag)
stripes (on menu bar)
Transparent command

Self-Testing Exercises

1. List four reasons why it's a good idea to include common elements of cards in a shared background.

2. Is it possible to have a background button in a two-card, one-background stack, that takes you back and forth between the two cards? Explain.

3. What do each of these HyperCard paint tool symbols represent?

    a.   b.   c.   d.

4. Describe three different ways you can select an irregularly shaped object in the current layer of a card.

5. How can you switch to FatBits without using the menu? How can you get back to "skinny bits"?

6. Describe the difference between relative reference and absolute reference to another card. Under what circumstances would each of these be most appropriate?

7. Describe the difference between the Rotate and Rotate Right commands. Under what circumstances is each appropriate?

8. What is the difference between the Lasso and the Selection rectangle?

Projects

1. Design a map of a finished dungeon game based on the game you developed in this session. Add several more rooms to the basic design. Make sure there are several dead ends and a single escape path; link some rooms with secret passages. Use your imagination. Using your design, complete the game by adding rooms, decorating them, and linking them. Test your game thoroughly; then have others test it for you.

2. Create a map of your city with a list of points of interest along the side or at the bottom. Make each one of those points of interest into a button which, when clicked, highlights the named point on the map. Put the map in the background and create one highlighted card for each item. Should the buttons be in the card layer or the background layer? Why? Variations: Do the same thing for your house, your state, the world, or whatever you can think of.

3. Make a line drawing of a familiar object on a HyperCard card. Select that object with the Selection rectangle and capture the screen image as a MacPaint file with the Command-Shift-3 keystroke combination.

Import that captured screen back into HyperCard and use it to create a demonstration of these effects in HyperCard's Paint menu: Fill, Invert, Darken, Lighten, Trace Edges, Rotate Left, Rotate Right, Flip Vertical, and Flip Horizontal. Your screen should list these commands down the left side in Chicago font. Clicking on any of the command names should change the screen so that (a) the command name is highlighted (inverted); (b) the selected part of the picture is transformed just as the command would transform it; and (c) an Undo button appears to take the user back to the previous card. Think carefully about what parts of the picture should be in the background before constructing this stack.

SESSION 5

Objectives

By the end of this session you should be able to

- Create a slide-show presentation with visual transition effects between slides
- Create presentations with different kinds of on-screen animation
- Create, edit, and install custom icons
- Add simple sound and musical effects to HyperCard stacks
- Understand the relationships among HyperCard objects, messages, and scripts
- Locate and understand common HyperTalk scripts in a HyperCard stack
- Write and edit simple HyperTalk scripts

BEHIND THE BUTTONS:

INTRODUCING HYPERTALK

The Problem

Your planet is in trouble. The climate of the Earth is changing dramatically as a result of short-sighted human activity. You've been asked to give a presentation at a local school assembly, and you'd like to share your knowledge and concerns about this vital issue. You want to back up your words with visual aids that will capture the attention and the imagination of your audience. The school has a device for projecting Macintosh screens so the audience can see them. Perhaps HyperCard can help.

Introduction

Like an acquaintance from another culture, HyperCard won't reveal its most interesting secrets until you learn a little bit of its language. The native language of HyperCard is **HyperTalk**, a programming language that's about as close to English as any you'll find. This session will introduce you to HyperTalk, first by observing scripts written by others, and then by creating your own. There's lots of new material here, so don't hesitate to break this session into shorter, more manageable sessions if you feel so inclined.

HyperTalk Revealed

Sending HyperTalk Messages

You may not be aware of it, but you've been using HyperTalk already. The **message box** that appears when you issue a Find command is designed for sending messages to HyperCard (and sometimes receiving messages from HyperCard). Those messages must be written in HyperTalk for HyperCard to understand them. So let's start the session by sending a HyperTalk message.

☐ **Start your computer and open HyperCard by double-clicking on your Home icon.**

☐ **Select Message from the Go menu (or press Command-M) to bring up the message box.**

☐ **Type the following, pressing Return at the end:**

```
Set UserLevel to 5
```

You're speaking HyperTalk now. When you pressed Return, you sent a message to HyperCard to reset the user level to level 5, scripting. If you don't believe it, go to the last card in the Home stack and see for yourself.

Let's try another HyperTalk message.

☐ **Type:**

```
the time
```

As soon as you press Return, HyperCard checks its watch and answers through the message box:

```
1:30 PM
```

> **time** is a HyperTalk **function**—a named value that is calculated when the statement (message) it is in executes. One way to call a HyperTalk function is to put the word `the` before it. Another is to follow the function name with parentheses like this: `time()`. When HyperCard sees either type of function call, it replaces the function with the current time according to the System clock.

The message box can be used as a calculator, too.

☐ **Type:**

```
510 * 340
```

HyperCard's answer:

```
173400
```

HyperTalk Calculations

Here's a list of the basic HyperTalk arithmetic operators, including examples with results:

+	add	$7 + 3.3 = 10.3$
−	subtract	$7 - 3.3 = 3.7$
*	multiply	$5 * 3.1 = 15.5$
/	divide	$5 / 2 = 2.5$
div	divide and truncate (chop off remainder)	$5 \text{ div } 2 = 2$
mod	modulo (remainder after integer division)	$5 \text{ mod } 2 = 1$
^	exponent	$5 ^\wedge 2 = 25$

When evaluating complex expressions with multiple operators, HyperTalk follows strict rules for ordering the operations:

1. **Operator precedence**. In a complex arithmetic expression, exponentiation is evaluated first, then multiplication and division (including `div` and `mod`), and finally addition and subtraction.

2. Left to right. Operators of equal precedence are evaluated in order from left to right.

3. Grouping. Parentheses may be used to override the first two rules by grouping operations; expressions inside parentheses are evaluated first.

Examples: `5 * 2 + 9 - 3 div 2 ^ 2` = 19,
but `5 * (2 + 9) - (3 div 2) ^ 2` = 54.

Eavesdropping with the Message Watcher

Even while you're typing these messages, HyperCard is sending messages of its own. A continuous stream of **system messages** provide a running commentary on the state of your computer as seen by Hyper-Card. You can monitor these messages with a tool called the **Message Watcher**. This window is part of the HyperTalk **debugging environment** that's provided to make it easier for you to find bugs (errors) in your stack scripts. We'll use the HyperTalk debugger later, but for now we just want to use the Message Watcher to monitor system communications. We'll invoke the Message Watcher with HyperTalk's show command.

> **show** and **hide** commands are used to make the message box, the menu bar, the Tools palette, windows, and other objects visible and invisible. (show can also be used to display a sequence of cards in rapid succession, as in show all cards or show 22 cards.)

☐ **Type:**

```
☐
show window "message watcher"
```

The Message Watcher window appears; you can move it around on the screen like any other window. It's empty because there are no HyperTalk messages currently being *used* for anything. Nonetheless, there are plenty of messages being sent.

☐ **Click on the Hide unused messages check box to turn it off.**

```
☐  Message Watcher
☐ Hide unused messages    ☐ Hide idle
(idle)                              ⇧
(idle)
(idle)
(idle)
(idle)
(idle)
(idle)
(idle)
(idle)
(idle)
(idle)                              ⇩
```

The Message Watcher should immediately start displaying a stream of **idle** messages. HyperCard is continually reminding itself that nothing's happening. We can turn off this idle chatter.

☐ **Click on the Hide idle check box to turn it on.**

☐ **Move the pointer over a button on the screen without clicking it; then move it off the button.**

```
┌─────────────────────────────────────┐
│ ▢ ░░░ Message Watcher ░░░░░░░░░░░░░░ │
├─────────────────────────────────────┤
│ ☐ Hide unused messages   ☒ Hide idle │
├─────────────────────────────────┬───┤
│ (idle)                          │ ⬆ │
│ (mouseEnter)                    │───│
│ (mouseWithin)                   │   │
│ (mouseWithin)                   │   │
│ (mouseWithin)                   │   │
│ (mouseWithin)                   │   │
│ (mouseWithin)                   │░░░│
│ (mouseWithin)                   │   │
│ (mouseWithin)                   │───│
│ (mouseWithin)                   │   │
│ (mouseLeave)                    │ ⬇ │
└─────────────────────────────────┴───┘
```

A series of system messages says that you moved the mouse pointer over a button (**mouseEnter**), then held it there for a while (**mouseWithin**), then moved it off the button (**mouseLeave**). (You might see a slightly different stream of messages, depending on whether you move the mouse over multiple buttons or fields.) As you'll soon see, HyperCard objects such as buttons can be programmed to use (respond to) messages like these. But the parenthesized messages you're seeing aren't used by any object in the stack; they're like radio broadcasts with no listeners. Let's send some messages that make things happen. But first, let's turn off the noise.

☐ **Click on the Hide unused messages check box in the Message Watcher window.**

☐ **Type:**

```
┌─────────────────────────────────────┐
│ ░▢░░░░░░░░░░░░░░░░░░░░░░░░░░░░░░░░░░░ │
├─────────────────────────────────────┤
│   show all cards                     │
│                                      │
└─────────────────────────────────────┘
```

As you type, HyperCard responds to each keystroke by sending a **keyDown** system message. Each keyDown message also includes the letter typed, but that information isn't visible in the Message Watcher window. The keyDown messages are being used to construct a command in the message box, so they aren't in parentheses. Pressing the Return key sends two messages: keyDown and **returnKey**. When the Return key is pressed, the typed message—show—is sent by the System. To make strings of messages easier to interpret, the Message Watcher window indents messages that result from previous messages.

```
┌──────────────────────────────────┐
│ □ ▒ Message Watcher ▒            │
├──────────────────────────────────┤
│ □ Hide unused messages  ⊠ Hide idle │
├──────────────────────────────────┤
│ keyDown                        ⬆  │
│ keyDown                           │
│ keyDown                           │
│ keyDown                           │
│ keyDown                           │
│ keyDown                           │
│ keyDown                           │
│ keyDown                           │
│ keyDown                        ▯  │
│   returnkey                       │
│   show                         ⬇  │
└──────────────────────────────────┘
```

HyperCard responds to the message by flipping quickly through the entire stack of cards.

☐ **Next, type:**

```
┌──────────────────────────────────────────────────────┐
│ ▒□▒                                                    │
├──────────────────────────────────────────────────────┤
│   go to stack "Pyramid"                                │
└──────────────────────────────────────────────────────┘
```

When you press Return, you may see the now familiar dialog box asking "Where is Pyramid?" Locate the stack you created in Session 3. (If you don't have that stack, just read along until we return Home.) The Message Watcher is flooded with new messages. You can scroll backward through the list of messages if you like, but don't expect to understand all of them. There are things going on behind the scenes that won't make sense to you at this point; that's why we're here.

Looking under a Button

Things don't happen accidentally in HyperCard; they happen because someone—or something—sends messages telling HyperCard to make them happen. In these examples, we told HyperCard what to do via the message box. When you click on a button, HyperCard responds by doing something, too. Let's peek under a button to see why HyperCard responds the way it does.

☐ **Select the Button tool from the Tools palette.**

The ever-vigilant Message Watcher tells you that a `choose` message has been sent.

☐ **Click on the Home button.**

☐ **Select Button Info... from the Objects menu.**

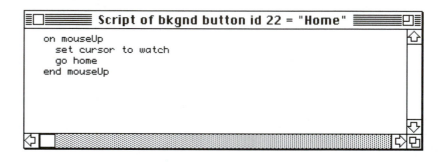

☐ **Click on the Script... button.**

When you click on that button, you're invoking HyperCard's script editor. The **script editor** is like a miniature word processor with special features to make working with scripts easier. The script editor responds to your click by opening a **script window** containing the HyperTalk script for this button.

```
 Script of bkgnd button id 22 = "Home"
on mouseUp
  set cursor to watch
  go home
end mouseUp
```

An English translation of the first line, **on mouseUp**, might be, "When the button is pressed, follow the instructions in order from the beginning to the end of this list." The list contains two instructions: one to temporarily change the pointer's symbol (**cursor**) so that it looks like a wristwatch and one to tell HyperCard to go to the Home card.

Notice that the go home command in this script has the same effect as the Home command in the Go menu. Scripts can be used to order HyperCard to do just about anything that can be done via HyperCard menus. However, set cursor to watch tells HyperCard to do something that has no menu equivalent: change a **property** of the HyperCard environment.

If you've programmed in a computer language such as BASIC or Pascal, you're probably thinking, "This looks a little like the programming language I've seen before, but there's something strange here. Where's the rest of the program?" If you've never seen a computer program before, you're probably just thinking that the whole thing is strange. Either way, a word of explanation is in order.

Objects and Messages

A program is a set of instructions that tells the computer what to do in the same way that a recipe tells a chef what to do. A program written in a **procedural language** such as BASIC or Pascal is structured like a recipe; the computer works through it, one step at a time, in the order specified by the program.

HyperTalk has many similarities to procedural Pascal and BASIC, but it also has many characteristics of an **object-oriented language**. A HyperCard stack is made up of **objects**—cards, fields, buttons, backgrounds, and the stack itself. Each object has a program—a **script**—that gives HyperCard instructions if the object receives a message. A script is made up of one or more **message handlers**. Each message handler tells HyperCard what to do if a particular message is received. A message handler takes the form

```
on message
  command(s)
end message
```

Translation: If the message *message* arrives at this object, obey the *command(s)* in this list.

To help clarify this, let's take a second look at the `on mouseUp` handler used in the Home button's script.

The **on mouseUp** handler tells HyperCard what to do when the system message `mouseUp` is received by the button. `mouseUp` is the most common message for HyperCard buttons, although it can be received by fields, cards, and backgrounds, too. `on mouseUp` is HyperTalk for "if the user presses and lets go of the mouse button while the pointer is on this button (or field, or card, or background), do everything listed between this statement and **end mouseUp**. (Although it might seem strange to specify that the action take place when the user lets go of the button, rather than when he or she presses the button, it makes sense. A mouse click consists of two actions—pressing and letting go—and it's not complete until both actions are done.)

In this example, the button receives the message and says, in effect, "I know what to do with this; my script tells me to go to the Home card, turning the pointer into a wristwatch until I'm there." HyperCard responds by turning on the watch and going Home; upon arrival at the Home card, the interaction is over.

Stacks, fields, and backgrounds can receive and respond to messages, too. How do all these objects keep their messages straight?

The HyperCard Object Hierarchy

As you point and click your way through a HyperCard stack, you're generating a flurry of messages that are passed upward through the HyperCard bureaucracy. For example, when you click anywhere on a card, the System sends a `mouseUp` message to the topmost button or field at the current mouse pointer location. This means, for example, that a button in the card layer will receive the message rather than a background button in the same location. If the script of the topmost button or field has a message handler telling it what to do `on mouseUp`, then the object accepts the message and performs the action. If there's no `on mouseUp` message handler in the script, the button or field passes the message on to the next button or field, whether in the card or the background layer. If the message passes through all buttons and fields in both layers without matching a handler in any script, it is sent to the card and compared with the card's script. If that script contains no appropriate handlers, the message is passed to the background, and then to the stack, and then in some cases to other stacks, and then to the Home stack, and finally, to HyperCard.

☐ **Close the script window by clicking on the close box in the upper left corner.**

☐ **Select the Browse tool and click on the Home button. Observe how each message in the script translates into an on-screen action. Notice also the messages scrolling through the Message Watcher window. Scroll backward through the messages until you see the `mouseUp` system message.**

The next two messages, set and go, were sent by the on mouseUp handler when it executed. The openStack message was sent by the System when the Home stack opened; the rest of the messages were sent as a result of scripts built into the Home stack. You'll learn more about these messages in due time.

☐ **Press the Tilde (~) key (or select Back from the Go menu) to return to the Pyramid stack.**

Examining the Script of a Linked Button

☐ **Select the Button tool and click on the button labeled "Click here to see inside."**

☐ **Hold down the Shift key while selecting Button Info....**

This is a shortcut to the script window.

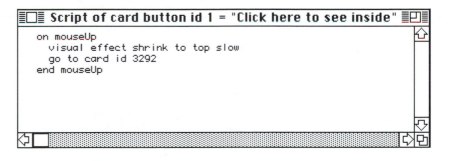

```
on mouseUp
   visual effect shrink to top slow
   go to card id 3292
end mouseUp
```

This button, like most buttons, has a single `on mouseUp` handler telling HyperCard what to do if the button is clicked. The handler says to implement a visual effect and go to the card assigned ID number 3292. (The number in the script probably won't be the same on your screen, but whatever it is, it's the ID number of the next card in the stack. You can check that by going to that card and selecting **Card Info...** from the Objects menu.) What does this number mean? Nothing; it's just a random ID number used for this kind of thing. HyperCard numbers every object you create; it's up to you to name those objects. By itself, the ID number 3292 tells you nothing about where that card is or what it does; that's why it's smart to give names to the things you create. If a card has a name, you can write scripts that say `go to card "Inside Pyramid"` instead of letting HyperCard say `go to card id 3292`.

☐ **Click on the script window's close box.**

If you're unclear about how the Button Info... button works, click it with the Browse tool while you watch the Message Watcher.

Checking the Script of a Relative Link

Let's check a button with a different kind of script.

☐ **Press Command-H (Home) and Command-4 (Last).**

☐ **Reselect the Button tool; then hold down the Shift key and double-click on the right-arrow button.**

You'll bypass the Button Info dialog box that way, and go straight to the script window.

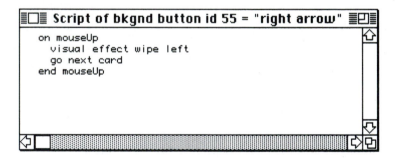

```
on mouseUp
   visual effect wipe left
   go next card
end mouseUp
```

When the mouse is clicked and released on this button, it sends a message to HyperCard to use a wipe left visual effect as a transition while going to the next card in the stack. There's no mention of a card

ID, just a reference to *next card*. This button script uses a logical reference, so that it will always go to the next card, no matter what that might be. Compare it with the absolute link in the button labeled "Click here to see inside" in the Pyramid stack.

☐ **Examine the script of the left-arrow button.**

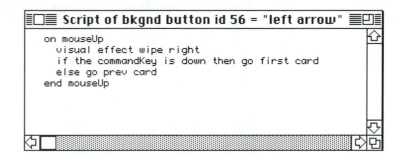

```
on mouseUp
  visual effect wipe right
  if the commandKey is down then go first card
  else go prev card
end mouseUp
```

This handler responds in different ways depending on whether the Command key is held down when the button received the mouseUp message.

> The **if structure** sends no messages. Instead, it tests for a specific condition and, if the condition is true, executes the command statement that follows. Alternate forms of the `if` structure allow multiple statements to be executed if the condition is true, or allow for a different set of statements to be executed if the statement is false. `if` structures allow programmers to build "intelligent" scripts that can respond to changes in their software and hardware environment.

☐ **Close the Message Watcher window.**

We won't need it for a while, but you can open it whenever you want to monitor the messages sent by your stack. Later in this session you'll learn how to use the Message Watcher with other debugging tools.

Break Point

Building a Dynamic Presentation

Let's build a stack to make a presentation, and use some simple scripts to give our stack some visual pizzazz.

Outlining the Problem

We know our audience won't learn much if we barrage them with facts and figures, so we have to carefully plan a few main points that we want them to remember. Here's one way to slice up the problem:

I. Global warming is a problem.

II. We're causing it.

III. It has serious consequences.

IV. We can do something about it.

We need to back up each of these points with some subpoints. We might flesh out our outline like this:

Global Warming: What Are We Doing to Our Planet?

I. What is global warming?

   A. We're changing the Earth's climate.

   B. The rate of change is greater than that of the glacial periods.

   C. We're changing the environment faster than we can predict the consequences.

II. How are we causing global warming?

   A. Burning fossil fuels produces carbon dioxide.

   B. Deforestation for fuel and grazing land eliminates carbon dioxide filters.

   C. Human activities produce other greenhouse gases (CFCs, methane, and so on).

III. What are the likely consequences?

   A. Heat waves, drought, and forest fires.

   B. Agricultural losses and famine.

   C. Rising sea level and flooding.

   D. Extinction of many trees and other species.

IV. What can we do?

   A. Reduce energy consumption.

   B. Recycle paper, metal, glass, and plastic.

C. Stop using plastic foam and CFC aerosols.

D. Eat less meat.

E. Plant more trees.

F. Work for public policies that encourage energy efficiency and discourage pollution.

This outline can be easily transformed into a **bullet chart**, one of the most frequently used forms of **presentation graphics**. Popular software packages such as Persuasion and More are designed to instantly create bullet charts from outlines like this one. While HyperCard demands more effort, it also allows more flexibility, provided you're willing to speak a little HyperTalk.

Creating a Starry Background

☐ **Create a new stack called Earth (remember to turn off the Copy current background check box).**

We're going to add an animated introduction later, and that introduction will have a different background than that of the rest of the stack. So let's save a place for the introduction with a single card. (This will save us considerable effort later, since there's no automatic way to insert a new card *before* the current card.)

Start with a background of stars.

☐ **Press Command-B (Background).**

☐ **Use the Paint Bucket to paint the background black.**

☐ **Select All of the background (using the command in the Paint menu or Command-A) and use the Lighten command in the Paint menu to produce a random star pattern.**

We'll use this starry pattern in two different backgrounds: one as a backdrop for animated sequences that will precede and follow our presentation, the other to frame our bullet charts. We can save a couple of steps later if we make a copy of the background now.

☐ **Press Command-C to copy the starry graphic to the Clipboard.**

Creating a Bullet Chart Background

☐ **Switch to the Browse tool and select New Background (*not* New Card) from the Objects menu.**

☐ **Press Command-V to paste the star-studded picture into the background.**

You're now looking at the new background of the second card. We want to put a field in this background, because that's the easiest way to have text in exactly the same location on every card.

☐ **Select the Field tool.**

☐ **Select New Field from the Objects menu.**

☐ Drag and stretch the field so it covers most of the window, leaving a one-quarter-inch starry frame around all four sides. (If you're working on a small-screen Mac, the menu bar will hide part of the frame.)

☐ Double-click on the field to reveal the **Field Info dialog box.**

```
┌─────────────────────────────────────────────┐
│                                               │
│  Field Name: [│                            ]  │
│  Card field number: 1                         │
│  Card field ID: 1                             │
│                                               │
│  ☐ Lock Text          Style:                  │
│  ☐ Show Lines         ○ Transparent           │
│  ☐ Wide Margins       ○ Opaque                │
│  ☐ Auto Tab           ● Rectangle             │
│  ☐ Fixed Line Height  ○ Shadow                │
│  ☐ Don't Wrap         ○ Scrolling             │
│  ☐ Don't Search                               │
│                                               │
│  ┌ Font... ┐                                  │
│  ┌ Script... ┐      ( OK )     ( Cancel )      │
│                                               │
└─────────────────────────────────────────────┘
```

There are several options here, most of which we can ignore for now.

☐ Type "bullet chart" to name the field.

This step is optional, but it's a good habit to establish.

☐ Click on Wide Margins, then click on Font... to open the Font dialog box.

☐ Select a font that's available in 18-point size in your system. (Helvetica, Geneva, New York, Palatino, and Times are likely candidates.) Click OK.

Fonts in the Field: A Cautionary Note

Your choice of fonts for field text should be based on more than just aesthetics. While paint text blends into the pixel pattern on the card or background after you create it, field text remains text forevermore. Field text is displayed on the screen using fonts stored in the computer's current System, which may or may not be the same fonts in the System that was used to create the stack. If the fonts that were used to create the text are not available on the user's System, the System substitutes another font. The results may be aesthetically unsatisfactory or worse. In some cases, substitute fonts may cause text to disappear from the screen because it won't fit in the field.

If you're building a stack that is to be displayed on different computers, you can avoid these potential problems by sticking to standard fonts that are installed in all Macintosh Systems. The only fonts that are required in every Mac System are Geneva 9 and 12, Monaco 9 and 12, and Chicago 12. But it's usually safe to assume that several other sizes of Geneva are installed. Other commonly used fonts are Times, Helvetica, New York, and Palatino.

If you must include something in an unusual font and you can't predict which computers will run your stack, (1) use paint text to do the typing, (2) install the font (provided it's in the public domain) in the stack (not recommended by Apple), or (3) provide the user with the font and instructions for installing it in the System.

☐ **Press Command-B to leave the background.**

☐ **Select the Browse tool, click in the field, and type this title page, using the Return key and the space bar to center the text vertically and horizontally:**

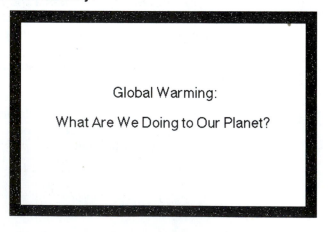

Creating a Dynamic Bullet Chart

We're going to create four bullet charts—one for each main point in the outline. We'd like to have the bulleted points appear on the chart one at a time, as we talk about them. So we'll start with a card containing only the first main heading.

☐ **Create a new card (Command-N) and type a title for the top of the card.**

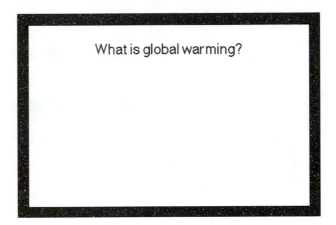

☐ **Copy this card and paste it.**

☐ **Add another line of text. To type a bullet (·), press Option-8.**

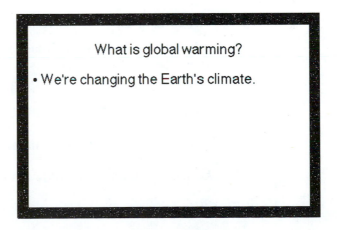

☐ **Repeat the process (Copy Card, Paste Card, type text) for each of these cards:**

```
What is global warming?

• We're changing the Earth's climate.

• The rate of change is greater than that of
the glacial periods.
```

```
What is global warming?

• We're changing the Earth's climate.

• The rate of change is greater than that of
the glacial periods.

• We're changing the environment faster
than we can predict the consequences.
```

Building a Background Button

Rather than link these cards one at a time, let's create one big background button that will allow us to advance through all of our "slides," complete with a visual effect.

☐ **Press Command-B to go to the background.**

☐ **Create a new button. Drag and stretch it to fill the entire screen.**

☐ **Make it transparent and hide the name.**

☐ **Click on Script....**

As you can see, the script doesn't tell HyperCard what to do when the mouse is clicked. It's up to us to insert instructions between `on mouseUp` and `end mouseUp`.

☐ **Type the middle two lines of this script:**

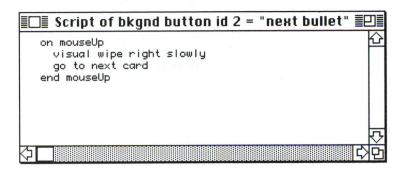

```
on mouseUp
    visual wipe right slowly
    go to next card
end mouseUp
```

(Window title: Script of bkgnd button id 2 = "next bullet")

The Syntax of Scripts

You can type scripts in any combination of upper and lowercase letters; it's all the same in HyperTalk. You don't need to worry about indentation either, because the HyperTalk script editor takes care of that automatically. But HyperTalk, like most programming languages, is picky about spelling, spaces between words, order of words, ends of lines, and other matters of **syntax**.

In general, each line of a script represents a single command or statement. If a command is too long to be visible on a single line, you can insert a **soft return** (typed Option-Return, appearing in the script as ¬) to tell HyperCard that the command is continued on the next line.

HyperTalk allows enough flexibility that it's possible to write ambiguous statements. Since ambiguity breeds unpredictability, it's important to avoid it whenever possible. Quotation marks (" ") are often used to group words and symbols together to eliminate ambiguity.

Some HyperTalk statements and scripts are clear and unambiguous to HyperCard, but not to people. These statements should be followed by **comments**—clarifying notes for human script readers. A double dash (--) in a script is a **comment marker**; everything that follows this symbol on the line is ignored by HyperCard; think of it as a stick-on note.

If you take liberties with syntax or mistype something, you're likely to see a dialog box with an error message when you try the button. If that happens, click on the Script... button in the dialog box and compare the script, line by line, with the original, editing the script as needed. Most of the traditional Macintosh editing techniques, including use of the Clipboard, work in the script editor.

☐ **Close the script window.**

A dialog box will ask you if you want to save changes to the script.

☐ **Click Yes.**

☐ **Press Command-B (Background).**

☐ **Press Command-1 (First) and Command-3 (Next).**

You're now looking at the first card of the presentation (not counting the unfinished introduction).

☐ **Select the Browse tool and click anywhere on the screen repeatedly to advance through the slides to the end.**

Notice the visual effect on card transitions. This time you typed the effect in the script rather than creating it in a dialog box, but it's there just the same.

Visual Effects in HyperTalk

Session 3 (page 111) includes a list of HyperCard visual effects. Any of these effects can be incorporated into a HyperTalk script with the `visual effect command`. The basic syntax of the `visual effect` command is:

```
visual [effect] effectName
```

The word *effect* is optional (that's what the brackets mean). To use the command, substitute an effect name for the italicized placeholder *effectName*.
   Examples:

```
visual effect iris open
```

```
visual dissolve
```

   You can add an optional speed specification after the effect name, provided you arrange the command in this order:

```
visual [effect] effectName [speed]
```

   Example:

```
visual effect barn door close very slowly
```

   Speed choices:

```
slow[ly]          very slow[ly]
```

```
fast              very fast
```

You can also specify the screen image HyperCard will use during the transition:

```
visual [effect] effectName [speed] [to image]
```

Example:

```
visual effect checkerboard slowly to black
```

Image choices:

```
black

white
```

```
gray
```

```
card          —the image of the destination card
```

```
inverse       —reverses the card image
```

Finally, you can include several visual effects in a row; they'll all happen in a sequence at the next go command. Experiment!

Rearranging Layers in the Background

Now it's time to add another card. You should currently be looking at the last card of the bullet chart sequence you just created.

☐ **Press Command-N (New Card) and move the pointer over the background field.**

Something is wrong; the pointer doesn't turn into an I-beam. Why? Because the full-screen button we created is standing between our pointer and the field, blocking our attempts at typing. But we can move the field in front of the button with another useful command.

☐ **Select the Field tool, click on the background field, and select Bring Closer from the Objects menu.**

Creating More Bullet Charts

We need to type three more complete slides of information.

☐ **Create the following cards.**

 If you're in a hurry, just create one of these cards. If you want to build a complete presentation, break each of these into several cards so the complete bullet chart builds one point at a time, like the first one.

How are we causing global warming?

• Burning fossil fuels produces carbon dioxide.

• Deforestation for fuel and grazing land eliminates carbon dioxide filters.

• Human activities produce other greenhouse gases (CFCs, methane, and so on).

What are the likely consequences?

• Heat waves, drought, and forest fires.

• Agricultural losses and famine.

• Rising sea level and flooding.

• Extinction of many trees and other species.

What can we do?

• Reduce energy consumption.
• Recycle paper, metal, glass, and plastic.
• Stop using plastic foam and CFC aerosols.
• Eat less meat.
• Plant more trees.
• Work for public policies that encourage energy efficiency and discourage pollution.

Adding a Card Layer Illusion

☐ **Go to the title card (the second card).**

☐ **Using the Button tool, select and copy the background button. (You don't need to go to the background to copy this button, since there are no buttons in front of it.)**

☐ **Paste it onto the card layer of this title card.**

The background button is still there, but on this card it's completely covered by the new card button. When the mouse is clicked on this card, the card button will intercept a `mouseUp` command before the background button can receive it. We can now change the script of the card button so that it has a different visual effect.

☐ **Hold down the Shift key and double-click on the button.**

☐ **Change the visual effect in the script from `wipe right` to `scroll down`.**

☐ **Press the Enter key.**

This single keystroke closes the script window and saves changes to the script.

☐ **Try the button (using the Browse tool).**

The scroll is effective for creating the illusion that we're moving the current card out of the way so we can see the next one, just as the wipe creates the illusion that we're writing text on the card.

☐ **If you decide to complete the bullet chart presentation, copy this button onto each *completed* bullet chart card (showing every point), excluding the final "What can you do?" card.**

Once the text is typed and checked on each card, there's one more step:

☐ **Using the Field tool, select the background field; select Send Farther from the Objects menu to return it to its original layer.**

Hiding the field behind the button will provide some security against accidental deletion of the text. We don't need to lock the text in the field, because there's no way to type in a buried field.

Break Point

Moving Pictures

Now it's time to add some **animation** at the beginning to capture the attention of the audience. The simplest kind of animation in HyperCard is familiar to every child: flipping through a stack of cards with slightly different pictures on them—**card-flipping animation**. Let's create a series of cards to make the Earth gradually appear and then dramatically go up in smoke. But before we can destroy the Earth we have to create it.

Creating an Earth Icon

We'll add the Earth to the picture by creating a button with a custom icon. HyperCard 2 includes an **icon editor** that allows you to draw your own icons and install them in your stack. Unfortunately, the icon editor lacks many of HyperCard's sophisticated paint tools, including the Oval tool we use to draw circles. To make up for its drawing deficiencies, the icon editor includes a **Pickup command** that allows you to grab any 32 x 32 pixel area from any card or background and turn it into an icon. So we can create our 32-pixel-wide circle with the Oval tool. But how can we control the size of the circle to that degree of precision? We'll start by creating a dummy icon to frame the area; the rest will be easy.

☐ **Press Command-1 (First).**

☐ **Use the Paint Bucket to temporarily paint the card layer white.**

☐ **Select Icon from the Edit menu.**

The icon editor is similar to the FatBits view of a painted scene; it allows you to edit every pixel of a 32 x 32 icon with a Pencil tool, a Selection rectangle, and several special menu items.

☐ **Name the icon "frame".**

The ID number has been arbitrarily assigned by HyperCard. You could change it, but why bother?

Special
Flip Horizontal
Flip Vertical
Frame
Gray
Invert
Mirror Horizontal
Mirror Vertical
Rotate 90°
Shadow

☐ **Select Frame from the Special menu.**

You've just drawn a 32-pixel square icon. That's all we need.

Icon Editor

Name: frame   ID: 27705

1 of 1

OK

Cancel

Edit
Undo   ⌘Z
Cut Text   ⌘H
Copy Text   ⌘C
Paste Text ⌘U
Clear Text
New Button

☐ **Select New Button from the Edit menu.**

We're out of the editor, looking at a new square button on the white card. We'll use it as a size guide for creating the circular icon we *really* want.

☐ **Drag the button close to the left edge of the window.**

 ☐ **Select from the Patterns palette one that looks like a cloud pattern on a distant planet.**

☐ **Double-click on the Oval tool to switch on the Draw Filled option, and click it again to select it.**

☐ **Position the cross hairs *exactly* on the upper left corner of the square icon and drag to the *exact* lower right corner. (Parts of the cross hairs will be white when they're in exactly the right position on each corner.)**

If you have trouble exactly positioning the cross hairs, you might want to do it with FatBits selected. Either way, you won't see what you're drawing because it's hidden by the button.

☐ **Select the Button tool, select the square button, and press Delete.**

 The button is gone, revealing the circle. This is the raw material we'll use to create the Earth.

☐ **Select Icon from the Edit menu.**

The only icon currently attached to this stack is the Frame icon. (The other icons you've used are attached to your Home stack and therefore are available in every stack.)

☐ **Select Erase from the Icon menu.**

We'll start fresh.

☐ **Rename the now empty icon "earth1" (type no space between *earth* and *1*).**

☐ **Select Pickup from the Icon menu.**

Icon	
Erase	
Pickup	**⌘P**
Keep	⌘K
Revert	
First	⌘1
Prev	⌘2
Next	⌘3
Last	⌘4
Find...	⌘F

The pointer becomes an icon-sized frame.

☐ **Position the frame so it exactly surrounds the patterned circle and click.**

You've captured your painted circle as an icon.

☐ **Use the icon editor's Pencil to change the patterns so they look more like random clouds; include a white crescent in the upper right part of the circle to simulate sunshine on the sphere.**

The window includes an actual-size representation to give you a better idea of what you're creating. Don't copy every pixel shown here; clouds aren't that exact. You may use Keep and Revert to save your work and double-back as you make changes.

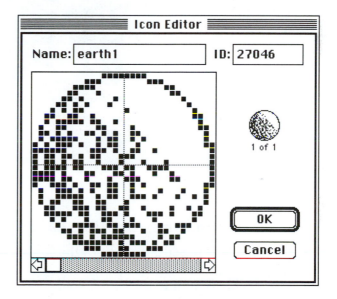

☐ **When you're happy with your icon, click OK.**

☐ **Double-click on the Eraser tool to erase anything left in this layer; then paint the whole layer black with the Paint Bucket.**

We'll start with this black card and fade into a view of the Earth from space. We'll put the Earth icon in the background.

☐ **Go to the background (Command-B).**

The stars are visible again.

☐ **Select the Button tool and select New Button.**

☐ **Double-click on the new button.**

☐ **Name the new button "earth", make it transparent, hide the name, and click on Icon....**

☐ **Select the earth1 icon and click OK.**

☐ **Reposition and reshape your button so it's in approximately the position shown here:**

Spraying Away Life as We Know It

Now you get to destroy the Earth with (what else?) an aerosol can.

☐ **Return to the card layer.**

Back to black.

☐ **Create a new card with the same background (Command-N).**

This card isn't painted black, so the Earth and stars are visible again.

☐ **Copy the current card, paste it, select the Spray Can and white paint, and spray in small circles around the Earth until it looks like a cloud. (While you're at it, experiment with the Paintbrush with different brush shapes and sparse patterns.)**

□ **Copy the current card, paste it, and enlarge the cloud.**

□ **Repeat the process several times, until the cloud fills the screen. Remember to paint behind the menu bar on the larger clouds, because we're going to turn it off later so our presentation fills the whole screen. (Press Command-Space to hide the menu bar and to bring it back later.)**

 Create as many cards as you want. The more images, the more convincing the animation.

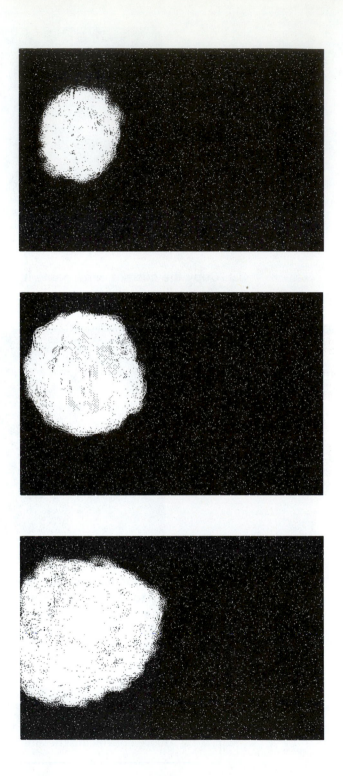

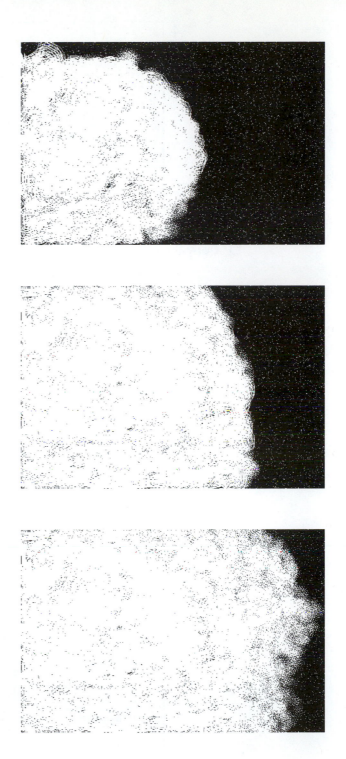

☐ **Copy the full-screen card and paste it; use the Spray Can to write:**

Remember that you can use the Revert command to erase the entire word if you aren't happy with it.

☐ **Copy and paste the card and add another word:**

☐ **One more time:**

Scripting an Animated Sequence

☐ **Try using the arrow keys to flip through these cards.**

The animation is a little jerky. We could link these cards, one at a time, and add scripts to dissolve from one card to another to smooth the transitions. But there's an easier, more effective way. We can put one button on the first card to start the show and add a script to that button that causes *all* of these cards to be displayed in order, with dissolve effects before each one. Here's how:

☐ **Go to the first card in the stack (Command-1).**

☐ **Create a new button, stretch and drag it to fill the screen, and double-click on it to bring up the Button Info dialog box.**

☐ **Name the button "blow up"; then click on Transparent, Show Name (to turn it off), and Script....**

☐ **Type the missing lines of this script:**

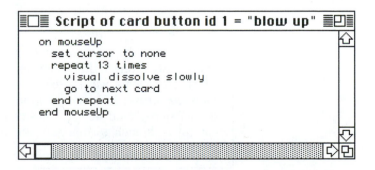

```
on mouseUp
   set cursor to none
   repeat 13 times
      visual dissolve slowly
      go to next card
   end repeat
end mouseUp
```

Depending on how many cards you have in your sequence, you might need to adjust the number in the `repeat` statement. Here's a rough translation of the script: "When the mouse is clicked, hide the cursor and repeat 'dissolve to next card' 13 times."

> **set** is a HyperTalk command for setting the properties of objects, windows, menus, and other HyperCard elements.
>
> `set [the]` *property* `[of element] to` *value*
>
> Every HyperCard object has properties: ID number, name, location, visibility, and so on. Some properties are unique to particular classes of objects. Buttons, for example, are the only objects that can have icons. Some properties, such as `cursor`, are **global**; they apply to the HyperTalk environment rather than to particular elements. Properties are often set by typing and clicking in dialog boxes. The `set` command allows you to automate the process of assigning a property to an object or the HyperTalk environment.

☐ **Select the Browse tool and click on the button to try the script.**

If the button works properly, the resulting sequence should be dramatic: The Earth gradually appears, then turns to a smoke cloud that overtakes the whole screen, revealing the title of the presentation, one word at a time. If it doesn't end on the right card, you'll need to change the number in the repeat line. When it is working properly, you'll find yourself staring at the Earth Under Fire card when the sequence ends.

> The **repeat** command tells HyperCard to repeat everything between `repeat` and `end repeat`. This form of the `repeat` statement repeats the enclosed statements a specified number of times.
>
> `repeat [for] n [times]`
>
> Another form repeats a set of commands until some condition is true:
>
> `repeat until` *condition*
>
> Still another repeats while a condition is true.
>
> `repeat while` *condition*
>
> `repeat` and `if` are examples of what computer scientists call **control structures**; they determine the flow of control in a script: which statements will be executed in what order. `repeat` is a **loop structure**; it causes program control to loop through a sequence of repeated steps. `if` is a **conditional structure**; it causes control to branch to different statements depending on present conditions.

Linking the Introduction to the Presentation

We need a button on this card to dissolve into the framed title card.

☐ **Create a full-screen, invisible button on the Earth Under Fire card, name the button "fade", and insert this script in the on mouseUp handler:**

```
visual dissolve slowly to black
visual dissolve slowly to card
go to next card
```

☐ **Go to the first card in the stack and test the presentation so far.**

Break Point

Animating with Icons

 This section contains more complex scripts than any you've seen so far. If you have no further interest in scripting in general and animation in particular, you may safely skip this section.

Creating a Spinning Planet

Once you start playing with HyperCard animation, it's hard to stop tinkering—there's always something that can be improved. In this presentation, for example, it could be argued that the Earth doesn't stay on the screen long enough for the audience to recognize it. Furthermore, the sequence might have more impact if the Earth rotated as a living, breathing planet should. Because we made the Earth a button with an icon, we can easily bring it to life by creating a few more icons showing different Earth views and writing a script telling the button to swap icons in rapid succession. This is called **icon animation**.

☐ **Go to the second card in the stack (the one with the visible Earth).**

☐ **Select Icon from the Edit menu.**

We're looking at the earth1 icon. Let's clone it.

☐ **Select Duplicate Icon from the File menu.**

File	
New Icon	⌘N
Close Icon Editor	⌘W
Duplicate Icon	**⌘D**
Quit HyperCard	⌘Q

It has a new ID number, but everything else is the same as our original.

☐ **Change the name of the new icon to "earth2".**

We want earth2 to look like earth1 rotated a little bit.

☐ **Hold down the Command key and drag a rectangle through the area in the center and to the left of the icon, roughly like this:**

You've selected an area of the picture. You can move that selection to the right, rather than trying to duplicate it with the Pencil.

☐ **Drag the selected area to the right about five pixels.**

☐ **Using a combination of selecting, dragging, and drawing, change some of the pixels in the remaining part of the icon, leaving the circular perimeter and the white crescent intact.**

Don't try to shift all the patterns in unison to the right; as long as some parts of the pattern shift rightward and others change randomly, you'll create the illusion of rotation with swirling clouds.

☐ **Select Duplicate Icon again.**

You'll be asked whether you want to save the changes to the earth2 icon.

☐ **Click Yes.**

☐ **Name the new icon "earth3" and change the cloud patterns in the same way.**

☐ **Repeat this process of duplicating and changing the icon one more time, creating an icon called "earth4". When you're finished, click OK to leave the icon editor.**

You have four Earth icons and one button; the next step is to add a script to the button telling it to rotate quickly through the icons, creating the illusion of movement.

☐ **Return to the card layer.**

☐ **Press Command-Option-C to open the script window for the card.**

☐ **Shrink the window so it's just large enough to display a few lines of text. (Use the size box in the lower right corner.)**

☐ **Type the following script:**

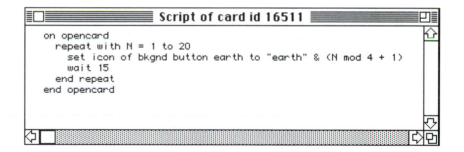

```
on opencard
   repeat with N = 1 to 20
      set icon of bkgnd button earth to "earth" & (N mod 4 + 1)
      wait 15
   end repeat
end opencard
```

This script contains several new HyperTalk words. Let's start by defining those words and then step through the script.

on **OpenCard** is a handler that sends a message when the current card is opened. Whenever the user goes to this card, the script in this handler will be executed.

This form of the `repeat` command tells HyperCard to repeat everything between `repeat` and `end repeat` using a variable as a counter. A **variable**, as its name suggests, can change in value. In this statement, the variable's value starts at a value (1) and is incremented (by 1) until it reaches the final value (20). With each increment the statements inside the `repeat` structure are repeated.

`&` is an operator for combining character strings by attaching them end to end. The result is another string. Examples: `"earth" & "quake"` yields `"earthquake"`; `"earth" & 1` yields `"earth1"`. Notice how the number is combined with the quoted string. In HyperTalk, a number is treated just like any other string of characters unless it's being used in an arithmetic operation.

The **wait** command tells HyperCard to wait a specified amount of time before proceeding. If no unit of time is specified, the default unit is the **tick**—one-sixtieth of a second.

So what is this script telling HyperCard to do when the card is opened? To execute the `set` statement 20 times, each time with a different value for the variable N, waiting one-fourth of a second after each execution. What, exactly, is the `set` statement doing? Telling Hyper-Card to attach an icon to the background button earth. Which icon? In order to determine that, HyperCard evaluates the numeric expression inside the parentheses and attaches the resulting number to the end of the character string "earth". The first time through, N has a value of 1, so (N mod 4 + 1) = (1 mod 4 + 1) = (1 + 1) = 2. The result of this calculation can be combined with the `"earth"` string, yielding `"earth2"`. This is the name of the icon the `set` statement attaches to the button called earth. The next time through the loop, N has a value of 2, so the set statement looks for the icon called `"earth3"` and attaches it to the button; then `"earth4"`; then `"earth1"` again. If this is confusing, never mind. HyperCard can do the calculations flaw-lessly, so you don't have to.

☐ **Test the script by saving the script, leaving the card, and returning.**

If all is well, you'll see the Earth's face change repeatedly for a few seconds. If it doesn't work, check the script and the icon names to make sure everything exactly matches what you've seen in this section.

☐ **Go to the beginning of the stack and click the button to start the card-flipping animation.**

Notice how the card flipping pauses when it reaches the Earth card. The `on openCard` handler temporarily takes control of HyperCard; when it's finished, control is passed back to the unfinished flipping script.

Creating Cards for a Finale

Let's use another kind of **button animation** to punctuate our conclusion.

☐ **Go to the second card (the Earth card) and select Copy Card. (You'll have to wait for the Earth to stop spinning).**

☐ **Press Command-4 (Last) and Command-V (Paste Card) *twice*.**

☐ **On the last card (the one you're looking at after the last Paste command), use paint text and a large display font to type the sentence shown here. To get the white-on-black effect, use the Selection rectangle to select the white area around the text and select Invert from the Paint menu. (If the text still doesn't show, press Command-S to select all card-layer painted objects; then select Opaque from the Paint menu).**

Finding the Mouse

☐ **Position the pointer so that it's fingering the Earth button.**

☐ **Press Command-M (Message), and type:**

```
the mouseloc
```

You just used the **mouseLoc** function to ask HyperCard where the mouse pointer is on the screen. When you press Return, HyperCard responds in the message box with a pair of numbers:

```
┌─────────────────────────────────────────────────┐
│ ▣□░░░░░░░░░░░░░░░░░░░░░░░░░░░░░░░░░░░░░░░░░░░░░░░░ │
│                                                   │
│   104,153                                         │
│  ................................................ │
└─────────────────────────────────────────────────┘
```

The card is made up of a 512 x 342 grid of pixels; each pixel has a unique address defined by two numbers: distance in pixels from the left, and distance in pixels from the top. The two numbers in the message box are the coordinates of the current mouse position. Those numbers represent the approximate location of the Earth button; the exact coordinates of that button can be retrieved, too.

☐ **Type:**

```
┌─────────────────────────────────────────────────┐
│ ▣□░░░░░░░░░░░░░░░░░░░░░░░░░░░░░░░░░░░░░░░░░░░░░░░░ │
│                                                   │
│   the loc of bg button earth                      │
│  ................................................ │
└─────────────────────────────────────────────────┘
```

> **loc** (or **location**) is a property that applies to buttons, fields, and windows. It is made up of a pair of numbers, separated by commas, representing the horizontal and vertical offsets of the object from the upper left corner of the card window.
> **bg**, like **bkgnd**, is an abbreviation for background.

The numbers that appear represent the offset coordinates of the center of the button. Now we'll see how HyperTalk can change that location automatically.

Scripting a Moving Button

☐ **Press Command-2 twice to go back to last bullet chart card.**

☐ **Create a full-screen invisible button named "finale", type the script shown here, and shrink the script window so it just frames the script.**

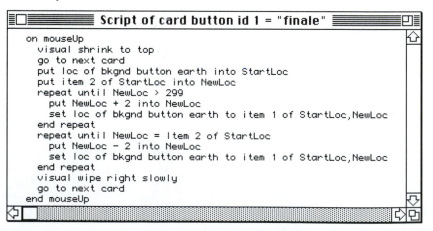

```
on mouseUp
  visual shrink to top
  go to next card
  put loc of bkgnd button earth into StartLoc
  put item 2 of StartLoc into NewLoc
  repeat until NewLoc > 299
    put NewLoc + 2 into NewLoc
    set loc of bkgnd button earth to item 1 of StartLoc,NewLoc
  end repeat
  repeat until NewLoc = Item 2 of StartLoc
    put NewLoc - 2 into NewLoc
    set loc of bkgnd button earth to item 1 of StartLoc,NewLoc
  end repeat
  visual wipe right slowly
  go to next card
end mouseUp
```

> **put** evaluates an expression and puts the result in a **container**—a variable, a field, the message box, or the current selection.
>
> An **item** is a group of characters (including punctuation, if any) separated by commas from other items. For example, item 1 of 144,153 is 144.

This script is telling HyperCard to perform these actions in order:

1. Use a visual effect to go to the next card (the first of the two new cards).

2. Copy the starting location of the Earth button into a variable called StartLoc. After this operation, StartLoc contains two numbers separated by a comma.

3. Copy the second number stored in StartLoc into another variable called NewLoc.

4. Repeat the following sequence, checking before each repetition to see whether NewLoc is greater than 299:

   a. Add 2 to the value of NewLoc; put the result back in the variable NewLoc, replacing the previous value. (Why 2? Because moving one pixel at a time takes too long on slower Macs.)

   b. Set the location property of the Earth button to the pair of numbers that includes the first item in StartLoc (which never changes from its starting value) and NewLoc (which has just been incremented by 1). The result of this substitution is that the horizontal position of the button remains unchanged, but the button moves two pixels down from its previous position.

   These two steps are repeated until NewLoc is greater than 299; that means that the button is now 300 pixels away from the top of the card. At this point, the next statement is executed.

5. Repeat the following sequence, checking before each repetition to see whether NewLoc is equal to the first of the two numbers stored in StartLoc:

   a. Subtract 2 from the value of NewLoc; put the result back in the variable NewLoc.

   b. Set the location property of the Earth button to the pair of numbers that includes the first item in StartLoc (still unchanged) and NewLoc (which has just been decreased by 1). The result of this substitution is that the horizontal position of the button remains unchanged, but the button moves two pixels down from its previous position.

This loop terminates when NewLoc equals its original value, and Earth is back where it belongs.

6. Wipe right into the next card—the one with the white-on-black concluding message.

If you find this confusing, don't feel alone. There's a lot happening here, and it's happening in a language that you've never seen before. Fortunately, HyperTalk comes with a tool that can help clarify this complex set of events: the HyperTalk debugger.

Using the HyperTalk Debugger

When you start writing longer scripts, bugs are inevitable. The HyperTalk debugger is designed to make it easy to track down and eradicate bugs. But even if your stack is completely bug-free, the debugger is a wonderful tool for learning how scripts work. You can use the debugger to slow the action down and observe messages and changes in variables while each script executes. Let's try it on the scripts we just created.

☐ **With the Finale button script window still open, click in front of the first line of the script and select Set Checkpoint from the Script menu.**

In the language of debugging, a **break point** is a spot in a program (script) where the execution of the program can be intentionally stopped so the programmer can see exactly what's going on at that instant, in the same way sports broadcasters use freeze-frame videos to analyze key plays in sporting events. In HyperTalk vernacular, break points are called **checkpoints**. When you selected the Set Checkpoint command, you told HyperCard to make the current line of the script into a checkpoint. (That's what the check mark means.)

✓ on mouseUp

☐ **Close the script window, saving the changes.**

☐ **Click on the card to execute the script.**

Since the first line of the script is a checkpoint, execution stops before it can get started, and the HyperTalk debugger takes over. The script reappears with a box around the checkpoint line.

The action is frozen until you tell the debugger what to do. That's what the bug in the menu bar is for.

```
✓ ┌─────────────────┐
  │ on mouseUp      │
  │    visual shrink to top
  │    go to next card
```

🐛 HyperTalk Debugger Menu Commands

The HyperTalk debugging environment is opened when Hyper-Card encounters a checkpoint, or when you click the debug window in a dialog box specifying a script error, or when you press Option-Command-Period while a script is executing. The **Debugger menu** (under the bug) offers several options, including one you've already tried.

```
┌─────────────────────────────┐
│ 🐛                          │
├─────────────────────────────┤
│ Step              ⌘S        │
│ Step Into         ⌘I        │
│ Trace                       │
│ Trace Into        ⌘T        │
│ Go                ⌘G        │
├─────────────────────────────┤
│ Trace Delay...              │
│ Clear Checkpoint  ⌘D        │
│ Abort             ⌘A        │
├─────────────────────────────┤
│ Variable Watcher            │
│ Message Watcher             │
└─────────────────────────────┘
```

Message Watcher shows (or hides) the Message Watcher window, which allows you to monitor messages as scripts execute. Check boxes allow you to hide idle messages and unused messages. (The Message Watcher can also be invoked by typing "mw" or "open window "message watcher"" in the message box, whether or not the debugger is operational.)

Variable Watcher shows (or hides) the Variable Watcher window, which allows you to monitor the contents of variables as the script executes. In essence, the Variable Watcher is a window into the computer's memory where variable values are stored. The variable watcher window also allows you to *change* the values for particular variables. (Like the Message Watcher, the Variable Watcher window can be viewed even if the debugger is turned off.

But when it's used without the debugger, it displays only global variables, so you can't see the values of any variables defined and used inside particular handlers. Global variables are discussed in the next session.)

Set/Clear Checkpoint (Command-D) adds (or clears) a checkpoint marker at the current line of the script. Each checkpoint stops the execution of the script and turns on the HyperTalk debugger.

Step (Command-S) allows you to walk through a script one statement at a time. By typing Command-S repeatedly, you can examine the results of each statement as long as you like, rather than trying to analyze things on the fly. If, in the course of stepping through a script, you cause another script to be executed (for example, the rotating Earth script is invoked when you go to the next card in the finale script), the second script is executed at normal speed before control is returned to the current script.

Step Into (Command-I) is like Step, except that it allows you to step into other scripts as they're invoked, rather than having them execute behind the scenes. For example, if you repeatedly Step through the finale script, the rotating Earth script window opens when you go to the card that contains that script, so you can continue stepping through that script until it is completed, at which time the finale script window reappears.

Trace and **Trace Into (Command-T)** are similar to Step and Step Into, except that they continue through the script(s) automatically, rather than waiting after each statement for input from you. Traces generally go too quickly to be of much use unless you slow the action by specifying a delay after each statement with the **Trace Delay** command. The Trace Delay dialog box allows you to specify the number of ticks (sixtieths of a second) to wait after each statement. Pressing **Command-Period** terminates any trace.

Abort (Command-A) turns off the debugger but leaves the current script window open.

Go (Command-G) turns off the debugger and closes the script window, allowing execution to continue from the point at which you entered the debugger.

Stepping through a Script

Let's use these menu commands to follow our scripts.

☐ **Select Message Watcher and Variable Watcher from the menu. Move the windows so you can still see the script and part of the card.**

☐ **Select Step Into.**

```
✓ on mouseUp
    visual shrink to top
  go to next card
```

The box moves to the second line of the script, the `visual` command. The keyboard shortcut is especially handy for this command.

☐ **Press Command-I (Step Into).**

```
✓ on mouseUp
    visual shrink to top
    go to next card
```

The box advances to the `go to next card` command.

☐ **Press Command-I again.**

```
on openCard
  repeat with N = 1 to 20
```

The next card is opened. Since that card has an `on openCard` handler in its script, control is temporarily transferred to that script, which now appears on the screen with a box around the first line.

☐ **Press Command-I two more times.**

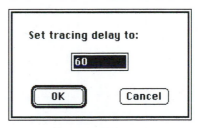

When we step past the `repeat` statement, the variable N appears in the Variable Watcher window, along with its initial value of 1. This value will be updated each time we go through the `repeat` loop, until N reaches a value of 20. Every variable change is recorded in this way in the Variable Watcher while the debugger is operating.

Tracing a Script's Actions

We could continue stepping through the scripts, but let's automate the process by turning on a trace.

☐ **Set Trace Delay to 60 ticks (one second).**

```
┌─────────────────────────────┐
│                             │
│   Set tracing delay to:     │
│                             │
│        ▐ 60        ▌        │
│                             │
│    ( OK )    ( Cancel )     │
│                             │
└─────────────────────────────┘
```

☐ **Select Trace or press Command-T.**

HyperCard will execute one statement each second until all invoked scripts have been completed. As the execution continues, you can monitor the current statement in the script, the messages being sent, changes in variables, and the resulting changes in appearance of the stack. (Of course, you may need to rearrange windows to see all these things.) If the action moves too fast (or too slow) for you, or if it fails to terminate, you can press **Command-Period** to stop execution at any time.

☐ **When your trace is completed, return to the last bullet chart and press the Finale button again. Experiment with the debugger by tracing and/or stepping through the script again until you're satisfied that you understand what's happening behind the scenes while the scripts execute. When you're finished, remove the checkpoint by selecting that script line and pressing Command-D.**

Debugging with the Debugger: Examples

The debugger is a wonderful tool for illuminating the inner workings of stacks. Use it to display script execution in slow motion. Add checkpoints to stop action in tricky places. Monitor variables and messages as they change. There are all kinds of possibilities. But the debugger is most useful for figuring out—and fixing—scripts that don't work.

If your scripts don't do what they're supposed to, use the debugger to look for problems and clues. What kind of clues? Here are two examples from the current stack.

Example 1: Suppose you accidentally mistype the name of the variable NewLoc at one point in the finale script, so that the statement inside the repeat loop says `Put NewLock + 2 into NewLoc`. When you click the button, the script stops executing before the last card appears. Instead of a moving Earth, HyperCard displays this dialog box:

```
Expected number here.

        ( Debug )   ( Script )   (( Cancel ))
```

Clicking on the Debug button takes us into the debugger with the suspicious statement outlined:

```
repeat until NewLoc > 299
   put NewLock + 2 into NewLoc
   set loc of bkgnd button earth to item 1 of StartLoc,NewLoc
```

In this case, HyperCard has zeroed in on the problem statement; all we need to do is press Command-A to abort the debugger and correct the misspelling. (HyperCard isn't always so accurate, but it does its best.)

Example 2: Suppose you mistype the same statement so it says `Put NewLoc + 2 into NewLock`. When you try to execute the script, the Earth icon fails to move and the script fails to stop. This is an example of an **endless loop**—a loop with no way of terminating. It's important to remember that you can terminate any script, any time, by typing Command-. (Command-Period). **Command-Option-Period** terminates the script and transports you immediately into the debugger at the current script line, so you can set a checkpoint at a suspicious location and start a trace with the two watcher windows open. In this case, a trace isn't necessary because we can see the smoking gun through the Variable Watcher window.

```
repeat until NewLoc > 299
    put NewLoc + 2 into NewLock
    set loc of bkgnd button earth
end repeat
repeat until NewLoc = Item 2 of
    put NewLoc - 2 into NewLoc
    set loc of bkgnd button earth
```

☐ ▓▓ **Variable Watcher** ▓▓▓	
mouseUp	
StartLoc	98,176
NewLoc	176
NewLock	178

Instead of two variables, the window displays three. Why not? That's what the script says. Since we're incrementing NewLock, and not NewLoc, it's safe to say that NewLoc will never reach 299, and the loop will never terminate on its own. Another case solved.

Use the debugger to trace any scripts you don't understand in the rest of this book. If you can't get a script to work after you type it in, use the debugger to help you locate the problem.

Singing Stacks

We've created an impressive finale for our presentation, but something is missing: sound. When you know a little HyperTalk, it's easy to add scripts that can make noise or play notes. Most musical scripts are attached to buttons, but we're going to set up a script to play a borrowed bit of Bach automatically when the final animation sequence begins.

Making a Musical Card

☐ **Go to the second-to-last card (the one with the Earth alone) and select Card Info... with the Shift key held down.**

This card, a copy of an earlier card, has a copy of that card's script. We'll replace it with something different.

☐ **Select all but the first and last lines of the script and replace them with the middle three lines of the script shown here:**

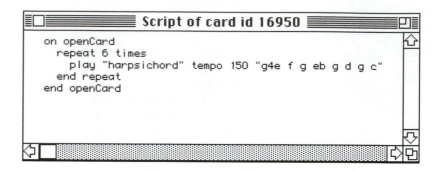

When the `openCard` message is received, this message handler tells HyperCard to repeat the play command six times.

☐ **Save the script; then leave the card and return to try it out.**

The key to this script is the **Play command**. If you can read standard musical notation, this command is fairly easy to interpret once you understand how it works. If you're not a musician, the command is, at best, cryptic. Either way, this brief description of the command should make its function clearer.

The Play Command

The play command takes the following form:

`play "voice" [tempo tempoValue] "notes"`

Here's a brief explanation of each element of the command:

    `voice` tells HyperCard what kind of sound to play. `harpsichord` and `boing` are built into HyperCard; if you want other sounds, you'll have to add **resources** (data) for those sounds using one or more of the tools described in Appendix A.

    `tempo` tells HyperCard how fast to play the sequence of notes. 100 is normal; larger numbers represent faster tempos.

    `notes` that make up the melody to be played may be represented by their letter names (*a* through *g*) separated by spaces, and followed by four optional characters: (1) accidentals (*b* for flat or # for sharp); (2) octave number, with 4 representing the octave for middle c; (3) the duration of the note (*w* for whole, *h* for half, *q* for quarter, *e* for eighth, *s* for 16th, *t* for 32nd, and *x* for 64th); and (4) . for dotted note or 3 for triplet.

Everything except accidentals stays in effect until changed, so you don't need to repeatedly specify note length or octave. In the example,

```
play "harpsichord" tempo 150 "g4e f g eb g d g c"
```

all of the notes are eighth notes (*e*) in the fourth octave.

HyperCard doesn't stop working while a sound is playing, so it's possible to combine audio and video effects to create simple multimedia presentations.

(Sounds may be distorted if you're not running HyperCard from a hard disk system; many other systems simply can't access information fast enough for distortion-free sound.)

Those are the basics of the Play command, but if you're serious about sound, there's much more to learn. Consult Appendix A for more sound information, including how to put your own real-world sounds into stacks.

Hiding and Showing the Menu Bar

Finally, as promised, we'll make sure the menu bar doesn't get in the way when we're viewing the presentation. We'll put handlers for this in the stack script, because we want the menu bar to disappear as soon as the stack is opened and reappear when the stack is closed.

The **on openStack** handler tells HyperCard what to do when the message openStack is received by the stack. openStack is a standard message sent by the System to each stack when it is opened. **closeStack** is sent when the stack is closed.

☐ **Press Command-Option-S to show the script for the stack, and type this script:**

```
on openStack
   hide menuBar
end openStack

on closeStack
   show menuBar
end closeStack
```

Always put things back the way you found them. If you hide the menu bar when the stack is opened, then show the menu bar when you close it. If you change the user level on openStack, then change it back on closeStack. And so on.

Bringing It Home

We have one more tiny script to write.

☐ **Put an invisible full-screen button on the last card and give it the following script:**

```
on mouseUp
  go Home
end mouseUp
```

☐ **Start at the beginning and test the whole stack.**

Enjoy the show!

Summary

In this session you went behind HyperCard's friendly front and learned a few words of HyperTalk, the scripting language of HyperCard. You learned how to send simple messages to HyperCard in the message box. You saw how the objects of HyperCard—buttons, fields, cards, backgrounds, and stacks—are controlled by scripts that interpret messages and execute commands. You used HyperTalk to add visual effects, animation, icon animation, button animation, and music to a stack. In the process, you learned enough about HyperTalk to easily learn more by examining other scripts, the HyperCard Help stacks, and other HyperTalk resources.

In the next session you'll learn more about HyperTalk by creating a nonlinear document using the powerful hypertext commands built into HyperCard 2.

Key Words

&
Abort command (Command-A,
  debugger)
animation

bg, bkgnd
break point
bullet chart
button animation

Card Info... command
card-flipping animation
checkpoint (break point)
closeStack message
Command-Option-Period
Command-Period
comment (in script)
comment marker (--)
conditional structure
container
control structure
cursor (property)
Debugger menu
debugging environment
div (arithmetic operator)
end mouseUp statement
endless loop
Field Info dialog box
Field tool
Frame command (icon editor)
function
global property
Go command (Command-G, debugger)
hide command
HyperTalk
icon animation
Icon command
icon editor
idle message
if structure
item
keyDown message
Lighten command
location (loc) property
loop structure
Message command (Command-M)
message box
message handler
Message Watcher
mod (arithmetic operator)
mouseEnter message
mouseLeave message
mouseLoc function
mouseUp message

mouseWithin message
New Field command
object-oriented language
objects
on mouseUp (handler)
on openCard (handler)
on openStack (handler)
operator precedence
Pickup command (icon editor)
Play command
presentation graphics
procedural language
property
put command
repeat command
resources
returnKey message
script
script editor
Script menu
script window
set command
Set/Clear Checkpoint commands (Command-D, debugger)
show command
soft return (Option-Return, ¬)
Spray Can
Step command (Command-S, debugger)
Step Into command (Command-I, debugger)
syntax
system messages
tick
time function
Trace command (debugger)
Trace Delay command (debugger)
Trace Into command (Command-T, debugger)
variable
Variable Watcher
visual effect command
wait command

Self-Testing Exercises

1. Explain what these script commands do:

   a. `visual wipe left slowly`

   b. `wait 30`

   c. `set cursor to watch`

   d. `play "boing"`

   e. `hide menuBar`

   f. `put Count + 1 into Count`

   g. `go to first card`

   h. `put 35 / 7 into Number`

2. Write a script to do each of the following:

   a. Have the computer make a "boing" sound 10 times when a button is clicked.

   b. Cause the screen (or card window) to slowly turn black when clicked.

   c. Calculate the sum of the first 20 integers when a button is clicked and display the result in the message box. (*Hint:* The last statement might read `put sum in msg`.)

3. Where might you use button scripts? Field scripts? Card scripts? Stack scripts? Describe the reasons for your decisions.

4. What happens when you press Command-M?

5. What is the difference between an object and a message?

6. Why does a button script generally contain the phrase `on mouseUp`?

7. What is syntax and how is it important in HyperTalk?

8. What does `the mouseLoc` mean?

9. Describe three methods of HyperCard animation. Give an example of an application for each type.

10. Describe how the HyperTalk debugger can be used to track down errors. What's another way to use the debugger?

11. What is the difference between Step and Trace in the debugger?

Projects

1. In the background of the bullet chart portion of the Earth stack, create a thermometer shape along the left edge of the screen. If you like, put an Earth icon in the bulb at the bottom of the thermometer. On the card layer, draw a line representing the temperature on the thermometer. Have it rise a little on each successive card, until you get to the "What can we do?" cards. Have the temperature drop for each new point on these cards.

2. Create buttons on your Home card that will automatically open each of the stacks you've created.

3. Modify the Dungeon stack (from Session 4) so that the bed's button causes the bed to move slowly, revealing the secret passageway underneath as it moves. Use card-flipping animation techniques. Copy the first card showing the bed and paste it. Remove the two buttons from this new card. Use the Lasso to select the bed and move it a small amount. Copy the new card and move the bed again. After you've created cards showing the complete bed-moving sequence, work *backward* through these cards, adding the pit in successively smaller segments to each card. Create a button on the first bed card to flip through the cards. (You will need to know how many cards are in the series when you script the button.) For a final touch, have the Bed button make a boing sound when you click it.

4. Add sound effects and animation to the Pyramid stack and the Dungeon stack. Be creative!

5. Create a card containing musical buttons. Make each play a different note. Using paint tools to create a keyboard and put the buttons on each note. Play a tune.

SESSION 6

By the end of this session you should be able to

- Create a hypertext document with dynamic links between text fields

- Create, modify, and write scripts to work with different kinds of HyperCard text fields

- Modify the HyperCard user interface by creating custom dialog boxes and pull-down menus

- Design a complex document with a linear structure, a tree structure, and a network structure

- Understand how different document structures can be used by different kinds of hypertext readers

- Apply the principles of software design and stepwise refinement to the process of building a HyperCard stack

CREATING HYPERTEXT:

NONLINEAR WRITING

The Problem

Your CS 101 instructor has asked you to produce a paper on basic computer anatomy. She wants you to write it in such a way that readers can either read it as a tutorial or use it as a reference to look up particular terms. She expects you to produce a document that presents an overview of the material but that allows the student to dig deeper into any concept to learn more. She also wants the paper to work as a reference guide for quickly looking up computer hardware terminology. This kind of flexibility isn't possible in a traditional term paper. Perhaps HyperCard can help.

Introduction

HyperCard is often described as Apple's brand of hypertext. But as you've seen in the last three sessions, HyperCard is, at its core, a kind of hypergraphics tool. Nonetheless, text manipulation is an integral part of HyperCard, and that's what we'll focus on during this session. In order to create a hypertext document that gives the user maximum flexibility, we'll design our document from the top down, filling in details as we go.

Designing Hypertext

Defining the Problem

When all is said and done, a computer is a tool for solving human problems. If we keep that in mind when we're working with HyperCard, it's easy to remember and apply one of the most important rules of thumb in programming:

> *Start by defining the problem clearly.* A program (or stack) with stunning graphics, elaborate special effects, impressive content, and mind-boggling structure is worth less than a simple stack that addresses and solves the problem at hand.

Our problem, described at the beginning of this session, is to create a document that can be used by CS 101 students to gain an understanding of how the basic parts of a computer function. Our readers, after a brief introduction, should be able to read the material sequentially, like a book, or explore particular topics in detail while ignoring others, or look up words for quick definitions and illustrations. We need a hypertext document.

(A word on vocabulary: **Hypertext**, as it was defined by its original champions, dealt mainly with text documents. Today, many hypertext systems include graphics as well as text. The creators of HyperCard insist that it is not a hyper*text* system, but a **hyper***media* system, because it allows the linking of cards containing text, graphics, and sound. The emerging consensus suggests that hypertext systems are limited to text, while hypermedia can include any form of information.)

The implicit assumption in the statement of our problem is that we are to use appropriate resources—in this case, HyperCard. (This may seem obvious, but it's still important. A HyperCard document would be of little use if no HyperCard-compatible computers were available to our potential audience. As standards develop across platforms, this restriction is likely to become less significant.)

Breaking the Problem into Pieces

The problem definition may seem clear, but it is vague in its generality. Computers don't tolerate vague, so we need to break the problem into more specific pieces.

After you've defined the problem (what you're trying to do), break it down into subproblems (how you're going to do it).

What, then, are the subproblems? If we were writing a traditional term paper, we might divide it into (1) introduction, (2) body, and (3) conclusion. We've agreed to throw out the traditional model, but before we do, let's examine each traditional component critically to see if it has a place in our hypertext document.

The introduction usually prepares the reader by (a) stating the goal(s) of the paper and (b) providing the necessary orientation for understanding the material in the paper. A hypertext reader needs to be prepared, too. A potential reader is not likely to browse through your stack if it's impossible to figure out what he or she is going to get out of it. Furthermore, since a hypertext document can be read in a variety of ways, it's especially important to make sure the reader is primed with whatever basic information is needed to make use of the stack: underlying assumptions, layout of the stack, and such. So our introduction might contain a title card, how-to-navigate-this-stack information, and a brief introduction of the concepts that will apply throughout the stack.

The body of a traditional term paper presents arguments, ideas, facts, quotations, and sources, tied together in prose that makes sense when read from beginning to end. In this case, we'll be presenting facts and ideas, but we can't assume that our reader will be plowing through the material sequentially. For some readers, the "body" of our hypertext document might be more like an encyclopedia than a term paper. So we need to make sure that each section makes sense whether reader approaches it from point A or point B. If the structure is complex, it's safest to make each section self-contained, assuming only that the reader has read the introduction.

The conclusion of a traditional term paper generally presents a summary of the main idea(s) so that the reader can see the forest as a whole after examining all the trees in the body. In many hypertext documents, there's no real conclusion, because there's no way to make sure the self-guiding reader ends the journey on a particular card. If our stack is strictly a reference stack (like a dictionary), we probably don't need to worry about a conclusion. But if the stack is to work as an introductory tutorial, too, we *may* want to guide readers through a closing card or two on their way home. We can defer that decision until we have a clearer idea of our structure.

Let's use these ideas to break the problem or project into pieces:

1. Introduction (title screen, background/overview, navigation instructions)

2. Body (details of computer components upon request)

3. Conclusion (if necessary and appropriate)

The components of this structure are still too vague for a computer to deal with, so we need to practice what's known as **stepwise refinement**. Stepwise refinement, like building the outline for a term paper, involves repeatedly breaking each component into smaller and smaller pieces until each piece is small enough to deal with easily.

Fleshing Out the Pieces

Let's start by considering the body, since that's the most important part of the stack and it will determine what the reader needs to be told in the introduction. The reader or user should be able to look at some kind of menu screen that shows the basic components of a computer and to click on each component to get more information about it. For example, the user might click on Output Devices to see a general description of output devices and a menu of buttons to click for more information about specific output devices: screen, printer, speaker, and so on.

Here's a map of what this part of the hypertext document might look like:

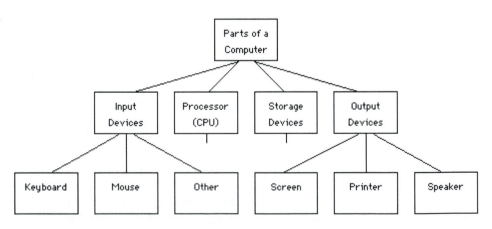

This is called a **tree structure**. (In computer science, trees are generally drawn with **roots** at the top and **branches** that grow downward.)

Unlike the network structure we used to create the dungeon stack, a tree structure has well-defined characteristics that make it predictable and easy to navigate. One advantage of a tree is that we can add more leaves to allow for more detailed descriptions or delineations. The user simply has to click on buttons to go deeper and deeper into the hierarchy and expose more details. Of course, we should provide a button on every card for returning to higher levels of the hierarchy, another button for returning to the main menu card, another button for returning to the Home card or quitting HyperCard, and (possibly) a fourth button for taking the user to a map that shows an overview of the stack.

We aren't going to enforce a rigid tree structure, though, because different readers have different needs. First-time readers should be able to read everything in sequential order so they don't miss anything; that means putting left- and right-arrow buttons on each card. Users who are really in a hurry might want to use the Find command to jump directly to a particular subject; that means including a Find button on each card. Since all of these buttons should appear on every card, we should consider putting them in the background.

What Goes in the Background?

- Which elements repeat themselves in your outline or map?

- Which elements could appear on most or all cards without causing unnecessary confusion or complication?

Any element that appears in the answer to either of these questions should be considered as a candidate for the background.

The introduction in our three-step outline should start with a title page that allows the user to quickly choose a path through the information. New users, in addition to needing some kind of how-to-use-this-stack information, may need an introduction to provide the background they need to understand the material in the document. In the interest of brevity, we'll bypass this introduction for now and assume that all readers have a basic understanding of computers. We can easily add an introduction later if the need arises. Our opening screen can be thought of as a title page with several options: Introduction (if we add one later), Main Menu (the tree-structured body), Find (quick search), Help (stack instructions), and Exit.

We might want to include a conclusion at some later time, but for now we just need to provide a way for the user to exit the stack gracefully. We'll include an Exit button in the background of every card.

Designing the User Interface

There's always a risk that too many buttons can overwhelm the user unless they're arranged in a clear, understandable way. Since we're using several buttons on every card, we can arrange the screen so that the universal buttons are all together in a row, and so that they all look and act the same way. For example, in this stack we'll arrange the buttons across the top of the background, and we'll make them all shadow-style buttons that auto-hilite when clicked. These kinds of details may seem unimportant, but they can make a tremendous difference to the people who will be using your creation.

> Design your card so that the buttons have a consistent look and feel, so the user knows what to expect when clicking them.

One way to determine what kinds of user interfaces work best is to look at stacks that work well and study their user interfaces. It's sometimes helpful to borrow directly from these stacks.

At this point in the planning process, we probably should study (and perhaps borrow from) the user interfaces of similar stacks that work well and, at the same time, notice what kinds of user interfaces don't work well. We may want to draw several prototype screens to experiment with different user interfaces and designs. We might find that some of our ideas don't work well when actually applied to paper or pixels, and have to come up with alternative approaches.

> Never be afraid to backtrack when designing a stack. It's almost never worthwhile to continue building on a flawed plan.

There are many more design decisions to be made, but let's use our fast-forward button to jump to the moment when we've completed the design and we're ready to actually build the stack. From that perspective, we can look back on those decisions that we bypassed.

Building a Background

Painting the Background

☐ **Open your Home stack.**

☐ **Select New Stack... from the File menu.**

☐ Name the stack "Computer Anatomy", locate the appropriate disk and folder in the dialog box, and click New.

☐ Go to the background layer and use the paint tools to draw an approximation of this background:

Building a Button Bar

The next step is to put a row of navigation buttons in the background.

☐ Select the Button tool and create a row of background buttons with the following names, properties, appearances, and visual effects. (Remember, it's easier to produce identically shaped buttons if you create one and clone it with Option-Drag.)

- Main Menu, Shadow style, Show Name, Auto Hilite, stretch from center effect.

- Find, Shadow style, Show Name, Auto Hilite, stretch from center effect.

- Exit, Shadow style, Show Name, Auto Hilite, iris close effect.

- Go Back, Shadow style, Auto Hilite, small return arrow icon, shrink to center effect.

- Go First, Shadow style, Auto Hilite, small first card arrow icon, shrink to center effect.

- Go Prev, Shadow style, Auto Hilite, small prev arrow icon, wipe right effect.

- Go Next, Shadow style, Auto Hilite, small next arrow icon, wipe left effect.

☐ Align the buttons in the white strip near the top of the background like this:

For now, the buttons don't need to do anything; we'll add scripts later.

Adding Fields to the Background

☐ Still in the background, select the Field tool and create these two fields (one in the button strip at the top and the other covering the rest of the card):

☐ Double-click on the upper field to bring up the Field Info dialog box. Name the field "Title" (the name is *not* optional; we'll refer to it in a script later), make it transparent, give it wide margins, and assign it a default font of 12-point Chicago.

☐ Name the larger field "Details", make it transparent, give it wide margins, and assign it a default font of 12-point Geneva.

The background is complete.

☐ Return to the card layer.

The first card in the stack will be a title page, complete with simple start-up instructions, a title headline, and a pop-up footnote.

Filling in the Blank

We'll use the smaller Title field to display the only instructions a novice user might need.

☐ **Select the Browse tool and type this in the Title field:**

Click on a button >->

We aren't going to use the large Details field on the first card, because we want a title in a large display font.

Painting a Title

A

☐ **Use the Paint Text tool to create a title and byline with an asterisk after your name. Use centered 18- or 24-point text in your choice of fonts (24-point Palatino is shown here).**

Click on a button >->	⟳	⇤	⇦	⇨	Main Menu	Find	Exit

Basic Computer Anatomy
a hypertext paper
by
Charles Babbage *

Bear in mind that paint text can't be edited once you click elsewhere or select another tool.

Creating a Pop-Up Field

Now it's time to add a dynamic footnote. We want a message to appear when the user clicks on the asterisk. That message will be in a **pop-up field**.

☐ **Create a field and position it in the white space below the painted text. Name the field "Thanks" (required) and give it a Shadow style.**

☐ **Using the Browse tool, type something like this in the field:**

> * with special thanks to my CS 101 instructor,
> without whom I never would have tackled this
> important and illuminating project.

If you decide to add a longer list of acknowledgements later, you can change the field style from shadow to scrolling. **Scrolling fields** have standard Macintosh scroll bars.

We don't want the user to be able to change this, so let's lock the text.

☐ **Select the Field tool again and lock the field via the Field Info... command.**

If we're going to have a button to make the field appear, we should also have a way to make the field disappear.

☐ **Open the field's script window and type this script:**

```
on mouseUp
  hide me
end mouseUp
```

> **me** in a script represents the object containing the currently executing handler.

The field should appear when the user clicks on the asterisk, so we'll put an invisible button there.

☐ **Use the Button tool to put a transparent button named "asterisk" on the asterisk.**

☐ **Script the button like this:**

```
on mouseUp
  set visible of card field "Thanks" to ¬
  not the visible of card field "Thanks"
end mouseUp
```

(Remember, the ¬ character is a soft return, created by typing Option-Return; its only purpose is to allow a single statement to stretch across multiple lines.)

In essence, this script says: If the Thanks card field is not visible, make it visible; if it's visible, make it not visible. A more accurate translation of the actual script might be "make the visibility property (called `visible`) of the Thanks card field the opposite of what that property is now."

If all is well, clicking on the asterisk should make the pop-up field appear. The field should disappear when the user clicks on the field or the asterisk.

☐ **Test the button and the field.**

Hiding Buttons with Buttons

Many of the buttons we created in the background are either irrelevant or inappropriate for the title page. All those choices are likely to overwhelm a first-time user of the stack. All we need on this card are a few simple choices: Go to the main menu, find a particular topic, and exit. (It's a good idea to have a Stack Overview or Help button, too, but we'll save that for a later project.) We can hide the other choices with an opaque do-nothing button on the card layer.

☐ **Create a button, make it opaque, name it "mask", hide the name, and drag/stretch it so that it covers all of the background icon buttons:**

Click on a button >->		Main Menu	Find	Exit

Stacking the Deck

Card 1 is done. Now we need to provide the Main Menu button with someplace to go. This is a background button that will appear on every card. No matter where we are in the stack, we want a click on this button to take us to the Main Menu card: the root of our hypertext tree. That means that the button should be hard-linked to that card with an absolute reference.

Making the Main Menu Card

☐ **Select the Button tool, double-click on the Main Menu button, and click on LinkTo....**

☐ **Press Command-N (New Card) and click on the This Card button.**

As usual, the new card shares a background with the previous card—buttons, fields, and all. You can't see the fields, but your browsing pointer should turn into an I-beam whenever it passes over them.

☐ **Locate each of those fields and fill them with the text shown here (with field text, using the Browse tool, *not* the Paint Text tool). Press Option-8 to type a bullet (·).**

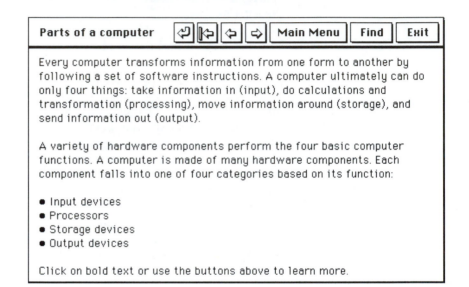

What bold text? The bold text you're about to add.

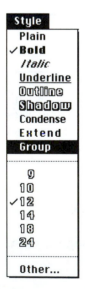

☐ **Double-click-drag to select the phrase *Input devices*. Then select Bold from the Style menu. Finally, with the phrase still selected, select Group from the Style menu.**

When you selected Bold, you saw the selected text change to boldface. Selecting Group caused no such cosmetic change. In truth, neither of these style changes is for cosmetic reasons. Later we're going to write a script for this field that will check to see whether the mouse is clicking on boldface text. We'll use bold as the cue for **hot text**: text that triggers a jump to another card in the stack.

> The Group style simply specifies that multiple words should be treated as a group when they're clicked, rather than as individual words.

☐ **Repeat the process of selecting, making bold, and grouping each of the remaining bulleted hardware categories:** *Processors,* *Storage devices,* **and** *Output devices.* **(There's no need to group** *Processors,* **since it's a single word.)**

- Input devices
- Processors
- Storage devices
- Output devices

This card indicates that there are four possible branches from this point, just as the map indicated. To save time and typing, we'll skip the first two branches and create cards for just the last two categories. We can always come back to this point and insert additional cards.

Before we finish with the Main Menu card, we should take care of one more detail. There's no point in having a button that links the Main Menu card to the Main Menu card; it's likely to just confuse the user. We can hide that button behind a do-nothing button, just as we did with the arrow buttons on card 1. But instead of making the button completely invisible, let's give it the name Main Menu and let it provide a "you are here" reference for the card; that way, the button can serve to orient, rather than disorient, the user.

☐ **Create an opaque button with a visible name "Main Menu"; place it directly on top of the Main Menu background button.**

This button doesn't do anything when clicked. It just serves as a visual reminder that the user is looking at the Main Menu card.

Creating Reference Cards

The main body of our hypertext document is to be tree structured, with buttons that allow the user to branch in several directions from a root menu. At the root level, we offer the reader four choices, corresponding to the four component types we've introduced.

Remember that some of our readers may want to read every card of the stack in order, from first to last. If we don't plan the order of the cards, sequential readers might find themselves being jerked from storage to output to processors to input devices. Such unplanned structure is confusing and disorienting, especially for beginners. We should plan a logical order and add cards in such a way that they end up in the order we planned.

Let's plan the stack so the sequential reader sees the branches in this order: Input, Processors, Storage, Output. The New Card command always inserts the new card after the current card, so we should create our cards in the order they're to be sequenced. If we decide to go back and add more cards later to provide additional branches, we should insert those cards, not at the end, but in the logical place for sequential readers.

The process of creating each of the remaining cards is the same as for the main menu card:

1. Create a new card for the next topic in the sequence.

2. Type the appropriate text into each of the two fields (remembering to use the Browse tool)

3. Apply Bold and (if necessary) Group styles to words and phrases that are to be hot text.

There's no need to explicitly link any of these cards. Readers will travel between cards with the arrow buttons, hot text, and Find button, none of which depends on absolute links.

☐ **Following the steps outlined above, create each of these cards.**

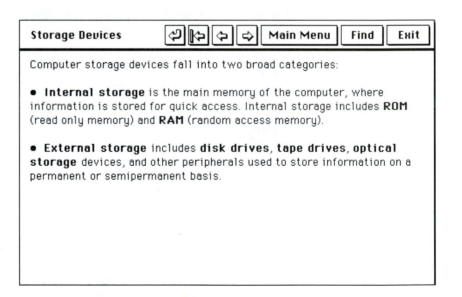

```
┌──────────────────────────────────────────────────────────────────┐
│ Output Devices      [↵][↤][⇐][⇒]  Main Menu   Find   Exit          │
├──────────────────────────────────────────────────────────────────┤
│ No amount of processing is of any value unless we have a way of    │
│ getting the results out of the computer. A typical computer has    │
│ three main forms of output:                                        │
│                                                                    │
│   • Monitor screens                                                │
│                                                                    │
│   • Printers                                                       │
│                                                                    │
│   • Audio output                                                   │
│                                                                    │
│                                                                    │
│                                                                    │
└──────────────────────────────────────────────────────────────────┘
```

```
┌──────────────────────────────────────────────────────────────────┐
│ Audio Output        [↵][↤][⇐][⇒]  Main Menu   Find   Exit          │
├──────────────────────────────────────────────────────────────────┤
│ Audio output from the computer takes several forms:                │
│                                                                    │
│   • synthesized sounds (music, speech, and sound effects)          │
│   mathematically generated  by the computer                        │
│                                                                    │
│   • digitized sounds (music, speech, and sound effects) copied     │
│   from real-world sounds                                           │
│                                                                    │
│   • MIDI data transmitted from the computer to synthesizers and    │
│   other electronic musical instruments                             │
│                                                                    │
│   • Computer control of audio/video multimedia equipment           │
│                                                                    │
└──────────────────────────────────────────────────────────────────┘
```

Scripting the Sequence Buttons

Let's activate the arrow buttons so a sequential reader can navigate the stack with them. These are all background buttons, but you can script them without leaving the card layer.

[⇐] ☐ **Select the Button tool and open the script window for the left-arrow button by holding down Command and Option while clicking on the button. Then complete its script like this:**

```
on mouseUp
  visual effect wipe right
  go to previous card
end mouseUp
```

☐ **Complete the script for the right-arrow button:**

```
on mouseUp
  visual effect wipe left
  go to next card
end mouseUp
```

☐ **Complete the script for the Go First button:**

```
on mouseUp
  visual wipe right
  go first
end mouseUp
```

☐ **Try the arrow buttons.**

Creating a Dead End

You should see a potential problem here: When you reach the last card of the stack, the right arrow abruptly transports you to the title card. There's no reason to introduce the potentially confusing concept of a wrap-around stack. It makes more sense to have a concluding card that has no visible right-arrow or Go Next button.

☐ **Create a final card at the end of the stack. Mask the right-arrow button with an opaque Do Nothing button.**

This card might contain a concluding summary, a picture of a complete computer system, or a list of references. For simplicity's sake, let's just add a simple message.

☐ **Type "You've reached the end of the stack." in the Details field.**

Break Point

Automatic Backtracking

This short stack now works for readers who want to traverse it from beginning to end. It's time to add hypertext scripts to allow for non-sequential navigation. One of the most important parts of creating a hypertext stack is providing the user with a simple, reliable way of backtracking. A document that allows readers to jump from one section or level to another must provide a way to jump back.

For example, if the reader of our stack has worked through the tree to the branch on MIDI, he or she should be able to go back up to the next highest level of the tree—Audio Output—without going all the way back to the root. That's what the Go Back button is for in this stack. Ideally, this button should be smart enough to know where you want to go when you press it, rather than mindlessly backtracking through every card you've visited. If you click it twice in a row, it should take you from MIDI to Audio Output to Output Devices, even if you've examined several branches of audio output in the meantime.

The problem becomes even more complex when we open up the possibility of jumping *between* branches of the tree. Suppose, for example, we decide to add a hot link from one of the audio input cards to the MIDI card, because MIDI is used for both input and output. The Go Back button can't be hard-linked to the Audio Output card; it needs to be flexible enough to return to your exact point of departure, *wherever that may be*. We can't create a telepathic return-arrow button, but we *can* create a button that takes the user back to a point in the stack that has been previously marked as the point of return. In this example, the script that dropped you down to the MIDI level should mark the Audio Output card (or the Audio Input card) before transporting you to MIDI.

Hot text and the Go Back button will work as a team. For example, you click on hot text—the word *MIDI* on the Audio Output card. This click effectively does two things: It makes a note of the current card (in the same way you might write down your page number before temporarily flipping to another reference in a book) and it jumps to the appropriate card—MIDI. You might, while you're at that level, decide to use the arrow buttons to explore some other audio output devices. When you're through, you click on the Go Back button. The Go Back button checks the note that was left when you last clicked on hot text (just as you might check your page number before returning to your original page) and returns to the marked spot. HyperTalk makes this possible with two commands.

Push and Pop Card

Each time HyperCard encounters a **push command,** it pushes a reminder onto its stack of reminders in memory. This reminder will tell HyperCard where to return when it's later told to pop a card off the stack. Here's the syntax:

```
push card
```

The **pop card** command, in its most commonly used form, takes you back to that point and deletes the note from the reminder stack. If the `push` command has been issued more than once, `pop card` returns to the last card for which a reminder was pushed onto the stack, and that reminder is removed from (popped off) the stack. This is the syntax of the basic `pop card` command:

```
pop card
```

This kind of reminder **stack** is not the same as a HyperCard stack; it's a special kind of **data structure** that allows information to be recovered in the opposite order that it was stored, so that the last item added to the stack is the first one removed. The conventional metaphor for a stack data structure is a spring-loaded stack of cafeteria trays, but a more appropriate metaphor might be an old-fashioned spindle for holding small paper notes.

The keyboard shortcuts for `push` and `pop card` are useful for navigating back and forth through such stacks during the stack development process. **Command-↓** (Command-down-arrow) pushes a reminder for the current card onto the memory stack; **Command-↑** (Command-up-arrow) pops the top reminder off the stack, returning you to that card.

That's the theory; here's how to make it happen.

Providing Many Happy Returns

Let's start by scripting the Go Back button.

 ☐ **Complete this script on the Go Back button.**

```
on mouseUp
   visual shrink to center
   pop card
end mouseUp
```

The pop card command will return to the card that was visible when the push card command was last issued. In order for this button to work properly, we need to modify the stack so a push card command is issued whenever the user clicks on hot text. We'll make the text hot by adding a script to the Details field.

Creating Hot Text

☐ **Type this script for the large Details field.**

```
on mouseUp
  get the clickText
  if the textStyle of the clickChunk contains bold ¬
  then
    lock screen
    push card
    find whole it in bg field "title"
    if the result is not empty then ¬
    answer "Missing card:" && It
    unlock screen with stretch from center
  end if
end mouseUp
```

In order to explain this script, we need to define several new HyperTalk terms:

---

get *expression*

The **get** command puts the value of any expression into the variable **It**. (**It** also serves as a destination for the ask, answer, and read commands.)

clickText is a function that returns the word in a field last clicked on by the user. (If the word has been specified to be part of a group, clickText returns the whole group.) **clickChunk** is a function that returns a chunk expression *describing* the word or group of words clicked in the field. A **chunk** is a piece of a character string represented as a chunk expression. For example, if the user clicks on the first word of the Main Text field on the Main Menu card, clickText returns the value "Every", while clickChunk returns the chunk expression "char 1 to 5 of bkgnd field 2". That is, clickText returns the content; clickChunk returns the description.

textStyle is a function that returns a list of the text styles (italics, bold, underline, outline, shadow, extend, condense, and/ or group) of a text string; in this script, the textStyle returns the styles of the text string contained in the clickChunk.

```
lock screen
unlock screen [with effectName]
```

the **lock screen command** sets the **lockScreen** global property to true, preventing HyperCard from updating the screen until the **unlock screen** command is issued, setting the lockScreen property back to false. Everything that happens between these two commands is hidden from the user.

```
find text [in field]
find chars text [in field]
find word text [in field]
find whole text [in field]
find string text [in field]
```

The **find command** comes in many variations, but they all do basically the same thing: search through all card and background fields in the stack for the specified text strings. This is the command that appears in the message box when you select the Find menu command. The find form finds the match only at the beginning of words. **find chars** finds matches anywhere within words. **find whole** searches for a specific word or phrase, including spaces. **find string** searches for strings, including spaces and punctuation, that don't necessarily start at the beginning of words. If the search is unsuccessful (the string is not found), the **result** function returns the explanatory message "Not found"; otherwise result returns an empty string. (result returns explanatory messages for unsuccessful completion of many HyperTalk commands).

bg, like bkgnd, is an abbreviation for background.

The simplest form of the **answer command** is used to create a dialog box containing a message with an OK button. (The answer command is discussed in more detail in a later example.)

&& concatenates (combines) two strings with a space between.

Let's walk through the script. Suppose the user clicks on the first word in the Details field on the Main Menu card. The clickText function returns "Every", so the get command puts "Every" in the local variable It. The clickChunk function returns the chunk expression "char 1 to 5 of bkgnd field 2", making the next statement begin

```
if the textStyle of char 1 to 5 of bkgnd field 2 ¬
contains bold then ...
```

It doesn't, so execution jumps to end if and end mouseUp. Nothing else happens.

Now suppose the user clicks on **Output Devices.** Because these two words are grouped, "Output Devices" is put in It by the get statement.

clickChunk returns "char 553 to 566 of bkgnd field 2", making the `if` statement

```
if the textStyle of char 533 to 566 of bkgnd field 2 ¬
contains bold then ...
```

Since it does contain bold, the statements between `if` and `end if` are executed. The screen is locked, the location of the current card is pushed onto the reminder stack, and the `find whole` command searches the background Title field on every card for text matching `It`; the search stops when it finds the Output Devices card. Because the search was successful, `result` returns an empty string, so the `answer` command is skipped. The screen is unlocked with a visual effect, revealing the Output Devices card with a box around the title.

Finally, suppose the user clicks somewhere on `Input Devices` on the Main Menu card. Because these two words are grouped, `clickText` returns "Input Devices", which is placed in `It`, and the `if` statement checks characters 506 to 518 of the field, which contain bold-face text. The screen is locked, the location of the current card is pushed onto the reminder stack, and the `find whole` command searches the background Title field on every card for text matching `It`—that is, "Input Devices". Since "Input Devices" isn't in that field on any existing card (because we haven't created an Input Devices card yet), `result` returns the message "Not found". The next statement checks to see whether `result` is empty; since it's not, the `answer` command puts together "Missing card:" and the contents of `It` (with a space between, as specified by the `&&` operator), and displays this dialog box:

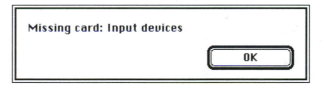

When the user clicks OK, the screen is unlocked with a visual effect and the `end if` and `end mouseUp` statements are processed.

The visual effect seems out of place here, since we're still on the same card. But this particular branch of the program isn't really designed for the user to see, anyway. When the stack is completed, there should be a card corresponding to every boldface word or phrase on every card. We've included this `if` statement more for the stack developer than for the user. As we're developing and testing the stack, the dialog box message can provide a helpful reminder that a card hasn't been created yet. The dialog box will also appear if the stack contains a spelling error that prevents a successful search. Even after the stack is theoretically completed and tested, it's probably a good idea to leave the `if` statement in the stack, just in case we've overlooked something.

The script won't work until we lock the text in the field, because the pointer turns into an I-beam whenever we place it over an unlocked field. It's important to lock both fields, anyway, to protect the information in those fields.

☐ **Lock the text in the two fields.**

☐ **Test the hot-text script. Try different combinations of hot-text clicks and Go Back button clicks to make sure they work as expected.**

You can use the debugger to slow the action so you can see exactly what happens as the script unfolds.

☐ **Put a checkpoint in the first line of the script. Turn on the Message Watcher and the Variable Watcher. Trace or Step through the script several times, reproducing the examples described in the last few paragraphs.**

Obviously, there are plenty of potential hot links on each of the cards we've created. For small items, we might want to include buttons that reveal pop-up footnotes rather than jump to another card. But other items lend themselves to cross-referencing with other cards. It's possible to turn this stack into a complex structure that's more like a network than a simple tree. But before you decide to build a labyrinthine stack, take a minute to consider a few issues.

The Hazards of Hypertext

Where am I? When links can take a reader to anywhere from anywhere, it's easy for the reader to become disoriented, wondering, "Where am I?" "How did I get here?" "How do I get back where I was?" "How do I get out of here?" Too much freedom can cause anxiety.

What's left? When you finish reading a book, you know you've read every page. Many hypertext documents leave the reader with the uneasy feeling that something important has gone unnoticed. Some HyperCard documents keep track of the reader's progress automatically, marking each completed session. Until you can build this kind of intelligence into your stacks, it's important to give your stack a structure that makes it easy for the reader to know what he or she has seen so far and what's left to see.

Which text is hot? It's easy to create hidden buttons on chunks of text—you did it on the title card of this stack. But buttons that aren't obvious to the user aren't generally a good idea. (They also

---

cause problems when you edit the text or use scrolling fields, because they don't stay with the text when it moves.) In this document, we've marked hot text with boldface. This makes it easier to write the hypertext scripts, but it also makes it easier for the reader to know where to click.

Try all of the buttons from several different locations in your stack. As you can see, we don't have a true tree structure, because you can get almost anywhere from almost anywhere else. But the casual user who's uncomfortable with all those choices can *use it* like a tree. Readers uncomfortable with the hypertext concept can continue flipping through the stack with the right-arrow button.

Break Point

Buttons That Talk Back

Scripting the Find Button

We still have to write a script for the Find button. Since there's a Find command in the menu, we could simply ask HyperCard to execute that command when the button is clicked with this script:

```
on mouseUp
   doMenu Find...
end mouseUp
```

> doMenu *itemName* [*menuName*] [without dialog]
>
> **doMenu** tells HyperCard to execute a menu command. It can be used to automate just about any menu action, provided the command is spelled correctly, including punctuation. (without dialog suppresses dialog boxes.)

When a button with this script is clicked, the message box pops up with the find command already typed, just as it would if you selected Find from the menu. But with a slightly more complex script, we can create a Find option that will be less intimidating to HyperCard novices:

Find   ☐ **Complete this script for the Find button.**

```
on mouseUp
  global StringToFind
  ask "What are you looking for?" with StringToFind
  if It is not empty then
    push card
    put It into StringToFind
    find StringToFind
  end if
end mouseUp
```

To understand this script we need another vocabulary lesson.

```
global variableList
```

Most variables are **local variables**—they are valid only within a single handler. As soon as the handler is executed, the local variables used in the handler cease to exist. A **global variable** is valid for all handlers in which it is declared with the **global command**. Global variables retain their values until they are changed or until the HyperCard session is terminated. Normally variables are declared global so they can be used in two or more handlers; in some cases (like this one) a variable is declared global so that its value can be retained until the same handler is executed later in the session.

```
ask question [with defaultAnswer]
ask password [clear] question [with defaultAnswer]
ask file [prompText] [with [default] filename]
```

The **ask command** displays a dialog box containing a question with a text box for receiving the user's typed answer. If a *defaultAnswer* string is included in the command, that string is highlighted in the text box when it appears. When the user clicks OK or presses Return, the text in the text box is put into the local variable It. (Other forms of the ask command are used for requesting passwords and creating standard file dialog boxes.)

Here's what happens now when a user clicks the Find button: Hyper-Card notes that StringToFind is to be a global variable and sets aside a space to keep track of that variable's value from this moment on. (Its current value is empty; it contains nothing.) The ask command displays this dialog box:

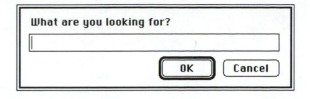

What are you looking for?

[   ]

[OK] [Cancel]

(If we had not declared StringToFind as a global variable, the text box would have contained "StringToFind" highlighted rather than just a flashing cursor, because HyperCard would have no way of knowing that StringToFind was a variable rather than just a text string.)

Suppose the user types "MIDI" and presses Return. The string "MIDI" is put into the local variable It. The If statement checks the value of It and determines that it is not empty. The current card is noted with the push card command so the user can use the Go Back button to return to that point. "MIDI" is copied from It into StringToFind by the put command. The find command then searches every field on every card until it finds a match for "MIDI".

When execution of the handler is done, the global variable StringToFind keeps its value, so that the next time the user clicks the Find button, the dialog box looks like this:

What are you looking for?

[MIDI   ]

[OK] [Cancel]

If the user types nothing, It is assigned "MIDI" once again and the script plays out the same as before. This provides a convenient way to do repeated searches for the same string.

☐ **Test the Find button at least twice. Use the debugger to trace the script if its operation isn't clear to you.**

Adding an Interactive Exit

The only button yet to be scripted is the Exit button. We can use the answer command to create a dialog box that provides exit choices.

Exit

☐ **Complete this script for the Exit button.**

```
on mouseUp
  answer "Are you sure you want to quit?" ¬
  with "Go Home" or "To the Finder" or "Cancel"
  if It is "Cancel" then
    exit mouseUp
  else
    if It is "Go Home" then
      go home
    else
      doMenu Quit HyperCard
    end if
  end if
end mouseUp
```

You've seen most of these statements before, but they're put together in a slightly different way. Before we walk through the script, let's fill in some details about the answer command and define the exit statement.

```
answer question [with reply [or reply2 ¬
[or reply3]]]
answer file [promptText][of type fileType]
```

answer is used to create a dialog box containing a message or question and one, two, or three buttons for the user's replies. If replies aren't specified, a single OK button appears in the box. The user's reply choice is stored in the variable It. (The answer file form shown here is used for displaying a standard file dialog box allowing the user to select a file.)

exit messageName

When HyperCard encounters the **exit command,** it terminates execution of the specified handler.

When the Exit button is clicked, the answer command displays this dialog box:

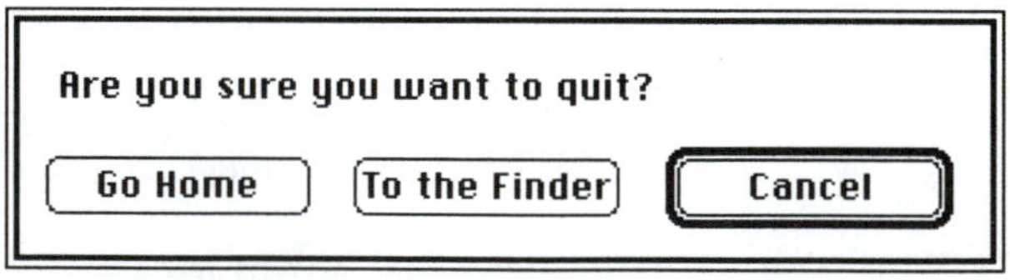

The option chosen by the user is stored in the local variable It. A **nested if structure** is used to compare the user's response with possible options and perform the appropriate action. If the user clicks Cancel, the handler is terminated by the `exit` statement; the dialog box disappears, and the user returns to the card where the Exit button was clicked.

If the user clicks Go Home, the first `if` statement is false, so the statements following `else` are executed. The first of those statements is another `if` statement, which checks to see whether It contains "Go Home". Since it does, the user is transported to the Home stack by the `go home` statement.

If the user clicks on the To the Finder button, both `if` statements test false, so the statement after the innermost `else` is executed: `doMenu` tells HyperCard to execute the menu command Quit HyperCard.

☐ **Test the Exit button.**

Break Point

Modifying the Menu Bar

 This section is optional; if you have no interest in modifying the menu bar or in advanced scripting techniques, pass it by.

Although it's far from complete, our stack now has a complete set of working buttons and fields. We've built a working user interface; we just need to add content cards. But before we dash off dozens of computer component cards, let's add one more wrinkle to the user interface: custom menus. HyperCard 2 makes it easy to modify the menu bar by adding new menus and menu items, deleting standard menus and menu items, and disabling existing menu items. This kind of power shouldn't be taken lightly, though.

The single greatest strength of the Macintosh menu bar is consistency. In well-designed Macintosh applications, menus are consistent with Macintosh standards, making it possible for new users of an application to feel immediately at home. Think carefully about the implications of your actions before you modify the menu bar. Don't confuse the user with unnecessary changes.

Designing the Stack Script

The Home stack, the Help stack, the Addresses stack, and the Appointments stack all have something that's missing in your stack: a custom stack menu. A well-designed stack menu can provide Macintosh veterans with a comfortable and consistent tool for navigating the stack. Let's build one.

Our stack has plenty of navigation options in the button bar. The most sensible approach is to duplicate those options in a Navigate menu, so users have a choice of navigation tools: menu or buttons. Suppose we want to create a menu that looks like the one shown here.

```
Navigate
  Title Card
  Main Menu
..................
  Find
  Exit        ⌘E
```

At the same time, we want to temporarily delete the Edit and File menus to avoid problems that might result when a naive user selects unfamiliar menu items. (Once again, this is not a decision that should be made lightly.) Using the same reasoning, we decide to disable some of the items in the Go menu that could put the first-time user in unfamiliar territory. Of course, if we cause the menu bar to change when the stack is opened, we should put everything back the way we found it when the stack is closed.

(It's possible to open another stack without closing this one; if we've changed the menu bar, we should think about what happens when our stack is temporarily **suspended** and another stack is opened. But since we're eliminating the File menu, we'll naively assume this isn't a problem and ignore the complications of coding for this situation. A more realistic approach was taken by the creators of Home, Help, Addresses, and the other standard stacks. Study those stack scripts for ideas on how to handle suspended stacks.)

Even with the Home command disabled in the Go menu, it's possible for the user to inadvertently go to the Home stack by clicking the Go Back button one time too many. Each click pops a card off the reminder stack; when all the cards are popped, Go Back takes the user Home. To minimize the chances of this happening, we should push the title card onto the stack, so that the Go Back button will take the user there before going Home.

While we're thinking about protecting the naive user, we might want to consider protecting our stack from the naive user. We can easily set the user level to browsing when the stack is opened, provided we make a commitment to return it to its former level upon exit.

We've discussed several things that should happen when the stack is opened. To keep everything straight, let's make a list of the things we'd like to have the stack do when it opens. We'll use **pseudocode**—a cross between a computer language (in this case, HyperTalk) and English:

```
on openStack
  lock screen
  lower user level
  add navigate menu
  delete other menus
  disable Go menu items
  push card
  unlock screen
end openStack
```

(If we lock the screen before we do everything else and unlock it when we're through, all of the cosmetic changes happen at once.)

Some of the statements (such as `lock screen`) are pure Hyper-Talk; others can be made into messages for soon-to-be-written handlers. Here's a refinement of the preceding handler in syntactically correct HyperTalk:

```
on openStack
  lock screen
  lowerUserLevel
  addNavigateMenu
  deleteOtherMenus
  disableGoMenuItems
  push card
  unlock screen
end openStack
```

We now need to write handlers that can intercept and make sense out of the following messages: `lowerUserLevel`, `addNavigateMenu`, `deleteOtherMenus`, and `disableGoMenuItems`.

Here's a handler for `lowerUserLevel`:

```
on lowerUserLevel
  global oldUserLevel
  get userLevel
  put It into oldUserLevel
  set userLevel to 1
end lowerUserLevel
```

This script, executed when the `lowerUserLevel` message is sent from the `on openStack` script, gets the current user level and puts it into the global variable `oldUserLevel`, where it remains until the stack is closed. (We'll write a script later to restore the original user level using this variable). The last command in this handler sets the user level to browsing level 1. At the `end lowerUserLevel` statement, execution returns to the `on openStack` script, ready for the next statement in that script.

Writing Menu Manipulation Scripts

Before we can write the menu-handling handlers, we need to learn a little more HyperTalk.

Menu Manipulation Commands and Properties

```
create menu menuName
delete menu
reset menuBar
```

The **create menu** command creates a menu with the specified name. The menu continues to exist until it is deleted with the **delete menu command,** or until the default HyperCard menus are reinstated with the **reset menuBar command,** or until the HyperCard session is ended. (The `delete menu` command can be used to delete standard HyperCard menus, too.) Menu creation and deletion commands are generally included in the stack script so the menus will exist while the stack is open.

```
put itemName preposition [menuItem of] menu ¬
[with menuMsg message]
```

This special form of the `put` command is used for putting new menu items in existing menus. The optional `with` clause specifies that a particular message be sent when the menu item is chosen; it's the easiest way to make the menu item functional. Here's an example for adding a new item (with a keyboard shortcut) to the Go menu:

```
put "Second" after menuItem "First" of menu "Go" ¬
with menuMsg "Go second card"
set the cmdChar of menuItem "Second" ¬
of menu "Go" to 5
```

The **cmdChar** property can be used to specify a command-key shortcut for any existing menu item.

```
disable menu
disable menuItem of menu
```

The **disable command** turns a menu or menu item gray and makes it inactive. Here's an example:

```
disable menuItem "Recent" of menu "Go"
```

For now, let's skip the message `addNavigateMenu` and work on `deleteOtherMenus` and `disableGoMenuItems`. The scripts are self-explanatory:

```
on deleteOtherMenus
  delete menu "Edit"
  delete menu "File"
end deleteOtherMenus

on disableGoMenuItems
  disable menuItem "Recent" of menu "Go"
  disable menuItem "Help" of menu "Go"
end disableGoMenuItems
```

Writing Custom Functions and Handlers

The `addNavigateMenu` handler is slightly more complex:

```
on addNavigateMenu
  show menuBar
  create menu "Navigate"
  put NavigateItems() into menu "Navigate" ¬
  with menuMessages NavigateMessages()
  set cmdChar of menuItem "Exit" ¬
  of menu "Navigate" to "E"
end addNavigateMenu
```

First, the script ensures that the menu bar is visible with the `show menuBar` command. Next, it creates a new menu called Navigate. The `put` statement puts the appropriate menu items in that menu and assigns messages to each of those items. But instead of listing all five items after `put`, we included a call to a **custom (programmer defined) function** called `NavigateItems`. This function, after we write it, will return the list of menu item names that belong here: `Title Card,Main Menu,-,Find,Exit`. Similarly, we've included a call to function `NavigateMessages`. This function will return the list of messages associated with the five menu items: `doMenu First, goMain, empty, doFind, DoExit`. When the `put` statement is executed, each of the function names is replaced by the value returned by the function. In effect, the statement says

```
put Title Card,Main Menu,-,Find,Exit into ¬
menu "Navigate" with ¬
doMenu First,goMain,empty,doFind,DoExit
```

In fact, we could have written the statement exactly like this from the beginning. But most seasoned programmers prefer to break large programs and statements into smaller modules by creating separate functions and message handlers. We've chosen to write a shorter, more readable `put` statement by including calls to two functions. Here's what the functions look like:

```
function NavigateItems
   return  "Title Card,Main Menu,-,Find,Exit"
end NavigateItems

function NavigateMessages
   return "doMenu First,goMain,empty,doFind,DoExit"
end NavigateMessages
```

This second function includes three more messages that have no corresponding handlers so far. Here are the missing handlers:

```
on goMain
   send mouseUp to bg button "Main Menu"
end goMain

on doFind
   send mouseUp to bg button "Find"
end doFind

on doExit
   send mouseUp to bg button "Exit"
end doExit
```

Notice that all three handlers do the same thing: send a `mouseUp` message to a background button. If the user selects Main Menu from the Navigate menu, the message `mouseUp` is sent to the background button Main Menu. This has exactly the same effect as a mouse click on that button; it's as if the computer clicked the button because you told it to via the menu. The button responds to the `mouseUp` message by pushing a card onto the stack and jumping to the Main Menu card with a visual effect transition.

> `send "`*`messageName [parameterList]`*`" [to `*`object`*`]`
>
> The **send command** sends a message to any specified object in the current stack or to another stack (but not to an object in another stack). If no object is specified, HyperCard is the object.

Covering Our Tracks

We've practiced stepwise refinement on the list of things to do when the stack is opened, and the result is a complete set of handlers and functions to set up the stack properly and modify the menu bar. All that remains is to create a set of scripts to handle the necessary housekeeping when the stack is closed.

Here's what we want to happen when we close the stack:

```
on closeStack
  set user level to old user level
  hide card field "thanks" on card 1
  reset menu bar
end closeStack
```

(We want to hide the card field credits so that it doesn't appear the next time the stack is opened. That way, every user who opens the stack has the same startup screen.) Converting pseudocode to HyperTalk, we have:

```
on closeStack
  global oldUserLevel
  set userLevel to oldUserLevel
  hide card field "thanks" on card 1
  reset menuBar
end closeStack
```

When the stack is closed, this script tells HyperCard to set the user level to the value stored in the global variable oldUserLevel; then to hide the credits field on the Title card; and finally, to reset the menu bar so it contains default HyperCard menus and nothing more.

Putting the Stack Script Together

Here, then, is the complete stack script:

```
on openStack
  lock screen
  lowerUserLevel
  addNavigateMenu
  deleteOtherMenus
  disableGoMenuItems
  push card
  unlock screen
end openStack

on closeStack
  global OldUserLevel
  set userLevel to OldUserLevel
  hide card field "thanks" of card 1
  reset menuBar
end closeStack
```

```
on lowerUserLevel
  global OldUserLevel
  get userLevel
  put it into OldUserLevel
  set userLevel to 1
end lowerUserLevel

--  MENU-HANDLING SCRIPTS  --
on addNavigateMenu
  show menuBar
  create menu "Navigate"
  put NavigateItems() into menu "Navigate"¬
  with menuMessages NavigateMessages()
  set cmdChar of menuItem "Exit" of menu "Navigate" ¬
  to "E"
end addNavigateMenu

on deleteOtherMenus
  delete menu "Edit"
  delete menu "File"
end deleteOtherMenus

on disableGoMenuItems
  disable menuItem "Recent" of menu "Go"
  disable menuItem "Help" of menu "Go"
end disableGoMenuItems

function NavigateItems
  return  "Title Card,Main Menu,-,Find,Exit"
end NavigateItems

function NavigateMessages
  return "doMenu First,goMain,empty,doFind,doExit"
end NavigateMessages

on goMain
  send mouseUp to bg button "Main Menu"
end goMain

on doFind
  send mouseUp to bg button "Find"
end doFind

on doExit
  send mouseUp to bg button "Exit"
end doExit
```

☐ **Type the script into the stack's script window. As you type, make sure the automatic indentation matches the indentation shown here. If it doesn't, you probably made a typing error. Check your typing and save the script.**

Adding a Temporary Script

Before you test the script, you should be aware of one potential problem: When you open the stack, almost all navigation commands will be disabled. This is fine for novice users, but it can be terribly inconvenient for you when you're debugging and refining the stack. How do you move around the stack if something is wrong with the script of the buttons you created? How do you modify the scripts when the user level has been set to browsing? To protect yourself from such potential problems, you can create a temporary button that allows you to undo some of the disabling commands.

☐ **Create a button somewhere near the bottom of the background. Name it "Emergency Override" and give it the following script:**

```
on mouseUp
  reset menuBar
  addNavigateMenu
  set userLevel to 5
end mouseUp
```

☐ **Test the openStack script by going to the Home stack and returning to the stack. Try out the modified menus. Test the closeStack script by using the Navigate menu to return Home. If you encounter any problems that require damage control, click on the Emergency Override button (or use the message box to reset the user level and the menu bar), fix the script errors, and retest. (The debugger might help you locate the errors.) If you don't understand how the scripts work, put a checkpoint at the beginning of the stack script and step/trace through the script, watching how variables, messages, and commands translate into actions.**

☐ **When the stack is thoroughly tested and debugged, delete the Emergency Override button.**

Missing Links

Keeping Track of Loose Ends

There is much to do before this stack is truly finished. In truth, a stack like this is never finished, because you can always think of some way to improve it.

> It's important to maintain an Unfinished Business List as you create large projects. The human brain can create loose ends much more efficiently than it can keep track of them.

Here's a To Do list that covers the most important missing features. We need to:

- Add a full-fledged introduction between the Title card and the Main Menu card, providing computer novices with the background they need to make sense of the rest of the stack.

- Complete the remainder of the Output branch (screens and printers). When we reach the leaves on each branch (leaves are cards that don't have branches, such as Dot Matrix Printer and Color Monitor), we might include pictures of the components being described. (You'll need to unlock the text in both fields to type information on the new cards, and lock them when you're through.)

- Complete the other three branches (Storage, Processors, Input).

- Add a conclusion for sequential readers of the stack. Most other users probably aren't interested in a conclusion, so we can just add information and/or pictures to the final card we've already created.

- Add graphics. Some cards, such as the root of the tree, could benefit from a little creative painting.

- Add a Help card and a Stack Map card, and add buttons to get to and from those cards.

- Add digitized sound effects. For example, you might include spoken comments, samples of sound output, or audio cues corresponding to page turning, jumping around, and other common actions.

Finally, the most important step of all:

> Test every button and feature of your stack carefully. Test the stack yourself; then ask members of your target audience to test it while you watch.

Critiquing Our Stack

By now, you may be thinking, "This stack has problems; I could design a better one myself." You're likely to have those kinds of thoughts even while you're turning your own design into reality. HyperCard invites experimentation, so stacks tend to evolve as they're being created. Halfway through a project you might come up with a better way to implement a particular feature. Whether you choose to modify your original design or stick with it, it's a good idea to take some time to critique your stack to see if it really achieves your original goals.

If we look at our stack critically, after testing it ourselves and with novice users, we might start a list of suggested improvements. For example:

1. The user interface is rather busy. Because we provided the user many ways of navigating the stack, it's possible for the user to lose track of what's been seen and what remains to be seen. We should consider ways for the user to mark his or her progress through the stack.

2. `closeStack` removes the menu we created, but what if we don't close the stack, but simply open another stack in a new window, instead? Our menu is still there, ready to send an error message if the user issues a menu command with it. We need a more sophisticated approach using the **suspendStack** and **resumeStack** system messages. (For a good example of how this might be implemented, examine the stack script for the HyperCard Help stack.)

This kind of criticism isn't always easy; when you've invested considerable time and energy in a project, it's hard to admit that it has structural flaws. But easy or not, critical analysis is important. Many serious stack designers take the process even beyond critiquing and fine tuning. Here's what those experts advise:

> When you've completed your rough draft of your stack, take an inventory of the ways that it might be improved. Then start over, building it a second time, applying what you learned the first time to your second stack. Repeat as needed.

HyperTalk Housekeeping

HyperTalk is a rich and powerful language with capabilities that go far beyond what we've covered here. You've had enough of a taste of HyperTalk to be well equipped to explore the language further. HyperTalk is the kind of computer language that encourages experimentation, and experimentation is a wonderful way to learn. But as you're exploring, remember that HyperTalk, like any powerful tool, can lead to problems as well as solutions.

Avoiding HyperTalk Hazards

- Use the Save a Copy... command regularly when you're working on an important stack. The more often you back up your work, the less work you'll lose if something goes wrong.

- Use the **Compact Stack command** after you've been working on a stack for a while. This command gets rid of pockets of **free space** that develop whenever you delete anything; the free space makes the stack slower and larger. (You can check the amount of free space in the Stack Info dialog box.)

- Plan ahead, and don't be afraid to backtrack or start over.

- Name everything with meaningful names, and write scripts that `Go to name` rather than `Go to number`. It's much easier to debug a script full of names than it is to debug a script full of numbers.

- Avoid duplicate names; HyperCard does not prevent two things from having the same name, so it's up to you.

- Use quotation marks to keep things together that belong together.

- Make your scripts as readable as possible, and add comments anywhere that the meaning or purpose of a statement isn't obvious.

- Use temporary scripts to help you debug your stacks. For example: When you're creating a stack with many links going in different directions (such as Dungeon or Computer Anatomy), it's easy to lose track of the card sequences. Add a field to each background, check its Field Info dialog box to see what number has been assigned to it, and create a background script like this:

```
on openCard
  put "Card" && number of this card into field 1
end openCard
```

Translation: When the card is opened, put a character string that's made up of "Card" and the number of the current card, separated by a space into field 1). In some stacks, such as Pyramid, this field might be useful as a permanent fixture. In other stacks, such as Dungeon, where you don't want the card number displayed, the script should be removed when the stack is finished.

- Use the **Comment** and **Uncomment** commands in the Script menu. Since you may need to resurrect temporary scripts during future debugging sessions, it's sometimes wise to deactivate them rather than delete them. Comment may be used to insert a comment marker at the insertion point; Uncomment deletes the preceding comment mark. If you select several lines of a script and use the Comment (or Uncomment) command, comment markers appear (or disappear) at the beginning of every selected line.

- Put scripts, buttons, and fields where they are most appropriate. If a button or field affects only one card, put it on that card. If something affects many cards with the same background, put it in the background. If it affects many cards with different backgrounds, put it in the stack. If it affects many different stacks, put it in a separate stack and reference that stack with the `startUsing` command (explained in the Help stack and in the Claris manual *HyperCard Reference*). Use a consistent method for deciding where to put scripts, so you can easily find them later.

- Don't reinvent the wheel unless you have to. The Claris version of HyperCard comes with stacks full of buttons, cards, backgrounds, and clip art that can be used in your stacks. Many commercial, shareware, and public domain programs include buttons, cards, and art designed for borrowing. If somebody has created a script that does what you want, and has given the world permission to copy it, feel free to do so. (However, it's important to respect copyright laws and the ethical underpinnings of intellectual property rights; don't borrow from copyrighted material without the author's permission.)

- Take advantage of the Claris HyperCard Power Tools if you have them. One especially useful tool for debugging allows you to export all of the scripts of your stack into a single text file so you can print it out and examine every detail.

- Use the right tool for the job. HyperTalk is an interpreted language, which means that the HyperTalk **interpreter** translates it on the fly, like an interpreter at the United Nations. Programs written in compiled languages, in contrast, are translated all at once into machine language by **compilers**, the way this book might be translated from English to Spanish. The tradeoff is between immediacy and speed; since it's an interpreter, HyperTalk produces relatively slow-running programs. (Technically, HyperTalk 2 scripts are *partially* compiled, but they're still no match in speed for fully compiled programs in other languages.) If your HyperCard stack needs speed—or some other feature or property that's not native to HyperTalk—you might be able to have the best of both worlds by including an **XCMD (external command)** written in Pascal or C in your stack. Writing XCMDs requires considerable programming skill, but borrowing XCMDs is easy. Many XCMDs are available in commercial and public domain packages.

- Learn from the masters. Study the best stacks that you can find; apply the programming techniques of those stacks to your own work. (A sampler of first-rate stacks is included in Appendix A.)

The Endless Stack

The scripts you've seen and written in this book should give you a feel for the basic mechanics of HyperTalk. You'll be surprised how much more you can learn by snooping in scripts of other people's stacks, consulting the Help stack to look up commands that are unfamiliar. The Help stack, like its printed counterpart, *The HyperCard Script Language Guide*, is designed to be a reference tool, not a tutorial. You may want a more systematic introduction to advanced HyperTalk scripting. Appendix A lists several such sources, as well as software tools specifically designed to facilitate the stack-building process.

There's no denying the power of HyperTalk as a tool for enhancing your scripts. But even if you never learn another word of HyperTalk, you'll be able to apply what you've learned in this book to build impressive and useful stacks. You now have the tools to make things happen. Go for it!

Summary

You've seen how to create nonlinear hypertext documents using Hyper-Card. Specifically, you combined several different structures—a sequence, a tree, and a complex network—into a document that can be read in several different ways. You learned many new HyperTalk commands, including several for building hypertext documents and others for customizing the HyperCard user interface. More important, you learned how to apply basic design principles to your work, so the stacks you create can accomplish the goals you've set for them.

Key Words

`&&`	custom (programmer defined)
`answer` command	function
`ask` command	data structure
`bg`	defining the problem
branch	`delete menu` command
chunk	`disable` command
`clickChunk` (function)	`doMenu` command
`clickText` (function)	`exit` command
`cmdChar` (property)	Field Info... command
Comment command	`find` (command)
Compact Stack command	`find chars` (command)
compiler	`find string` (command)
concatenate	`find whole` command
`create menu` command	free space

`get` command	`push` command (Command-↓)
`global` command	`reset menuBar` command
global variable	`result` function
Group style	`resumeStack` message
hot text	root
hypermedia	scrolling field
hypertext	`send` command
interpreter	stack (data structure)
`It`	stepwise refinement
local variable	Style menu
`lock screen` command	`suspendStack` message
`lockScreen` (property)	suspended (stack)
nested if structure	`textStyle` (function)
`pop card` command	tree structure
(Command-↑)	Uncomment command
pop-up field	`unlock screen` command
pseudocode	XCMD (external command)

Self-Testing Exercises

1. What kind of structure (linear, tree, or network) is most appropriate for a stack that

    a. Provides users with a list of legislators, with options for seeing the voting record of each one?

    b. Guides users through a walking tour of your town, highlighting main scenic attractions along the way?

2. What happens when a button in the card layer covers a button in the background layer?

3. What happens when a field in the card layer covers a field in the background layer?

4. What happens when a button in the card layer covers a field in the background layer?

5. What happens when a field in the card layer covers a button in the background layer?

6. What is hot text?

7. What is the variable `It` used for?

8. What is the difference between a local variable and a global variable? When is it appropriate to declare a variable as global?

9. What is the relationship between the `push` and `pop card` commands? Give examples of how they can be used in stack scripts.

What are their keyboard shortcuts, and how might the shortcuts be useful?

10. What is the difference between the `ask` command and the `answer` command? Give examples of how each might be used.

11. Why would you lock text? How?

12. What is a function? Give examples of built-in functions and user-defined functions.

13. The following HyperTalk commands contain words you haven't seen before. What do you think each statement does?

    a. `set textFont of field "bullet chart" to Times`

    b. `set textSize of word 1 of field "bullet chart" to 18`

    c. `set textAlign of field "bullet chart" to center`

    d. `set textFont of button 1 to Helvetica`

    e. `set textStyle of button 1 to italic, extend`

    f. `set autoHilite of button 2 to true`

    g. `set style of button 1 to radioButton`

    h. `put the number of cards into msg`

    i. `put the number of windows into msg`

14. What do the following handlers do? (If you have trouble figuring something out, type it in and try it out.)

    a.
    ```
    on getName
       ask "What is your name"
       put it into yourName
       if yourName is empty then exit getName
       put "Hello Welcome to HyperCard, " & ¬
       yourName into the message box
    end getName
    ```

    b.
    ```
    on nonsense
       ask "Give a starting number for Bozo"
       put it into Bozo
       repeat 10 times
         add 1 to Bozo
       end repeat
       put "The answer is " & Bozo into ¬
       message box
    end nonsense
    ```

c.
```
on mouseUp
    ask "Enter a temperature in Fahrenheit"
    put Fahrenheit(it) into temp
    put "The Centigrade temperature is: " & ¬
    temp into msg
end mouseUp
function Fahrenheit temperature
    return (temperature - 32) * 5/9 ¬
    -- Fahrenheit to Centigrade
end Fahrenheit
```

d.
```
on mouseUp
    get the clickText
    if the textStyle of the clickChunk ¬
    contains bold then
        put char 1 of word 1 of field "my name" ¬
        & char 1 of word 2 of field "my name" ¬
        into msg
    end if
end mouseUp
```

e. (*Hint:* This handler contains some unfamiliar words, but it's not hard to figure out. Assume there's a picture of a car in the card layer at location (100, 320), and that the background layer contains the rest of the picture of a city street. This technique is sometimes called *paint animation*.)

```
on mouseUp
    choose select tool
    type "s" with commandkey
    doMenu opaque
    set dragspeed to 70
    drag from 100, 320 to 400, 320
    choose browse tool
end mouseUp
```

15. Write a script for a button that, when clicked, causes HyperCard to do the same thing that it does when you select the following menu items:

    a. New Card

    b. Recent

    c. Message

    d. Quit HyperCard

16. Write a handler to create a menu named Other Stuff when the stack is opened. Include the following items in the menu:

    a. Userlevel to Scripting

    b. Play a Song

    c. Get Card Info

17. Write handlers for each of the menu items in question 16.

Projects

1. Complete as many of the items on the To Do list at the end of this session as you can.

2. Add page numbers to your stack using the trick described in the box called "Avoiding HyperTalk Hazards."

3. Add and implement a Help button on the first card: (a) with a pop-up field, (b) by going to the last card in the stack (remember to provide a way to get back).

4. Add a glossary to the Computer Anatomy stack. Underline words and phrases in the main text that appear in the glossary, and write a script for the field that links those words and phrases to the glossary entries.

5. As an alternative to a glossary, add pop-up definitions to underlined words in the text.

6. Modify the Pyramid stack from Session 3 so that it displays informative pop-up fields when buttons are clicked.

7. Modify the Map stack (Project 6, Session 3) so that it displays fields describing particular areas when those areas are clicked.

8. Write an interactive story that allows users to click on buttons to choose different paths through the story.

9. Create a stack to catalog your collection of tapes, records, or CDs. Include fields for artist, title, music category, favorite tracks, and comments. Borrow and/or create buttons to find and sort cards in your stack. After entering data for several recordings, test both of these buttons.

10. Create a glossary of terms for a specific field of study (computers, hypermedia, biology, anthropology, or whatever), with each term defined and/or illustrated on a single card. Create cross-links that connect related terms, so that readers can jump from definition to definition instantly. For example, if the card for *disk drive* includes

the term *peripheral*, that term should have a button that links to a card for *peripheral*.

11. Make a genealogy stack that includes at least three generations. Develop a plan before you actually start to create the stack. Include in the background five text fields: name, birth date, birth place, interesting information, and date of death. Think about the field attributes carefully in terms of their function. (Should any of these fields scroll?) Design a good-looking background; allow space for several card buttons. In the card layer create the following buttons where appropriate: Mother, Father, Spouse(s), and Child(ren). (Why should these buttons be in the card layer?) Link each button to the appropriate card. If the button has nowhere to go, display a message to that effect using a pop-up field. Finally, when you have completed the stack, critique it as if someone else had created it and you were the user.

APPENDIX A

HYPERCARD SOURCES AND RESOURCES

HyperCard 2 in a Hurry was designed to give you a quick but thorough introduction to HyperCard, version 2.0 and beyond. If you decide to work seriously in software development with HyperCard, you'll want to learn more about HyperCard and other tools that extend your powers as a stack builder. This appendix surveys software and hardware tools for adding graphics, animation, sound, scripts, and other enhancements to your stacks. In addition, it describes an assortment of exemplary stacks available through commercial and public domain channels so you can see how professionals and serious amateurs are putting Hyper-Card to work. (Addresses and phone numbers for all software sources are listed at the end of this appendix.) Finally, this appendix lists several books that you can use to expand your knowledge of HyperCard and HyperTalk.

Graphic Tools

A stand-alone graphics program can be a useful accessory for Hyper-Card stack developers, HyperCard paint tools notwithstanding. There are three reasons why you might want to use a separate graphics program with HyperCard:

1. HyperCard's Import Paint... command can access only the top part of a standard Macintosh paint file, so most clip art pictures and digitized images must be edited and manipulated with a paint program before they can be imported into HyperCard.

2. Many graphics programs have tools and options that go far beyond HyperCard's painting capabilities. By creating images in one of these

programs and importing the results into HyperCard, you can often save time and produce more artistic stacks.

3. HyperCard 2 includes a `picture` command that makes it possible to display color or gray-scale pictures in their own windows, but HyperCard has no capability for producing or editing these pictures. A color graphics program is a useful tool for creating those images.

Several popular graphics programs are available for the Macintosh. Here are a few worth knowing about:

- MacPaint (Claris Corporation) was originally designed by Bill Atkinson, the creator of HyperCard, so it shares many features, tools, and menus with that program. If you're comfortable drawing in HyperCard, MacPaint will feel like home from the minute you double-click its icon. Unfortunately, the aging MacPaint is short on features when compared with almost every other paint program on the market; it has little to offer that you don't already have in HyperCard.

- Studio/1 (Electronic Arts) is a reasonably priced black-and-white paint program with built-in animation capabilities. With an overall design similar to Studio/8 and Studio/32 (see below), Studio/1 provides an array of tools and tricks that make the toolboxes in HyperCard and MacPaint look conspicuously underpowered. Custom brushes, dithered gradients, editable Bezier curves, and a host of other features allow you to quickly create graphic effects that would take hours to produce in HyperCard.

- Amazing Paint (CE Software) is another popular paint program with more features and a lower price than MacPaint. Its feature list looks like a wish list for frustrated MacPainters: multiple undos, mouse magnification, specialized selection tools, on-screen measurement, and more, all bundled in one of the friendliest user interfaces you'll find in any paint package.

- DeskPaint (Zedcor) provides an incredible array of sophisticated black-and-white and 24-bit color painting tools in the convenience of a desk accessory. Because it's a DA, DeskPaint is always available in the Apple menu. This makes it easy to edit and import clip art, scanned images, and other paint files without leaving HyperCard. DeskPaint is bundled with DeskDraw, a useful object-oriented drawing DA. It can also be purchased as part of Desk, an all-purpose collection of powerful applications in DA form.

- UltraPaint (Deneba Software) and SuperPaint (Silicon Beach Software) are two popular paint programs that combine the best features of paint and draw programs, so you can work with objects or pixels, depending on your needs. UltraPaint includes a number of features not found in SuperPaint, including full-color capabilities, but Super-

Paint still enjoys great popularity because of its seniority; it was the first paint program to challenge MacPaint as the standard Macintosh paint application. Both programs are more expensive than the ones listed so far, but less expensive than typical high-end, professional color graphics programs.

- Studio/8 and Studio/32 (Electronic Arts) are representative of the high-end color paint programs used—and praised—by professionals. Studio/8 is designed for producing 8-bit (256-color) images; the more expensive and feature-laden Studio/32 is an exquisite tool for creating "true color" (32-bit) images. (While it's possible with Studio/32 to create or edit 32-bit images on any color Mac, you can't see all of the colors without a 32-bit video board.) Of the two, Studio/32 is undeniably more powerful, but either program is capable of producing breathtaking color pictures.

- Kid Pix (Brøderbund) was originally designed as a color graphics toy for preschool Mouseketeers. As a productivity tool for serious artists, it's no match for Studio/32. Nonetheless, Kid Pix is arguably the most original paint program since MacPaint. It's certainly the most fun. Recommended for kids of all ages.

- MacDraw Pro (Claris Corporation), Canvas (Deneba Software), Freehand (Aldus Corporation), and Illustrator (Adobe Systems, Inc.), are among the most popular and powerful professional graphics programs for the Macintosh. All of these programs are best at manipulating on-screen objects rather than tweaking pixels. Freehand and Illustrator use Adobe's PostScript page description language for creation of objects; MacDraw and Canvas are based on the Macintosh's resident QuickDraw system, and are therefore more appropriate for use with HyperCard.

- DeltaGraph (Delta Point, Inc.) is a specialized tool for turning numbers into quantitative charts and graphs. If your stack needs a bar chart, line chart, pie chart, or scatter chart, DeltaGraph can automatically create it for you in a fraction of the time that it would take you to draw it with HyperCard's paint tools. For that matter, so can Excel, Microsoft Works, Wingz, DeskCalc (part of Zedcor's Desk), and a number of other spreadsheet and presentation graphics programs. But if you don't need a spreadsheet, DeltaGraph offers considerably more flexibility for producing unique, eye-catching charts with ease. The program's command language provides even more flexibility for HyperCard users. Using the language, you can issue a series of commands from within HyperCard to invoke DeltaGraph, pass it the necessary data for creation of a chart, and accept the resulting chart back into your stack—all automatically.

- Image Grabber (Sabastian Software), SnapJot (Trillium Software), and Exposure (Preferred Publishers) are special-purpose utilities for capturing whatever you see on the Macintosh screen in a black-and-white or color picture file. When the standard key combination Command-Shift-3 won't do the job, one of these will. Exposure is more complex, more feature-laden, and more expensive than the other two.

If you aren't artistically inclined, you can use professionally drawn clip art in your stacks. If you can't find what you need in the public domain, you'll probably find it in a commercial collection. High-quality bit-mapped art packages are available in collections such as Wet Paint (Dub'l Click Software) and Click Art (T-Maker Software). There are dozens of other collections, including several massive collections on CD-ROM (compact disk read only memory, described in more detail in the section called "Multimedia Makers"). For example, Down to Earth! (Wayzata Technology) contains *hundreds* of detailed drawings from nature that look great printed at 300 dots per inch or displayed on screen at 72 dots per inch. Like many CD-ROM collections, it includes a HyperCard-based index to simplify the process of locating and opening pictures. For more information on clip art, check *Macworld* magazine's annual review of clip art collections or Peachpit Press's definitive reference, *Canned Art: Clip Art for the Macintosh*, by Erfert Fenton and Christine Morrissett (Berkeley, CA: 1990).

Scanners and Digitizers

With a good scanner it's possible to digitize hand-drawn pictures, photographs, and other images from noncomputer sources so they can be edited and imported into HyperCard. It's important, though, to be aware that copyright laws and intellectual property rights apply when you're scanning published materials. Scanners vary widely in price and features. Here are three of particular interest to HyperCard users:

- Apple Scanner (Apple Computer), is one of many gray-scale flatbed scanners on the market. (Flatbed scanners read face-down pages like a photocopier does.) It's capable of scanning images at much higher resolution than you can see on the Macintosh screen. Its distinguishing feature from the point of view of a HyperCard user is the included HyperScan software that allows you to control the scanner directly from HyperCard. The current Apple Scanner won't scan color images; you'll need to spend quite a bit more for that capability. In fact, the Apple Scanner's gray-scale scanning capabilities are very limited when compared to most competitors. The Apple Scanner's gray-scale performance can be improved considerably with ThunderWorks software from competing scanner manufacturer Thunderware.

- ThunderScan (Thunderware) turns an ImageWriter printer into an input device by temporarily replacing the ribbon with a photoelectric cell that can pick up images from paper fed through the printer. It's dreadfully slow and inaccurate with fine detail, but it's priced at a fraction of the cost of a flatbed scanner and it does the job.

- LightningScan (Thunderware) and ScanMan (LogiTech), between ThunderScan and Apple Scanner in price and capability, are two hand-held scanners similar in appearance, capability, and price. Each scanner quickly sucks up a five-inch-wide image when it's rolled across a page like a tiny information vacuum cleaner. The main differences between these two units are in the software. Since software revisions happen often, you'll make the most informed choice if you try both before you buy.

- MacVision Video Digitizer (Koala Technologies) is an inexpensive hardware/software combination that allows the Macintosh to accept video input from a standard video camera, video recorder, or laser disc, and turn that input signal into a standard monochrome Macintosh graphic image. (A more expensive color version should be available by the time you read this.) The digitizing process is slow and the results often require tweaking, but the process is impressive nonetheless.

Animation Aids

In Session 5 you learned several ways to animate HyperCard stacks. These animation effects are illustrated, along with others, in the public domain stack by Jeremy Ahouse called Animation Help (a *Macworld* SuperStacks award winner). Although HyperCard offers plenty of possibilities for making moving pictures, it places clear limitations on the artist or programmer interested in serious animation. Fortunately, several special-purpose software tools are available for creating more sophisticated animation, and it's generally easy to display the results inside a HyperCard stack. Here are some noteworthy examples:

- ADDmotion (Motion Works) is a software tool specifically designed to extend the multimedia capabilities of HyperCard 2. Since it's installed as a series of XCMDs directly into HyperCard, ADDmotion is a natural choice for creating color animation with sound effects in HyperCard. ADDmotion includes a 24-bit color paint module that allows you to create and edit color pictures without leaving Hyper-Card. These pictures become backgrounds and "actors" for animated sequences. ADDmotion's Media Controller palette makes it easy to put up to 100 actors into motion at a time. Animated sequences can be controlled by keyboard and mouse events, and they can be sequenced to include sound effects and control of external devices such as synthesizers and CD players. Sequences created with ADDmotion can be distributed royalty free, including the ADDmotion runtime XCMD that allows any HyperCard 2 stack to play them back.

- Studio/1 (Electronic Arts) combines a black-and-white paint program with an easy-to-use animation builder. In order to display Studio/1 animated sequences (with sound effects) in HyperCard, you need to install a series XCMDs, but Studio/1 comes with a stack that automates the installation process. These XCMDs provide HyperCard with the vocabulary to open Studio/1 files and play them without leaving HyperCard (provided the Studio/1 files are in the same folder as the current stack). With a minimal amount of scripting, you can create on-screen buttons that control the speed and direction of the animation the way infrared remote buttons control a VCR.

- Director (MacroMind) is an expensive, high-end package that does far more than basic animation; it's a multimedia program that stretches the limits of the Macintosh hardware. Director is regarded by many as the standard against which other animation and multimedia programs should be measured. A series of XCMDs make it possible to play Director movies from within HyperCard (if the movie file and the MacroMind Player file are in the same folder as the current stack). But with Director's interactive capability and built-in scripting language you might find that you can do everything you need without even using HyperCard!

- MediaTracks (Farallon Computing) is a special-purpose tool for recording, editing, and playing back sequences of Macintosh screen movements. It's ideal for anyone creating how-to-do-something-on-a-Macintosh tutorials. Sounds can be added to recorded sequences with MediaTracks, so it's easy to add voice-over instructions to visual sequences. Finished sequences can be triggered from inside a HyperCard stack. MediaTracks is available as a stand-alone application or as part of the MediaTracks Multimedia Pack, which includes the MacRecorder digitizer and sound-editing software, described in the next section. (The MediaTracks Multimedia Pack is available in a CD-ROM version as well as a floppy disk version.)

- InterFace and HyperAnimator (Bright Star Technology) are designed to make it easy to create animated talking heads on your computer screen. Facial expressions and lip movements can be synchronized with digitized sounds to produce amusing and impressive, if not completely realistic, effects. To fully master either package, you'll need to learn the underlying scripting language. Hyper-Animator is considerably less expensive, but it lacks many of the advanced features of InterFace. Both packages include several sample "characters."

- Swivel 3D and Swivel 3D Professional (Paracomp) are designed for creating realistic three-dimensional color visualizations on your two-dimensional computer screen. The models you create can be moved and rotated just like real 3D objects, and parts can be linked together with defined mechanical properties. This makes it possible to attach a sliding door to a building or a head to a torso so that the parts work together just as they would in the real world. Swivel 3D's Tween panel allows you to create smooth animated sequences using 3D models and view those sequences from different perspectives; you can even watch from the moving object's point of view! Unlike the other packages listed here, Swivel 3D and Swivel 3D Professional don't include XCMDs for automatic replay within HyperCard, but there are several ways to display sequences created in these applications from your HyperCard stack. For example, you can paste the pictures directly onto HyperCard cards via the Macintosh Scrapbook, or, for more realism, you can import entire sequences directly into ADDmotion or Director for playback via HyperCard XCMDs. 3D animation work is time consuming, but the results can be stunning. (Paracomp also markets 3D clip art called Swivel Art for users who don't want to build their own creations.)

Sound Resources

HyperCard comes with two sounds built in: boing and harpsichord. As you explore HyperCard stacks, you're likely to run across buttons that play other sounds, ranging from symphonic strings to Sylvester and Tweety Bird. It's possible to copy those buttons and paste them into your stacks, but the copied buttons won't play sounds in the new stack because they lack resources. Every sound in HyperCard is stored as part of a resource. (Resources are also used to store icons, XCMDs, and other data used by HyperCard and other programs.)

Resources can't be copied like buttons; they have to be moved with special tools. The most widely available program for moving resources is ResEdit, a tool used by Macintosh software developers for creating and modifying resources. But ResEdit can be a dangerous tool in the hands of the uninitiated, because it provides the power to destroy a stack or a System with a click of the mouse. Two safer and friendlier tools for copying resources are Resource Mover, included in the Power Tools collection in the Claris HyperCard package, and Steve Maller's public domain program ResCopy. Both programs allow you to copy sound resources from other stacks into your stack. Once you've done that, you can play those sounds in a variety of ways with the `play` command. A growing number of stacks take care of the resource copying automatically.

Probably the most important tool for anyone serious about Hyper-Card sound is a sound recorder. While many newer Macintoshes include sound input hardware and software, the great majority of Macs are designed only with sound *output* in mind. For those machines, an add-on sound input device is necessary for creating custom sounds.

Farallon's MacRecorder is by far the most popular sound accessory for the Macintosh. MacRecorder is a reasonably priced mouse-sized device that allows you to capture any sound as a digitized sound resource that can be used in HyperCard, MediaTracks, or other programs. Two models are available; both attach to the modem port of the Macintosh and include built-in microphones. The MacRecorder Sound System includes jacks for connecting the device directly to external microphones and other electronic sound sources; the less expensive MacRecorder Voice Digitizer has no input jacks. The MacRecorder Sound System package also includes SoundEdit software (also available separately), which allows you to add echoes, play the sound backward, bend it, change the tempo, or modify it in a number of other ways. Both products include HyperSound software, which makes child's play of recording sounds and porting them directly into your stacks as ready-to-push buttons.

With a sound input device such as MacRecorder and a little creativity you can add a powerful audio dimension to your stacks. There's just one catch: Sounds take up *lots* of disk space. An otherwise tiny stack can expand to fill a floppy disk with the addition of just a few digitized sounds. The sound-editing software provided by Apple and Farallon allow you to compress sounds so they take up less disk space (with some cost in fidelity), but even compressed sounds add significant storage overhead to a stack. So if disk space is at a premium, here's some sound advice: Choose and use sounds sparingly.

MultiMedia Makers

The growing popularity of CD-ROM (compact disk read only memory) as a storage medium opens up all kinds of possibilities for multimedia and other data-intensive applications. Because a CD-ROM disk, which looks like an audio compact disk, can hold hundreds of floppy disks worth of information, sound and graphics no longer need to be limited by the comparatively small capacities of typical magnetic disks. This larger capacity isn't free; CD-ROM access is slower than that of a magnetic hard disk, and CD-ROMs aren't erasable. But for applications that require access to massive amounts of information, CD-ROM has no equal in today's market. And HyperCard is commonly used to create a front end (user interface) for accessing that data.

Many CD-ROM drives can also play audio compact disks, opening up the possibility of controlling access to high-fidelity audio CDs by computer. Because audio CDs are nothing more than digital storage media, the data from those disks can be manipulated just like any other data. With CD Audio Stack (The Voyager Company) or HyperCard CD Audio Toolkit (Apple Programmers and Developers Association or APDA), it's easy to create stacks that can rapidly access and play any passage from any portion of any track on a CD at the click of a button. (At press time, the products listed in this paragraph and the next have not been upgraded for version 2 of HyperCard, but revisions are likely to be available by the time you read this.) For examples of how this kind of tool is being used in products today, see the section "Prime Examples."

Along similar lines, it's possible to control a videodisc player with the Voyager Video Stack (The Voyager Company) or the HyperCard Videodisc Toolkit (APDA). This won't work unless your videodisc player has a computer control interface, not commonly found on players marketed for home use. (The Voyager Company sells a hardware product called The BOX that allows you to use their software with many home consumer videodisc players.) In addition, the lack of standardization among manufacturers makes it important that you know what kind of player you're writing for. But if you can overcome the hurdles, you can use HyperCard to produce truly interactive video.

Another multimedia track that's now open to HyperCard stack builders is electronic music. Synthesizers, samplers, and other digital instruments today are all capable of communicating with each other—and with computers—because of a standard interface called MIDI (musical instrument digital interface). By connecting a MIDI interface to one of the Macintosh serial ports, you give it the capability of talking to just about any modern electronic musical instrument. This means that you can use your Macintosh as a sequencer—a sort of multitrack digital tape recorder for composing and arranging electronic music. Professional sequencing software can cost many hundreds of dollars. Fortunately, low-cost software such as EZ Vision (OpCode Systems), Trax (Passport), and Deluxe Recorder (Electronic Arts) have features aplenty for most users, but not so many as to overwhelm amateurs. These sequencers accept input from the Mac's standard input devices or from a MIDI-equipped music keyboard, and play back the edited output files via any MIDI synthesizer or other sound source. All three are capable of working with standard MIDI files, so each can produce files that can be read by other MIDI software.

If you don't have the time, talent, or keyboard for creating a sequenced MIDI file, you can buy professionally arranged MIDI files for hundreds of popular and classical pieces from Passport's Music Data Company. You're certain to find many of your favorites in the ever-growing Music Data catalog. If you want hot-sounding original music (without many of the copyright restrictions that are attached to popular hits), consider OpCode's library of prerecorded Music Clips. MIDI files from any source may require some tweaking before they'll work with your particular synthesizer unless you have an industry standard sound source such as Roland's MT-32. You can make the necessary adjustments with a sequencer, or you can do it from within HyperCard using new products from OpCode and Passport.

OpCode's MIDIplay and Passport's HyperMusic can play standard MIDI files from any source (or combination of sound sources), including files you create with any sequencer. HyperMusic's main stack has a friendly interface with an on-screen mixer and a jukebox that includes ready-to-play MIDI recordings of several popular songs. MIDIplay has no jukebox, but its database-like interface makes it easy to catalog songs for your multimedia library based on key words. The MIDIplay package includes a sampler of original MIDI music rather than popular hits. Both programs include mixers for adjusting sounds and easy-to-use tools for installing MIDI-controlling buttons in your own stacks. If you have only 1 megabyte of RAM, your choice is limited by the fact that HyperMusic requires a 2-megabyte system.

Like CD audio, MIDI makes it possible to produce stunning audio sounds and effects that simply aren't possible with the Macintosh's limited internal audio tools. (For a basic introduction to MIDI technology, check out OpCode's excellent HyperCard stack called The Book of MIDI.)

General Goodies

Some HyperCard tools are hard to classify, but harder still to ignore. Here are a few:

- HyperDA (Symmetry Software) is a desk accessory that allows you to open and use HyperCard stacks on a standard Macintosh without quitting other applications. If you don't use MultiFinder or System 7, HyperDA is a good way to keep in touch with HyperCard while you do other things.

- Reports 2.0 (Nine to Five Software) takes up where HyperCard's report generator leaves off. With Reports, HyperCard comes close to competing directly with expensive dedicated database programs. If you need to print customized form letters, free-form reports, reports with complex calculations, preprinted forms, or other custom print-outs, Reports can make your life easier.

- HyperSpeller (Foundation Publishing) is an add-on spelling checker for HyperCard. If you're a poor speller working with text-intensive stacks, a spelling checker can save you a lot of time and embarrassment. HyperSpeller is a batch spelling checker—it checks for errors in a batch of selected text. If your spelling is truly terrible, you might prefer a general-purpose spelling checker such as Spelling Coach Professional (Deneba Software). In its current incarnation, Spelling Coach Professional won't check HyperCard files in batch mode. But Coach's interactive spelling checker works with any Macintosh application. The interactive checker beeps immediately whenever you type a word that's not found in the dictionary. (Spelling Coach Pro also offers on-line definitions in its dictionary, as well as an on-line thesaurus.)

- QuicKeys (CE Software) isn't designed specifically for HyperCard, but it's the kind of tool every HyperCard stack builder should know about. With QuicKeys, you can automate all of those repetitive tasks that take so much time and mental real estate. Need to copy a string of cards from one stack to another? Perform the operation on a single card while QuicKeys is recording, and the rest of the job is reduced to a few keystrokes. Once you've tried QuicKeys, you'll wonder how you got along without it.

HyperTalk Helpers

Many software tools are available to assist you as you build stacks, so you don't need to do everything the hard way. Some are power tools to make the script-writing process easier and to improve the quality of finished stacks. Others are packages of prefabricated buttons, art, cards, and XCMDs that can easily be incorporated into stacks. Still others are basic utilities to make the stack construction process simpler. Here are some examples:

- ScriptEdit (Somak Software) is a supercharged replacement for HyperCard's built-in script editor and debugger. Pop-up menus in every script window provide instant access to every built-in HyperTalk message, key word, command, function, property, and constant. The ScriptEdit editor includes a host of features for streamlining the editing process. An Objects window displays a dynamic list of every object in the current stack; a double-click on any object in that list opens a window for editing the related script. ScriptEdit is a real time saver for serious scripters.

- Dialoger Professional (Heizer Software) provides XCMDs to simplify the process of creating true Macintosh-style dialog boxes. With Dialoger, it's possible to create dialog boxes that go far beyond the limitations built into HyperTalk's `ask` and `answer` commands. If you need dialog boxes with scrolling editable text, pop-up menus, grouped radio buttons, styled text, color pictures, icons, or other exotica, Dialoger Professional is the right tool for the job.

- HyperCom (Gava Corporation) allows you to send HyperTalk messages to other systems on an AppleTalk network using `tell`, a new HyperTalk command. HyperCom can be licensed for any number of networked Macs.

- HyperCard Serial Communications Toolkit and HyperCard AppleTalk Toolkit (APDA) are Apple's programming tools for accessing the Mac serial ports and communicating via AppleTalk. (Neither has been rewritten for HyperCard 2 at press time.)

- Wild Things (Language Systems) is a good place to start if you want to learn how to create XCMDs and XFCNs. The package includes 40 ready-to-use XCMDs and XFCNs that do everything from animation to trigonometry. The documentation discusses the routines in detail, and complete source code is included.

- CompileIt! (Heizer Software) is a compiler to convert HyperTalk scripts into XCMDs or XFCNs (external functions). CompileIt! is useful for speeding up overall stack performance, protecting scripts so they can't be bootlegged, saving time on character manipulations and integer calculations, and for accessing the Macintosh ToolBox ROM routines. To fully master CompileIt! requires considerable technical know-how, but the package includes a debugger called DebugIt! that makes the troublesome process of finding errors easier.

In addition, there are hundreds of public domain and shareware tools, buttons, cards, and art collections available via electronic bulletin boards and user groups. Many of these are of questionable quality, but there are treasures aplenty for those who are willing to dig.

Beyond HyperCard

When HyperCard was introduced in 1987, it was a breakthrough product unlike anything that had come before. Since then, HyperCard has inspired several imitators on various computer platforms. Even the venerable Apple II now has a version of HyperCard with features similar to those of the original Macintosh HyperCard. Why should you consider using an alternative to HyperCard 2? You might find that the feature set of another product more closely meets your specific needs. But more importantly, some HyperCard alternatives allow your creations to be used by those who don't have access to Macintoshes. In fact, many HyperCard stacks can be converted by these alternatives into documents that can be used on IBM-compatible computers.

Here, then, are a few HyperCard alternatives worth knowing about:

- SuperCard (Silicon Beach Software), developed as an alternative to HyperCard 1.2, shares many features with HyperCard 2. Many users still prefer SuperCard, though, for a number of reasons, not the least of which is the ability to include color on cards, rather than on separate pictures.

- Plus (Spinnaker Software) is another color program that was designed for users who weren't happy with HyperCard 1.2. In its current incarnation, Plus lacks the debugger, multiple-window capability, and customizable menus found in HyperCard 2. However, Plus has several convenient object types and other programming features not supported by HyperCard. The biggest plus for Plus, though, is the fact that it comes in versions for both Macs and IBM-compatible computers running Windows. Since these two versions use identical file structures, Plus stacks created on either platform can be run on the other. What's more, Plus can read HyperCard 1.2 stacks and convert them to Plus format, making it indirectly possible to run HyperCard stacks on Windows PCs. (The next version of Plus should be able to read and convert HyperCard 2 stacks.)

- ConvertIt! (Heizer Software) is a utility that allows you to convert your HyperCard 1.2 stacks (a HyperCard 2 version is in the works) into ToolBook "books" for use on a Windows-equipped PC. Since a run-time version of ToolBook ships with every copy of Windows, ToolBook is likely to become the de facto standard for hypermedia in the Windows world. The process of translating a stack with ConvertIt! is painfully slow, and it's not 100 percent effective; there are simply too many differences between the two environments for everything to cross over intact. Still, ConvertIt! provides stack builders with an opportunity add several million people to their potential audience.

Prime Examples

Imitation may be the sincerest form of flattery, but it's also a great way to learn. Thousands of stacks have been created since HyperCard was introduced in 1987. Many of these stacks have modest price tags; others are available free through public domain software channels. By snooping through some of these stacks, studying their design, and analyzing their scripts, you can learn tricks and techniques that you aren't likely to find in books. Here's a highly subjective list of stacks that are particularly noteworthy.

- Bird Anatomy (public domain, available from Berkeley Macintosh User Group, or BMUG, and elsewhere). A comprehensive study of bird anatomy, complete with sound effects. A good model for educational stacks. A commercial version, available from The Voyager Company, sports many enhancements, including a companion videodisc.

- Bomber (Inline Design) is a flight-simulation game that answers the question, "Can HyperCard be used to create an arcade-style game?" The impressive effects were created without a single XCMD or XFNC.

- CD Companion Series, including Beethoven's Symphony No. 9 and Stravinski's *Rite of Spring* (The Voyager Company), and Warner Audio Notes Series, including Mozart's *Magic Flute* and Beethoven's String Quartet (Warner New Media)—these packages illustrate how music education can be brought to life with a combination of CD audio and HyperCard. Using any of these stacks in a CD-ROM-equipped machine, you can take an interactive tour of some of the world's great music, watching text, graphics, and background information unfold on your computer screen while high-quality digital audio pours from your stereo speaker, all controlled by your mouse.

- The Dream Machine and other titles (The Voyager Company), and Martin Luther King and other titles (ABC News Interactive, distributed by Optical Data Corporation) are state-of-the-art examples of HyperCard-controlled videodiscs. Dream Machine is a stunning, glitzy exploration of cutting-edge computer graphics with a HyperCard front end that turns the sequential tour into a direct-access reference tool. The ABC News titles use TV news clips, film footage, maps, and other documents to make TV into a truly interactive medium. Many other titles from these two companies cover topics from AIDS to van Gogh.

- The Editorial Advisor (Petroglyph) is an on-line reference for writers and editors. This cleverly designed, cross-referenced set of stacks is organized in such a way that it's easy to check with the experts on issues of style.

- EarthQuest (EarthQuest) is an ambitious stack designed to provide students with an interactive tool for exploring ecology, biology, geography, astronomy, and a number of other interrelated topics. This highly interactive and entertaining stack links everything with almost everything else. The package also includes an impressive Global Warming stack designed by volunteers from Apple Computer.

- The Freedom Trail (public domain, Boston Computer Society, also available on the BCS PD-CD, described in the next section) is a *Macworld* SuperStacks award winner created by volunteers of one of the largest and most active Macintosh user groups in the world. If you're interested in American history, Boston, or educational hypermedia, study this stack.

- If Monks Had Macs and Passing Notes (public domain, available from BMUG)—considered together as a single entity, these two award-winning stacks become a massive hypertext tour de force that's both inspiring and mind boggling. A crisscross catalog of ideas with a medieval flavor.

- Links to the Past I and II ($25 donation to SMILE) were created by junior high American Indians during two-week math camps at Oregon State University. Each stack graphically illustrates several native American legends. The results, while far from professional, show the kinds of amazing creations that motivated kids can produce with just a few hours of Macintosh/HyperCard training.

- The Manhole and Cosmic Osmo (Activision) define the state of the art in interactive nonverbal hypermedia. Originally designed for preschoolers, these massive stacks are great fun for anybody with a playful spirit. The Manhole has an Alice-in-Wonderland kind of magic that's 100 percent HyperCard, whereas Cosmic Osmo is more of a science-fiction–cartoon spoof with lots of VideoWorks animation sequences seamlessly woven in. Both are available in multidisk packages or in greatly enhanced CD-ROM versions. The Cosmic Osmo CD-ROM, weighing in at more than 100 megabytes (making it the largest entertainment software package anywhere), was chosen by *MacUser* magazine as the best recreational program of 1990.

User Groups and Bulletin Boards

Many of the best HyperCard stacks, clip art collections, and other useful software tools are available for free or with a pay-if-you-like-it understanding. User group libraries and electronic bulletin boards (BBS) are good sources for public domain software and shareware.

User groups have different policies on public access to their libraries. The Berkeley Macintosh User Group (BMUG), one of the largest in the world, maintains a large, well-organized collection of public domain and shareware programs on disks that may be purchased by members and nonmembers for a nominal fee. Their occasional catalogs are excellent tools for sorting through the mountains of free and almost-free software for the Macintosh. The best of BMUG software can be found in PD-ROM, a CD-ROM packed with stacks, sounds, graphics, games, applications, and miscellany, all tied together with a well-designed navigation stack. The Boston Computer Society (BCS) Macintosh User Group is the East Coast equivalent of BMUG. Their library is well organized, and their impressive PD-CD, another CD-ROM collection, is revised often so it includes the latest and greatest shareware and public domain software.

Macintosh user groups offer far more than a software library. They can be a valuable source of answers, ideas, and other kinds of support that are difficult to package on a disk. In addition, many user groups publish newsletters with folksy tips and tidbits that are often overlooked by *Macworld, MacUser,* and *MacWeek.* (To see a good example, send a dollar for a sample issue of *Mouse Droppings,* the sassy newsletter of the Corvallis Macintosh User Group, 1420 SW Crest Circle, Waldport, OR 97394.) To locate the user group nearest you, call Apple's User Group Hotline: 800/538-9696, ext. 900.

Heizer Software's Stack Exchange isn't really a user group, but it does provide a valuable service by acting as a clearinghouse for inexpensive stacks. The quality of Heizer stacks is, on the average, higher than that of public domain and shareware collections, but the cost is considerably lower than most commercial packages.

Electronic bulletin boards are also a good source of stacks, software tools, and HyperCard information. But since most of these services cost several dollars per hour in connect charge, they're not usually the cheapest stack source. Three of the most popular nationwide public information utilities with Macintosh bulletin boards are CompuServe (800/848-8199 or 614/457-0802), America OnLine (800/227-6364 or 703/893-6288), and GEnie (800/638-9696).

No single book can tell you everything you need to know to take full advantage of HyperCard. Each book listed here has something to offer for anyone serious about HyperCard stack development.

HyperCard Script Language Guide: The HyperTalk Language (Santa Clara, CA: Claris, 1990). This is the official Claris guide to HyperTalk. It's the definitive reference book for serious HyperTalk programmers. It comes with the Claris version of HyperCard.

The Complete HyperCard Handbook, Third Edition, by Danny Goodman (New York: Bantam Books, 1990). The first edition of this book was released the day HyperCard was introduced to the world, and this book is still the most popular HyperCard book on the market. The first third will be review for you, but the rest is packed with detailed information on HyperTalk, complete with many sample scripts and suggestions. This is an excellent alternative—or supplement—to the Claris reference manual.

HyperCard Developer's Guide, by Danny Goodman (New York: Bantam Books, 1988). This book takes up where *The Complete HyperCard Handbook* leaves off, covering advanced stack design, advanced HyperTalk concepts, resources, and XCMDs. It hasn't yet been revised for version 2 of HyperCard, but much of the information is still relevant.

Cooking with HyperCard 2.0, by Dan Winkler and Scott Knaster (New York: Bantam Books, 1990). This entertaining book of HyperTalk "recipes" written by two of the masters (Winkler wrote HyperTalk) is full of good ideas. The accompanying disk includes all the scripts, so you don't need to type them in yourself.

HyperCard Stack Design Guidelines (Reading, MA: Addison-Wesley, 1987). This official Apple publication covers the human side of stack development. If you care about the user interface of your creations, read this book carefully.

Sources of Software and Hardware

Activision
P.O. Box 7287
Mountain View, CA 94039
800/227-9759 or 415/960-0518

Adobe Systems, Inc.
1585 Charleston Road
P.O. Box 7900
Mountain View, CA 94039
415/961-4400

Aldus Corporation
411 First Avenue South
Seattle, WA 98104-2871
206/622-5500

Apple Computer
20525 Mariani Avenue
Cupertino, CA 95014
408/996-1010

Apple Programmers and Developers Association (APDA)
20525 Mariani Avenue
Cupertino, CA 95014
408/996-1010

Berkeley Macintosh User Group (BMUG)
1442A Walnut St. #162
Berkeley, CA 94709
415/849-9114

Boston Computer Society (BCS)
Macintosh User Group
48 Grove Street
Somerville, MA 02144
617/625-7080

Bright Star Technology
1450 114th Avenue SE, Suite 200
Bellevue, WA 98004
206/451-3697

Brøderbund
17 Paul Drive
San Rafael, CA 94903-2101
800/527-7273 or 415/492-3500

CE Software
P.O. Box 65580
West Des Moines, IA 50265
515/224-1995

Claris Corporation
5201 Patrick Henry Drive
Box 58168
Santa Clara, CA 95052-8168
415/960-1500

Corvallis Macintosh User Group
1420 SW Crest Circle
Waldport, OR 97394

Delta Point, Inc.
200 Heritage Harbor, Suite G
Monterey, CA 93940
408/648-4000

Deneba Software
7855 N.W. 12th St., Ste. 202
Miami, FL 33126
800/622-6827 or 305/594-6965

Dub'l Click Software
9316 Deering Avenue
Chatsworth, CA 91311
818/700-9525

EarthQuest
125 University Avenue
Palo Alto, CA 94301
415/321-5838

Electronic Arts
1820 Gateway Drive
San Mateo, CA 94404-2497
415/571-7171

Farallon Computing
2000 Powell St.
Emeryville, CA 94608
415/596-9100

Foundation Publishing
14228 Shore Lane
Prior Lake, MN 55372
612/445-8860

Gava Corporation
1001 4th Ave. Plaza, Suite 3200
Seattle, WA 98154
206/784-4736

Heizer Software
P.O. Box 232019
Pleasant Hill, CA 94523
800/888-7667 or 415/943-7667

Inline Design
5 West Mountain Road
Sharon, CT 06069
203/364-0063

Koala Technologies
70 N. Second Street
San Jose, CA 95113
408/287-6278

Language Systems
441 Carlisle Drive
Herndon, VA 22070
703/478-0181

LogiTech
6505 Kaiser Drive
Fremont, CA 94555
415/795-8500

MacroMind
410 Townsend, Suite 408
San Francisco, CA 94107
415/442-0200

Motion Works
#300-1334 W. 6th Ave.
Vancouver, BC
Canada V6H 1A6
604/732-0289

Nine to Five Software
3360 Mitchell Lane, Suite 105
Boulder, CO 80301
303/443-4104

OpCode Systems
3641 Haven, Suite A
Menlo Park, CA 94025-1010
415/369-8131

Optical Data Corporation
30 Technology Drive
Box 4919
Warren, NJ 07060
201/668-0022 or 800/524-2481

Paracomp
1725 Montgomery Street, 2nd
Floor
San Francisco, CA 94111
415/956-4051

Passport
625 Miramontes St.
Half Moon Bay, CA 94019
415/726-0280

Petroglyph
123 Townsend St., Suite 345
San Francisco, CA 94107
415/979-0588

Preferred Publishers
5100 Poplar Ave.
Memphis, TN 38137
901/683-3383

Sabastian Software
P.O. Box 70278
Bellevue, WA 98007
206/861-0602

Silicon Beach Software
P.O. Box 261430
San Diego, CA 92126
619/695-6956

SMILE
c/o Sue Bordon
Administration Building
Oregon State University
Corvallis, OR 97331

Somak Software
535 Encinitas Blvd., Suite 113
Encinitas, CA 92024
619/942-2556

Spinnaker Software
1 Kendall Square
Cambridge, MA 02139
800/826-0706 or 617/494-1222

Symmetry Software
P.O. Box 13914
Scottsdale, AZ 85267-3914
800/624-2485

T-Maker Software
1973 Landings Dr.
Mountain View, CA 94043
415/962-0195

Thunderware
21 Orinda Way
Orinda, CA 94563-2565
415/254-6581

Trillium Software
21W171 Coronet Rd,
Lombard, IL 60148
708/916-9360

The Voyager Company
1351 Pacific Coast Highway
Santa Monica, CA 90401
800/446-2001

Warner New Media
3500 Olive Avenue
Burbank, CA 91505
818/955-9999

Wayzata Technology
P.O. Box 87
16221 Main Avenue
Prior Lake, MN 55372
800/735-7321 or 612/460-8438

Zedcor
4500 E. Speedway, Suite 22
Tucson, AZ 85712

APPENDIX B

ASK DOCTOR HYPER:
A BEGINNER'S HYPERCARD TROUBLESHOOTING GUIDE

Home

HyperCard won't open, or it quits unexpectedly, or it doesn't allow me to perform necessary operations. What's wrong?

You probably don't have enough available memory. If you're sure that the machine you're using has *at least* 1 megabyte of memory (2 megabytes with System 7), make sure MultiFinder is not operating and the RAM cache is turned off.

When I double-click on HyperCard, it responds by asking me, "Where is Home?" Why?

HyperCard needs to have a Home stack to open. It looks for Home in the immediate neighborhood, and if it can't find it, it asks for help. Locate the Home stack using the dialog box (as explained in Session 1) and double-click on it.

I can't find a button for the _____ stack in my Home card. Where is it?

It's probably nowhere. The Home card is not a complete directory of all your stacks, like the Macintosh Finder. Home includes buttons to launch some stacks. If you want your Home card to include buttons to open other stacks, you have to install them yourself.

When I click on the _____ button on the Home card, HyperCard asks me, "Where is _____ ?" Why?

HyperCard looks for stacks in the folders where it has found them before. It keeps this information on one card of the Home stack. If the stack isn't in one of those folders, it will probably ask you to help find it. As long as you don't move that stack later, HyperCard will know next time where to look for it.

Menus

The menu bar is missing. How do I get it back?

To make the menu bar disappear or reappear, press Command-Space bar.

I have only three (or four) menus. What's wrong?

Your user level is probably set to one of the first three levels. If you need to create stacks or modify buttons, fields, or scripts, set the user level to authoring or scripting.

I see seven menus, but the Objects menu is missing. Where is it?

A paint tool is selected, so the Objects menu has been replaced by the Paint menu, the Options menu, and the Patterns menu. To see the Objects menu, select one of the three tools at the top of the Tools menu or palette.

I can't find the Paint menu, the Options menu, or the Patterns menu. How can I get them back?

Click on any of the paint tools. See previous answer.

Getting Around

When I select Recent from the Go menu, I see the cards in my stack, but they aren't in the right order. How can I rearrange them?

Your cards may, in fact, already be in the right order. Recent doesn't show you the cards in stack order, but in the order in which you last visited them. Recent is like a roll of film you use to take a snapshot of each new card that you visit.

Typing

When I move the pointer over text that I want to edit, it doesn't turn into an I-beam. Why?

The text is probably paint text, which can't be edited like field text, but must be repainted instead. Another possibility is that the text is in a locked field; check the Field Info dialog box for the field. A third possibility is that a button is sitting on top of the field; hold down the Option and Command keys to see if a button is outlined there.

I know that one of the cards has the phrase "XYZ" written on it; I've seen it. But when I issue a Find "XYZ" command, HyperCard just beeps at me. Why can't it find that phrase?

The Find command *will* find the card with "XYZ" on it, but only if (1) "XYZ" is on a card in the *current stack*, (2) "XYZ" is *field text*, not paint text; and (3) the field that contains "XYZ" has not been scripted to prevent searches. If HyperCard can't find a phrase, then you can be sure that one of these three conditions hasn't been satisfied.

Painting

When I try to erase my picture, part of it won't go away. Why?

The Eraser tool removes only painted material from the current layer. The part that you can't erase is probably either an icon, which can be removed only with the Button tool, or painting on the background, which can be erased only after you switch to the background (Command-B).

When I try to move an object that I've drawn, I have trouble separating it from its surroundings. Why won't it move easily like objects in Works or MacDraw?

HyperCard's graphics are bit-mapped (like MacPaint), rather than object-oriented (like MacDraw). In plain English, that means that whatever you paint is stored in the computer as just a collection of dots on the screen. When you add a new graphic flourish to your card, the computer initially sees it as a separate flourish, so you can remove it with the Undo command or select and edit it with the Select command. But as soon as you do anything else, the flourish ceases to exist as a separate entity; it becomes just another part of the bit-mapped dot pattern that makes up the graphics of the card. From that point on, it can be edited only as part of the bigger picture.

I created a new card and redesigned its background to show something different than what's on the other cards in the stack. To my dismay, I found out too late that the new background is now on all the old cards. Where did I go wrong?

The New Card command assigns the background of the current card to the new card, so if you change the new card's background, you're also changing all other cards with that background. Instead of selecting New Card, you should have selected New Background. That command creates a new card, too, but it assigns it an all-new background that's completely unrelated to the background of the other cards in the stack.

APPENDIX C

HYPERCARD MENUS

General Menus

File		
New Stack...		Creates a new stack
Open Stack...	⌘O	Opens an existing stack
Close Stack	⌘W	Closes current stack
Save a Copy...		Saves a copy of current stack on disk (recommended before making major changes)
		The next two menu items are visible when any paint tool is selected
Import Paint...		Imports the top left corner of a selected paint document; pastes it as a card graphic
Export Paint...		Creates a MacPaint document from the current card and background picture
		Only one of the following two menu items is visible at any time
Compact Stack		Eliminates free space caused by deleting objects; makes stack smaller and faster
Convert Stack...		Converts older stack to HyperCard version 2.0 format (necessary before stack can be changed)
Protect Stack...		Allows you to limit access, prevent changes, and control user level within stack
Delete Stack...		Deletes all cards in the current stack and takes you to the Home stack
Page Setup...		Controls printer features and layout of printouts on page
Print Field...		Prints field text on the current card with a variety of options
Print Card	⌘P	Prints current card
Print Stack...		Provides several options for printing the current stack
Print Report...		Provides options for printing text-only reports from current stack
Quit HyperCard	⌘Q	Returns to the Finder

Edit

The last five menu items are visible only at the painting, scripting, and authoring user levels

Undo	⌘Z	Undoes the last editing or painting action
Cut	⌘H	Removes currently selected text, picture, icon, button, or field and places it in Clipboard
Copy	⌘C	Places a copy of currently selected text, picture, icon, button, or field in Clipboard
Paste	⌘U	Places Clipboard contents (text, picture, icon, button, or field) in current position
Clear		Removes currently selected text, picture, icon, button, or field
New Card	⌘N	Inserts a new card with the current background after the current card
Delete Card		(Command-Delete) Deletes the current card, revealing the next card in the stack
Cut Card		Deletes the current card and places a copy (including background) in the Clipboard
Copy Card		Copies current card (including background) into the Clipboard
Text Style...	⌘T	Displays dialog box for controlling text style, font, size, justification, and spacing
Background	⌘B	Switches between card layer and background layer
Icon...	⌘I	Opens icon editor for adding, editing, or deleting icons in current stack

Go

Back	⌘~	Takes you back one card (to the one most recently visited)
Home	⌘H	Takes you to the first card of the Home stack
Help	⌘?	Takes you to the first card of the Help stack, if available
Recent	⌘R	Presents the 42 most recent cards in the dialog box; click on one to go there
First	⌘1	Takes you to the first card of the current stack
Prev	⌘2	Takes you to the card before this card in the current stack
Next	⌘3	Takes you to the card after this card in the current stack
Last	⌘4	Takes you to the last card of the current stack
Find...	⌘F	Displays the message box containing Find command; type characters and press Return
Message	⌘M	Displays the message box; type command or message and press Return
Scroll	⌘E	Displays the scroll window, allowing you to scroll around partially visible cards
Next Window	⌘L	Moves to the next open stack

Tools

Visible only at painting, scripting, and authoring user levels; see Tools table inside back cover

Font

Visible only when Browse, Button, or Field tool is selected, except at browsing user level; changes font of field text

Style

Visible only when Browse, Button, or Field tool is selected, except at browsing user level; changes size and style of field text

Objects | Visible only at authoring and scripting user levels when Browse, Button, or Field tool is selected

Button Info... — (Double-click on button with Button tool selected) Displays Button Info dialog box

Field Info... — (Double-click on field with Field tool selected) Displays Field Info dialog box

Card Info... — Displays Card Info dialog box

Bkgnd Info... — Displays Background Info dialog box

Stack Info... — Displays Stack Info dialog box

> If you hold down Shift while selecting any of these five commands, you're taken directly to the script window

Bring Closer ⌘+ — Brings a selected button or field one level closer

Send Farther ⌘- — Sends the selected button or field one level farther

New Button — Creates a new button; double-cllick button to display Button Info dialog box

New Field — Creates a new field; double-cllick field to display Field Info dialog box

New Background — Creates a new card with a new, blank background

Home Menu (available only from the Home stack)

Home

New Link to Stack... — Allows you to add a button to the Home stack that opens another stack

New Link to Application... — Allows you to add a button to the Home stack that opens an application program

New Link to Document... — Allows you to add a button to the Home stack that opens a document and application

Rename This Card... — Renames a Home card and associated buttons for moving to the card

Reorder Cards... — Allows you to reorder Home cards and move buttons to reflect the new order

Home Cards — Takes you to the first Home card in the Home stack

Preferences — Takes you to the Preferences card for setting user level and other options

Search Paths — Takes you to the first of three Search Path cards in the Home stack

Reports Menus (available only after selecting Print Reports... from the File menu)

Reports

New Report ⌘N   Displays a dialog box for creating and naming a new report template (Command-N)

Items   Available only after selecting Report Items... from the Edit menu

New Item ⌘N   Creates an item for a report (Command-N)

Item Info... ⌘I   Allows you to specify the contents and appearance of an item in a report (Command-I)

Edit   Report Version

Undo ⌘Z

Cut ⌘H   Cuts the selected item in the Report Items dialog box

Copy ⌘C   Copies the selected item in the Report Items dialog box

Paste ⌘U   Pastes the selected item in the Report Items dialog box; pastes a report template copied or cut from another stack

Clear   Clears the selected item in the Report Items dialog box

Delete Report   Completely removes a report template

Cut Report   Moves a report template from one stack to another

Copy Report   Copies a report template to move to another stack

Report Items... ⌘E   Allows you to define the items for a report

Report Name...   Displays dialog box to to rename an existing report template

Icon Menus (visible only when icon editor is active)

File

New Icon ⌘N   Creates a new icon

Close Icon Editor ⌘W   Closes the icon editor

Duplicate Icon ⌘D   Makes an exact copy of current icon

Quit HyperCard ⌘Q   Quits HyperCard and returns to the Finder

Edit

Undo	⌘Z	
Cut Icon	⌘H	Removes the current selected icon from the stack and copies it to the Clipboard
Copy Icon	⌘C	Puts a copy of the current selected icon in the Clipboard
Paste Icon	⌘V	Pastes icon from the Clipbard into the icon editor
Clear Icon		Permanently removes icon from the stack
New Button		Creates a new button with the new icon

Power Keys ↓

Icon

E	Erase		Erases whole image of current selected icon
	Pickup	⌘P	Turns pointer into snapshot tool for capturing graphic image (with a click) as a new icon
	Keep	⌘K	Saves changes to icon without leaving icon editor
R	Revert		Reverts to last saved image of the icon, discarding any changes made since last save
	First	⌘1	Takes you to first icon in current stack
	Prev	⌘2	Takes you to the previous icon in the current stack
	Next	⌘3	Takes you to the next icon in the current stack
	Last	⌘4	Takes you to the last icon in the current stack
	Find...	⌘F	Lets you search for a specific icon by name or ID

Special

H	Flip Horizontal	Flips icon horizontally around an imaginary center axis
V	Flip Vertical	Flips icon vertically around an imaginary center axis
F	Frame	Draws a border around the icon
G	Gray	Dims the icon
I	Invert	Inverts icon: black pixels become white and white pixels become black
M	Mirror Horizontal	Makes the right half of the icon a mirror image of the left half
H	Mirror Vertical	Makes the bottom half of the icon a mirror image of the top half
[ ]	Rotate 90°	Rotates the icon 90 degrees
S	Shadow	Draws a shadow to the right and bottom of the image

Script Menus (available only in the script editor)

File

Close Script	⌘W	Closes script and saves changes (Command-Option-click)
Save Script	⌘S	Saves the current script and stays in the editor
Revert to Saved		Reverts to the last saved version of the script
Print Script	⌘P	Prints selection or entire script
Quit HyperCard	⌘Q	Quits HyperCard and goes to Finder

Script

Find...	⌘F	Searches script for a specified word or phrase
Find Again	⌘G	Searches script for the next occurrence of specified text
Find Selection	⌘H	Searches script for the next occurrence of currently selected (highlighted) text
Scroll to Selection		Displays portion of script where the insertion point is or where text is selected
Replace...	⌘R	Changes a word or phrase in script to word or phrase that you specify
Replace Again	⌘T	Changes the next occurrence of the specified text
Comment	⌘-	Places a double hyphen before the selected text or lines
Uncomment	⌘=	Removes any double hyphens from the selected text or lines
Set Checkpoint	⌘D	Places a checkmark in the left margin before a statement in the script (Set Checkpoint changes to Clear Checkpoint when cursor is on line with a checkpoint)

Go   Used to navigate between stack and script windows

Debugger Menu (available only when debugger is active)

Step	⌘S	Steps to the next line in the current handler
Step Into	⌘I	Steps to next executed line in any handler
Trace		Traces through current handler without user interaction
Trace Into	⌘T	Traces execution through all handlers to completion (or next checkpoint)
Go	⌘G	Exits debugger and continues running the script from the current line
Trace Delay...		Sets delay time in ticks between steps of a trace
Clear Checkpoint	⌘D	Toggles between Set Checkpoint and Clear Checkpoint (see Script menu)
Abort	⌘A	Stops the handler and exits the Debugger
Variable Watcher		Opens the Variable Watcher window
Message Watcher		Opens the Message Watcher window

Paint Menus (visible only when a paint tool is selected)

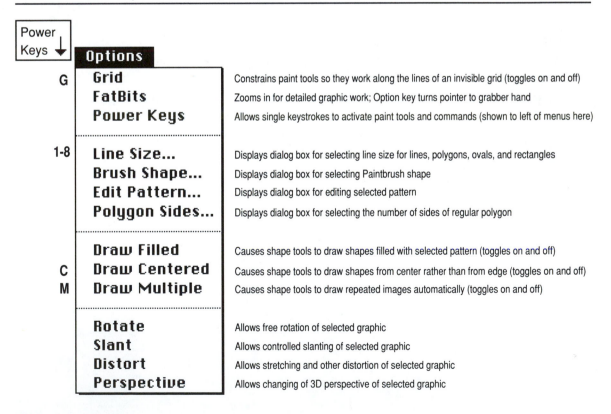

Power Keys ↓

Options

Power Keys	Option	Description
G	**Grid**	Constrains paint tools so they work along the lines of an invisible grid (toggles on and off)
	FatBits	Zooms in for detailed graphic work; Option key turns pointer to grabber hand
	Power Keys	Allows single keystrokes to activate paint tools and commands (shown to left of menus here)
1-8	**Line Size...**	Displays dialog box for selecting line size for lines, polygons, ovals, and rectangles
	Brush Shape...	Displays dialog box for selecting Paintbrush shape
	Edit Pattern...	Displays dialog box for editing selected pattern
	Polygon Sides...	Displays dialog box for selecting the number of sides of regular polygon
	Draw Filled	Causes shape tools to draw shapes filled with selected pattern (toggles on and off)
C	**Draw Centered**	Causes shape tools to draw shapes from center rather than from edge (toggles on and off)
M	**Draw Multiple**	Causes shape tools to draw repeated images automatically (toggles on and off)
	Rotate	Allows free rotation of selected graphic
	Slant	Allows controlled slanting of selected graphic
	Distort	Allows stretching and other distortion of selected graphic
	Perspective	Allows changing of 3D perspective of selected graphic

Power Keys ↓			
Paint			
S	**Select**	⌘S	Selects the most recently drawn shape or figure
A	**Select All**	⌘A	Selects the entire card picture (or background picture)
F	**Fill**		Fills the selection (or last shape drawn) with the current pattern
I	**Invert**		Inverts the selected picture (black to white, white to black)
P	**Pickup**		Copies underlying image in the currently selected shape
D	**Darken**		Makes selected area of picture slightly darker
L	**Lighten**		Makes selected area of picture slightly lighter
E	**Trace Edges**		Outlines the black in the selected picture (or in the entire picture)
[	**Rotate Left**		Rotates the selected picture or the last drawn object 90 degrees left
]	**Rotate Right**		Rotates the selected picture or the last drawn object 90 degrees right
V	**Flip Vertical**		Flips the selection or the last drawn object vertically
H	**Flip Horizontal**		Flips the selection or the last drawn object horizontally
O	**Opaque**		Makes the selected area of the card picture opaque
T	**Transparent**		Makes the selected area of the card picture transparent
	Keep	⌘K	Saves all the current card or background graphics
R	**Revert**		Reverts the graphics to the last saved version (undoes everything done since)

W
B

Other patterns have no power key equivalents

APPENDIX D

HYPERCARD KEYBOARD COMMANDS AND MENU EQUIVALENTS

Action	Keyboard Command	Menu Equivalent
General		
Copy selection to Clipboard	⌘-C	Edit: Copy
Cut selection to Clipboard	⌘-X	Edit: Cut
Paste selection in Clipboard	⌘-V	Edit: Paste
Undo last action (with exceptions)	⌘-Z	Edit: Undo
Cancel current action (such as printing)	⌘-Period	
Access full File menu from user level below painting	⌘ when selecting menu	
Quit HyperCard, return to Finder	⌘-Q	File: Quit HyperCard
Navigation		
Go to the Home stack	⌘-H	Go: Home
Go to the Help stack (when available)	⌘-?	Go: Help
Go to the first card in this stack	⌘-1 or up-arrow	Go: First
Go to the last card in this stack	⌘-4 or down-arrow	Go: Last
Go to the previous card in this stack	⌘-2 or left-arrow	Go: Prev
Go to the next card in this stack	⌘-3 or right-arrow	Go: Next
Go back through the previously viewed cards	~, Esc, or down-arrow	
Go forward through retraced cards	up-arrow	
Open a new stack	⌘-O	File: Open Stack...
Open a new stack in a new window	⌘-Shift-O	
Close an open stack	⌘-W	File: Close Stack
Move between open stacks	⌘-L	Go: Next Window

Action	Keyboard Command	Menu Equivalent
Store current card's location for quick return (push)	⌘-down-arrow	
Return to stored location (pop)	⌘-up-arrow	

Show

Show most recent 42 cards visited	⌘-R	Go: Recent
Show message box	⌘-M	Go: Message
Show message box with Find	⌘-F	Go: Find
Show or hide Tools palette	Option-Tab	
Show or hide Patterns palette (paint tool selected)	Tab	
Show or hide the menu bar	⌘-Space bar	
Show all buttons (Browse or Button tool selected)	⌘-Option	
Show all fields (Field tool selected)	⌘-Option	
Show all fields and buttons (Browse tool selected)	⌘-Shift-Option	
Show scroll window	⌘-E	Go: Scroll
Show Text Styles dialog box	⌘-T	Edit: Text Style...
Show size box in bottom right of window	⌘-Shift-E	

Tools

Select Browse tool	⌘-Tab	Tools: Browse tool
Select Button tool	⌘-Tab-Tab	Tools: Button tool
Select Field tool	⌘-Tab-Tab-Tab	Tools: Field tool
Select Browse tool and leave background layer	⌘-Shift-Tab	

Objects

Bring field or button all the way to the front	⌘-Shift-Plus	
Send field or button all the way to the back	⌘-Shift-Minus	
Move a button or field closer relative to another	⌘-Plus	Objects: Bring Closer
Send a button or field back relative to another	⌘-Minus	Objects: Send Farther
Go to/from the background layer	⌘-B	Edit: Background
Paste miniature picture of card from Clipboard	⌘-Shift-V	
Create a new card	⌘-N	Edit: New Card
Delete the current card	⌘-Delete (⌘-Backspace)	Edit: Delete Card
Print Card	⌘-P	File: Print Card

Fields

Select all text in current field	⌘-A	
Paste field, text included with field	⌘-Shift-V	
Revert field to previous contents	⌘-Shift-Z	
Boldface all selected text in a field	⌘-Shift-B	
Condense all selected text in a field	⌘-Shift-C	
Change all selected field text to default format	⌘-Shift-D	

Action	Keyboard Command	Menu Equivalent
Make all selected text in a field into plain text	⌘-Shift-P	
Shadow all selected text in a field	⌘-Shift-S	
Extend all selected text in a field	⌘-Shift-X	
Change selected field text to next font (alphabetically)	⌘-Shift-F	
Group all selected text in a field (for hot text)	⌘-Shift-G	
Italicize all selected text in a field	⌘-Shift-I	
Outline all selected text in a field	⌘-Shift-O	
Underline all selected text in a field	⌘-Shift-U	
Make all selected text in a field a smaller font size	⌘-Shift-<	
Make all selected text in a field a larger font size	⌘-Shift->	
Decrease the height of the field's line	⌘-Shift-Minus	
Increase the height of the field's line	⌘-Shift-Plus	
Go to the next field on a card	Tab	
Go to a previous field on a card	Shift-Tab	

Reports

Action	Keyboard Command	Menu Equivalent
Create a new report	⌘-N	Reports: New Report
Show Item Info dialog box	⌘-I	Items: Item Info...
Create item for a report	⌘-N	Items: New Item
Show Report Items dialog box	⌘-E	Edit: Report Items...

Paint

Action	Keyboard Command	Menu Equivalent
Show opaque areas (paint tool selected)	Option-O	
Select the last graphic object created	⌘-S	Paint: Select
Select all of the graphics on this layer	⌘-A	Paint: Select All
Save current picture for next Revert	⌘-K	Paint: Keep
Revert to picture saved with last Keep	⌘-R	Paint: Revert
Enter or leave FatBits	⌘-F	Options: FatBits
View only the card picture	Option-D	
Undo most recent action (paint tool selected)	Tilde (~)	

Icons

Action	Keyboard Command	Menu Equivalent
Open the icon editor	⌘-I	Edit: Icon...
Pick up an image to edit as icon	⌘-P	Icon: Pickup
Save changes without leaving icon editor	⌘-K	Icon: Keep
Go to first icon in current stack	⌘-1 or ⌘-left-arrow	Icon: First
Go to previous icon in current stack	⌘-2 or left-arrow	Icon: Prev
Go to next icon in current stack	⌘-3 or ⌘-right-arrow	Icon: Next
Go to last icon in current stack	⌘-4 or right-arrow	Icon: Last
Search for a specific icon by name or ID	⌘-F	Icon: Find...
Create a new icon	⌘-N	Icon: New Icon
Completely remove the selected icon	⌘-Delete	
Duplicate an icon	⌘-D	Icon: Duplicate Icon
Select part of an icon picture	⌘-Drag	

Action	*Keyboard Command*	*Menu Equivalent*
Peel off a copy of the selected icon	Option-Drag	
Paste *picture* of icon from Clipboard	⌘-Option-V	
Close the icon editor	⌘-W	Icon: Close Icon Editor

Scripts

Edit current card script	⌘-Option-C	
Edit current background script	⌘-Option-B	
Edit current stack script	⌘-Option-S	
Open button or field script (Button or Field tool selected)	⌘-Option-click on object	
Select entire line	Triple-click	
Select entire script	⌘-A	Edit: Select All
Set (or remove) a checkpoint	⌘-D or Option-click	Script: Set (or Clear) Checkpoint
Clear all checkpoints that are set	Shift-Option-click on checkpoint	
Find text	⌘-F	Script: Find...
Find next occurrence of same text	⌘-G	Script: Find Again
Find current selection	⌘-H	Script: Find Selection
Find and replace text	⌘-R	Script: Replace...
Replace next occurrence of same text	⌘-T	Script: Replace Again
Comment current line or selected lines	⌘-Hyphen	Script: Comment
Uncomment current line or selected lines	⌘-Equals	Script: Uncomment
Print selection or entire script	⌘-P	File: Print Script
Save the current script	⌘-S	File: Save Script
Close script without saving changes	⌘-Period	
Close script and save changes	Enter, ⌘-W, ⌘-Option-click	File: Close Script
End of HyperTalk statement	Return	
Wrap line without return character (soft return)	Option-Return	
Format script	Tab	
Enter debugger while script is running	⌘-Option-Period	

Debug

Step one line at a time through current handler	⌘-S	Debug: Step
Step one line at a time through current and called handlers	⌘-I	Debug: Step Into
Trace without delays through all handlers	⌘-T	Debug: Trace Into
Continue running script at next command	⌘-G	Debug: Go
Set (or remove) checkpoint	⌘-D	Debug: Set (or Clear) Checkpoint
Exit Debugger, abort handler	⌘-A	Debug: Abort

APPENDIX E

A HYPERTALK DICTIONARY

This appendix lists and defines, in alphabetical order, all of the Hyper-Talk vocabulary words introduced in this book, plus many not included in the main text. Each entry includes a number referring to the page of this book containing an example and/or more complete explanation. More than half of HyperTalk's native vocabulary is included here. The HyperTalk words omitted from this list are, for the most part, either special-purpose words of little interest to the typical HyperCard user or trivial words with obvious meanings (for example, two). A more complete list is published in the *HyperCard Script Language Guide* (Santa Clara, CA: Claris, 1990).

Term	Category	Meaning	Page
abs	Function	Returns the absolute value of a number.	
add	Command	Adds the value of an expression to a value in a container.	
after	Preposition	Used with the put command, directing HyperCard to append a new value following any preexisting value in a container.	
all	Adjective	Specifies total number of cards in stack to show cards command.	
answer	Command	Displays a dialog box with question and reply buttons.	242, 247–248
answer file	Command	Presents the standard dialog box for locating a file; used for opening files of a specified type.	

Term	Category	Meaning	Page
any	Ordinal	Special ordinal used with object or chunk to specify a random element within its enclosing set.	
arrowKey	System message	Sent to current card when an arrow key is pressed.	
ask	Command	Displays a dialog box with a question and default answer.	246–247
ask file	Command	Presents the standard dialog box for locating where to save a file; used for saving files.	
ask password	Command	Displays a dialog box with a field for a password.	
autoHilite	Property	Determines whether or not the specified button's `hilite` property is affected by the message `mouseDown`.	
average	Function	Returns the average value of numbers in a list.	
background	Object	Generic name of background object; used with specific designation (`go to next background`). Also used to specify containing object for buttons and, optionally, fields (`background button 2`).	242
beep	Command	Causes the Macintosh to make a beep sound.	
before	Preposition	Used with `put` command, directing HyperCard to place a new value at the beginning of any preexisting value in a container.	
bkgnd	Object	Abbreviation for `background`.	
bg	Object	Abbreviation for `background`.	
blindTyping	Property	Allows typing into the Message box when it's hidden.	
bottom	Property	Determines or changes the value of item 4 of the `rectangle` property when applied to the specified object or window.	
bottomRight	Property	Determines or changes items 3 and 4 of the value of the `rectangle` property when applied to the specified object or window.	
browse	Tool	Name of tool from Tools palette; used with the `choose` command or returned by the `tool` function.	
brush	Property	Determines the current brush shape.	
brush	Tool	Name of tool from Tools palette; used with the `choose` command or returned by the `tool` function.	
btn	Object	Abbreviation for `button`.	
bucket	Tool	Name of tool from Tools palette; used with the `choose` command or returned by the `tool` function.	
button	Object	Generic name of button object; used with a specific designation (`hide button one`).	
button	Tool	Name of tool from Tools palette; used with `choose` command or returned by the `tool` function.	

Term	Category	Meaning	Page
card	Object	Generic name of a card object; used with a specific designation (`go to card "fred"`). Also used to specify containing object for fields and, optionally, buttons (`card field "date"`).	
cd	Object	Abbreviation for `card`.	
center	Adjective	Specifies center alignment of text in a field.	
centered	Property	Determines whether shapes are drawn from the center or from the corner.	
char[acter]	Chunk	A character of text in any container or expression.	
choose	Command	Changes the current tool.	173
click	Command	Causes same actions as clicking at a specified location.	
clickChunk	Function	Returns chunk information about text that is clicked.	241
clickLine	Function	Returns line information about text that is clicked.	
clickLoc	Function	Returns location of most recent click.	
clickText	Function	Returns text information about word or group phrase that is clicked.	241
closeBackground	System message	Sent to current card just before you leave the current background.	
closeCard	System message	Sent to current card just before you leave it.	
closeField	System message	Sent to unlocked field when it closes.	
closeStack	System message	Sent to current card just before you leave the current stack.	217, 259
close file	Command	Closes a previously opened disk file.	
commandKey	Function	Sent to current card when a combination of the Command key and another key is pressed.	
commandKeyDown	System message	Returns the Command key.	
commands	Property	Returns a list of the commands associated with the buttons in a palette XCMD.	252
compound	Function	Computes present or future value of a compound interest-bearing account.	
controlKey	Command	Sends the `controlKey` system message.	
controlKey	System message	Sent to current card when a combination of the Control key and another key is pressed.	
create menu	Command	Creates a new menu with the specified name.	252
create stack	Command	Creates a new stack with the specified name and background.	
cursor	Property	Sets image appearing at pointer location on screen. You can only set `cursor`; you can't get it.	
curve	Tool	Name of tool from Tools palette; used with the `choose` command or returned by the `tool` function.	
date	Function	Returns a string representing the current date.	

Term	Category	Meaning	Page
debug checkpoint	Command	Sets a checkpoint in a script to invoke the built-in debugger.	
delete (text)	Command	Removes a chunk of text from a container.	
delete (menu)	Command	Deletes a menu without a dialog box.	252
delete (menu items)	Command	Deletes a menu item without a dialog box.	
dial	Command	Generates touch-tone sounds through audio output or a modem attached to serial port.	
disable	Command	Disables the specified menu or menu item.	252
diskSpace	Function	Displays the amount of free space available on the disk containing the current stack.	
divide	Command	Divides the value in a container by the value of an expression.	170
do	Command, Keyword	Sends the value of an expression as a message to the current card.	
doMenu	Command	Performs a specified menu command.	
doMenu	System message	Sent to the current card when any menu item is chosen.	245, 249
dontSearch	Property	Determines whether a card, background, or background field can be searched by the find command.	
dontWrap	Property	Determines whether the text in a field wraps onto the next line.	
down	Constant	Value returned by various functions to describe the state of a key or the mouse button.	
drag	Command	Performs same action as a manual drag.	
dragSpeed	Property	Sets pixels-per-second speed at which the pointer moves with the drag command.	
else	Keyword	Optionally follows then clause in an if structure to introduce an alternative action clause.	
empty	Constant	The null string; same as the literal " ".	
enable	Command	Enables the specified menu or menu item.	
enabled	Command	Determines whether the specified menu or menu item is enabled.	
end	Keyword	Marks the end of a message handler, function handler, repeat loop, or multiple-statement then or else clause of an if structure.	175
enterKey	Command	Sends contents of the Message box to the current card.	
enterKey	System message	Sent to the current card when the Enter key is pressed unless the text insertion point is in a field.	
eraser	Tool	Name of tool from Tools palette; used with choose command or returned by the tool function.	
exit	Keyword	Immediately ends execution of a message handler, function handler, or repeat loop.	248–249

Term	Category	Meaning	Page
exp	Function	Returns the mathematical exponential of its argument.	
false	Constant	Boolean value resulting from evaluation of a comparative expression and returned from some functions.	
field	Container	Generic name of field container; used with specific designation (`put the time into card field "time"`).	
field	Object	Generic name of field object; used with specific designation (`get name of first field`).	
field	Tool	Name of tool from Tools palette; used with the `choose` command or returned by the `tool` function.	
filled	Property	Determines the Draw Filled setting.	
find	Command	Searches card and background fields for text strings derived from an expression.	242
first	Ordinal	Designates object or chunk number one within its enclosing set.	
fixedLineHeight	Property	Determines whether or not a field has fixed line spacing.	
foundChunk	Function	Returns a chunk expression describing the text found with the `find` command.	
foundField	Function	Returns an expression describing the field the text was found in with the `find` command.	
foundLine	Function	Returns an expression describing the line the text was found in with the `find` command.	
foundText	Function	Returns the text found with the `find` command.	
function	Keyword	Marks the beginning of a function handler. Connects the handler with a particular function call.	
get	Command	Puts the value of an expression into the local variable `It`.	241
global	Keyword	Declares specified variables to be valid beyond current execution of current handler.	246, 319
go	Command	Takes you to a specified card or stack.	174, 177
grid	Property	Determines the Grid setting.	
help	Command	Takes you to the first card in the stack named Help.	
height	Property	Determines or changes the vertical distance in pixels occupied by the rectangle of the specified button or field.	
hide	Command	Hides the specified window from view.	171
hide groups	Command	Hides the gray underline displayed beneath text by the `show groups` command.	
hide menuBar	Command	Hides the HyperCard menu bar.	

Term	Category	Meaning	Page
hilite	Property	Determines whether a specified button is highlighted.	
icon	Property	Determines the icon that is displayed with a specified button.	
ID	Property	Determines the permanent ID number of a specified background, card, field, or button.	
idle	System message	Sent to the current card repeatedly whenever nothing else is happening.	171
if	Keyword	Introduces a conditional structure containing statements to be executed only if a specified condition is true.	179, 202
in	Operator	Used with the comparison operators `is in` and `is not in`.	
in	Preposition	Used as a connective preposition in chunk expressions. For example, `card 12 in this stack`.	
into	Preposition	Used with the `put` command, directing HyperCard to replace any preexisting value in a container with a new value.	
It	Container	Local variable that is the default destination for the `get`, `ask`, `answer`, `read`, and `convert` commands.	241
item	Chunk	A piece of text delimited by commas in any container or expression.	209
items	Chunk type	Specifies items as type of chunk to the `number` function.	
keyDown	System message	Sent to the current card when a key is pressed.	172
lasso	Tool	Name of tool from Tools palette; used with the `choose` command or returned by the `tool` function.	
last	Ordinal	Special ordinal used with object or chunk to specify the element whose number is equal to the total number of elements in its enclosing set.	
length	Function	Returns the number of characters in the text string derived from an expression.	
left	Adjective	Specifies left-justified alignment of text in a field.	
left	Property	Determines or changes the value of item 1 of the `rectangle` property when applied to the specified object or window.	
line	Chunk	A piece of text delimited by return characters in any container.	
line	Tool	Name of tool from Tools palette; used with the `choose` command or returned by the `tool` function.	
lineSize	Property	Determines the thickness of lines drawn with line and shape tools.	

Term	Category	Meaning	Page
loc[ation]	Property	Determines the location at which a window, field, or button is displayed.	208
lock screen	Command	Prevents updating of the screen from card to card.	242
lockScreen	Property	Determines whether the screen is updated when moving from card to card.	
lockText	Property	Determines whether text editing is allowed in a specified field.	
mark	Command	Marks cards.	
marked	Property	Determines whether or not a specified card is marked.	
max	Function	Returns the highest-value number from a list of numbers.	
me	Object	The object containing the executing handler.	232
menuMsg	Property	Determines the message to be sent by a specified menu item.	
menu	Function	Returns a list of the menu items in a specified menu.	
message [box]	Container	The Message box.	175
messageWatcher	Property	Determines the message watcher to use.	
mid[dle]	Ordinal	Special ordinal used with an object or chunk to specify the element whose number is equal to one more than half the total number of elements in its enclosing set.	
min	Function	Returns the lowest-value number from a list of numbers.	
mouse	Function	Returns state of the mouse button: up or down.	
mouseClick	Function	Returns whether the mouse button has been clicked.	
mouseDown	System message	Sent to a button, unlocked field, or the current card when the mouse button is pressed down.	
mouseEnter	System message	Sent to a button or field when the pointer is first moved inside its rectangle.	172
mouseH	Function	Returns the horizontal offset in pixels of the pointer from the left edge of the card window.	
mouseLeave	System message	Sent to a button or field when the pointer is first removed from its rectangle.	172
mouseLoc	Function	Returns the point on the screen where the pointer is currently located.	207
mouseStillDown	System message	Sent to a button, unlocked field, or the current card repeatedly when the mouse button is held down.	
mouseUp	System message	Sent to a button, unlocked field, or the current card when the mouse button is released after having been previously pressed down within the same object's rectangle.	175, 176

Term	Category	Meaning	Page
mouseV	Function	Returns the vertical offset in pixels of the pointer from the top of the screen.	
mouseWithin	System message	Sent to a button or field repeatedly while the pointer remains inside its rectangle.	172
msg [box]	Container	The Message box.	
multiple	Property	Determines whether multiple images are drawn with a shape tool.	
multiply	Command	Multiplies the value in a container by the value derived from an expression.	
multiSpace	Property	Determines the space between objects drawn when the multiple property is true.	
name	Property	Determines the name of a stack, background, card, field, button, menu, or menu item.	
newBackground	System message	Sent to the current card as soon as a background has been created.	
newButton	System message	Sent to a button as soon as it has been created.	
newCard	System message	Sent to a card as soon as it has been created.	
newField	System message	Sent to a field as soon as it has been created.	
newStack	System message	Sent to the current card as soon as a stack has been created.	
next	Keyword	Ends execution of current iteration of a repeat loop, beginning next iteration.	
next	Object modifier	Used with card or background to refer to the one following the current one.	
number	Function	Returns the number of buttons or fields on the current card or background, the number of marked cards, the number of HyperCard menus, the number of menu items in a menu, the number of windows in HyperCard, or the number of a specified type of chunk within a value.	
number	Property	Determines the number of a background, card, field, or button.	
open	Command	Launches the specified application.	
openBackground	System message	Sent to a card when you go to it and its background is different from the one you were formerly on.	
openCard	System message	Sent to a card when you go to it.	205, 206
openField	System message	Sent to an unlocked field when you place the insertion point in it for text editing.	
open file	Command	Opens the specified file for a read or write command operation.	
openStack	System message	Sent to a card when you go to it and it's in a stack different from the one containing the card you were formerly on.	177, 217
optionKey	Function	Returns the state of the Option key: up or down.	

Term	*Category*	*Meaning*	*Page*
oval	Tool	Name of tool from Tools palette; used with the `choose` command or returned by the `tool` function.	
palette	Command	Invokes the specified palette XCMD.	
pass	Keyword	Ends execution of a message handler or function handler and sends the invoking message or function call to the next object in the hierarchy.	
pattern	Property	Determines the Paint pattern.	
pencil	Tool	Name of tool from Tools palette; used with the `choose` command or returned by the `tool` function.	
pi	Constant	The mathematical value pi to 20 decimal places, equal to the number 3.14159265358979323846.	
picture	Command	Displays the specified picture file in an external window.	
play	Command	Starts the HyperCard sound-playing feature.	
poly[gon]	Tool	Name of tool from Tools palette; used with the `choose` command or returned by the `tool` function.	
polySides	Property	Determines the number of sides created by the Regular Polygon tool.	
pop card	Command	Returns you to last card saved with the `push card` command.	240, 241
powerKeys	Property	Provides keyboard shortcuts of commonly used painting actions.	
prev[ious]	Object modifier	Used with `card` or `background` to refer to the one preceding the current one.	
print	Command	Prints the specified file.	
print card	Command	Prints the current card or a specified number of cards beginning with the current card.	
push	Command	Saves the identification of a specified card in a LIFO memory stack for later retrieval.	240, 241
put	Command	Copies the value of an expression into a container.	209, 252
quit	System message	Sent to the current card when you choose Quit HyperCard from the File menu (or press Command-Q), just before HyperCard goes away.	
random	Function	Returns a random integer between 1 and the integer derived from a specified expression.	
read	Command	Reads a file previously opened with the `open file` command into the local variable `It`. See also `write`.	
rect[angle]	Property	Determines the rectangle occupied by a specified window, field, or button.	
rect[angle]	Tool	Name of tool from Tools palette; used with the `choose` command or returned by the `tool` function.	

Term	Category	Meaning	Page
reg[ular] poly[gon]	Tool	Name of tool from Tools palette; used with the `choose` command or returned by the `tool` function.	
repeat	Keyword	Introduces a `repeat` loop, an iterative structure containing a block of one or more statements executed multiple times.	202, 206
reset menuBar	Command	Reinstates the default values of all the HyperCard menus and removes any user-defined menus.	252
reset paint	Command	Reinstates the default values of all the painting properties.	
reset printing	Command	Reinstates the default values of all the printing properties.	
result	Function	Returns the status of commands previously executed in the current handler. See the `result` function.	242
resume	System message	Sent to the current card when HyperCard resumes running after having been suspended.	
resumeStack	System message	Sent to the current card when HyperCard returns to a stack.	259
return	Keyword	Returns a value from a function handler or message handler.	
returnKey	Command	Sends any statement in the Message box to the current card.	
returnKey	System message	Sent to current card when the Return key is pressed.	172
right	Adjective	Specifies right-justified alignment of text in a field.	
right	Property	Determines or changes the value of item 3 of the `rectangle` property when applied to the specified object or window.	
round	Function	Returns the number derived from an expression, rounded off to the nearest integer.	
round rect[angle]	Tool	Name of tool from Tools palette; used with `choose` command or returned by the `tool` function.	
save stack	Command	Saves a copy of the specified stack with a specified name.	
script	Property	Retrieves or replaces the script of the specified stack, background, card, field, or button.	
select	Tool	Name of tool from Tools palette; used with `choose` command or returned by the `tool` function.	
selectedChunk	Function	Returns a chunk expression describing the selected text in a field.	
selectedField	Function	Returns an expression describing the field the selected text is in.	

Term	Category	Meaning	Page
selectedLine	Function	Returns an expression describing the line in a field where the selected text is.	
selectedText	Function	Returns the selected text in a field.	
selection	Container	Currently selected area of text in a field.	
send	Keyword	Sends a specified message directly to a specified object.	254
set	Command	Changes the state of a specified global, painting, window, or object property.	177, 202
sharedHilite	Property	Determines or sets whether a background button shares the same highlight state on each card.	
sharedText	Property	Determines if a background field shares the same text on each card. If set to true it also sets the dontSearch property of the field to true.	
shiftKey	Function	Returns the state of the Shift key: up or down.	
show	Command	Displays a specified window or object.	170–171
show groups	Command	Displays a gray line under all text with a textStyle property of group.	
show cards	Command	Displays a specified number of cards in the current stack.	
showLines	Property	Determines whether or not the text baselines are visible in a field.	
show menuBar	Command	Displays the menu bar if it was hidden.	
showName	Property	Determines whether or not the name of a specified button is displayed in its rectangle on the screen.	
showPict	Property	Determines whether or not a specified card or background picture is displayed.	
show titleBar	Command	Shows the title bar of the current card window if it was hidden.	
sort	Command	Puts all of the cards in a specified stack in a specified order.	
sound	Function	Returns the name of the sound that is currently playing.	
space	Constant	The space character (ASCII 32); same as the literal " ".	
spray [can]	Tool	Name of tool from Tools palette; used with the choose command or returned by the tool function.	
sqrt	Function	Returns the square root of a number.	
stack	Object	Generic name of stack object; used with specific name (go to stack "help").	
startUp	System message	Sent to the current card (first card of the Home stack) when HyperCard first begins running.	
startUsing	Command	Specifies a stack to add to the message-passing hierarchy.	

Term	Category	Meaning	Page
stopUsing	Command	Specifies a stack to remove from the message-passing hierarchy.	
style	Property	Determines the style of a specified field or button.	
subtract	Command	Subtracts the value of an expression from the value in a container.	
suspend	System message	Sent to the current card when HyperCard is suspended by launching another application with the open command.	
suspendStack	System message	Sent to the current card when you leave an open stack to go to another.	259
tabKey	System message	Sent to the current card or a field when Tab key is pressed.	
target	Function	Indicates the object that initially received the message that initiated execution of the current handler.	
text	Tool	Name of tool from Tools palette; used with the choose command or returned by the tool function.	
textAlign	Property	Determines the alignment of characters created with the Paint Text tool, or those in a field, or those in the name of a button.	
textArrows	Property	Determines the functions of the arrow keys.	
textFont	Property	Determines the font of characters created with the Paint Text tool, or those in a field, or those in the name of a button.	
textHeight	Property	Determines the space between the baseline and characters created with the Paint Text tool or those in a field.	
textSize	Property	Determines the size of Paint text, or text in a field, or text in the name of a button.	
textStyle	Property	Determines the style of Paint text, text in a field, text in the name of a button, or text of a menu item.	241
the	Special	Precedes a function name to indicate a function call to one of the built-in functions of HyperCard. You can't call a user-defined function with the. Also allowed, but not required, to precede special container names (the Message box) and properties.	169
then	Keyword	Follows the conditional expression in an if structure to introduce the action clause.	
this	Modifier	Used with card, background, or stack to refer to the current one.	
ticks	Function	Determines the number of ticks since the Macintosh was turned on or restarted.	
time	Function	Returns the current time as a text string.	169

Term	Category	Meaning	Page
to	Preposition	Used to specify ranges (`3 to 5`), connect a message to its destination when used with `send`, specify a format for the `convert` command, assign a container for the `add` command, and connect values to object properties.	
tool	Function	Returns the name of the current tool.	
top	Property	Determines or changes the value of item 2 of the `rectangle` property when applied to the specified object or window.	
topLeft	Property	Determines or changes items 1 and 2 of the value of the `rectangle` property when applied to the specified object or window.	
traceDelay	Property	Determines or changes the delay between the execution of lines of HyperTalk during a debugger trace.	
true	Constant	Boolean value resulting from evaluation of a comparative expression and returned from some functions.	
trunc	Function	Determines the integer part of a number.	
type	Command	Inserts the specified text at the insertion point.	
unlock screen	Command	Allows updating of the screen.	242
unmark	Command	Unmarks the specified marked card.	
up	Constant	Value returned by various functions to describe the state of a key or the mouse button.	
userLevel	Property	Determines the user level from 1 to 5.	
visible	Property	Determines whether or not a window, field, or button appears on the screen.	233
visual	Command	Sets up a specified visual transition to the next card opened.	213
wait	Command	Causes HyperCard to pause before executing the rest of the current handler.	206
wideMargins	Property	Determines whether or not additional space is displayed in the margins of a specified field.	
width	Property	Determines or changes the horizontal distance in pixels occupied by the rectangle of the specified button or field.	
within	Operator	Tests whether or not a point lies inside a specified rectangle.	
word	Chunk	Piece of text delimited by spaces in any container or expression.	
words	Chunk type	Specifies words as type of chunk to the `number` function.	
write	Command	Copies specified text into a specified disk file starting at a specified point.	
zero	Constant	String representation of the numerical value 0.	

GLOSSARY

actual parameters: See **parameters.**

algorithm: A step-by-step procedure for solving a problem or accomplishing a task. Writing HyperTalk handlers or programs in other languages often begins with figuring out a suitable algorithm for a task.

background: A type of HyperCard object; a template shared by a number of cards. Each card with the same background has the same picture, fields, and buttons in its background layer. Like other HyperCard objects, every background has a script. You can place handlers in a background script that you want to be accessible to all the cards with that background.

background button: A button that is common to all cards sharing a background. Compare with **card button.**

background field: A field that is common to all cards sharing a background; its size, position, and default text format remain constant on all cards associated with that background, but its text can change from card to card. Compare with **card field.**

background picture: The graphics in the background layer; the entire picture that is common to all cards sharing a background. You see the background picture by choosing Background from the Edit menu. Compare with **card picture.**

Browse tool: The tool you use to click buttons and to set the insertion point in fields.

button: A type of HyperCard object; a rectangular "hot spot" on a card or background that responds when you click it according to the instructions in its script. For example, clicking a right arrow button with the Browse tool can take you to the next card. See also **background button, card button.**

Button tool: The tool you use to create, change, and select buttons.

card: A type of HyperCard object; a rectangular area that can hold buttons, fields, and graphics. All cards in a stack are the same size. Each layer can contain its own buttons, fields, and graphics.

card button: A button that belongs to a card; it appears on, and its actions apply to, a single card. Compare with **background button.**

card field: A field that belongs to a card; its size, position, text attributes, and contents are limited to the card on which the field is created. Compare with **background field.**

card picture: A picture that belongs to and which applies only to a specific card. Compare with **background picture.**

chunk: A piece of a character string represented as a chunk expression. Chunks can be specified as any combination of characters, words, items, or lines in a container or other source of value.

chunk expression: A HyperTalk description of a unique chunk of the contents of any container or other source of value.

command: A response to a particular message; a command is a built-in message handler residing in HyperCard. See also **external command.**

Command key: The key at the lower-left side of the keyboard that has a propeller-shaped symbol. This key also has an Apple symbol and is sometimes called the *Apple key.*

comments: Descriptive lines of text in a script or program that are intended not as instructions for the computer, but as explanations for people to read. Comments are set off from instructions by symbols called delimiters, which vary from language to language. In HyperTalk, two hyphens (– –) indicate the beginning of a comment.

constant: A named value that never changes. For example, the constant empty stands for the null string, a value that can also be represented by the literal expression " ". Compare with **variable.**

container: A place where you can store a value (text or a number). Examples are fields, the Message box, the selection, and variables.

control structure: A block of HyperTalk statements defined with keywords that enable a script to control the order or conditions under which specific statements execute.

current: (adj) Applies to the card, background, or stack you're using now. For example, the current card is the one you can see on your screen.

debug: To locate and correct an error or the cause of a problem or malfunction in a computer program, such as a HyperTalk script.

delimiter: A character or characters used to mark the beginning or end of a sequence of characters; that is, to define limits. For example, in HyperTalk double quotation marks act as delimiters for literals, and comments are set off with two hyphens at the beginning of the comment and a return character at the end.

descriptor: The combination of an object's generic name, immediately followed by its particular name, number, or ID number.

dynamic path: A series of extra objects inserted into the path through which a message passes when its static path does not include the current card. The dynamic path comprises the current card, current background, and current stack. Compare **static path.**

expression: A description of how to get a value; a source of value or complex expression built from sources of value and operators.

external command (XCMD): A command written in a computer language other than HyperTalk but made available to HyperCard to extend its built-in command set. External commands can be attached to a specific stack or to HyperCard itself. See also **external function.**

external function (XFCN): A function written in a computer language other than HyperTalk but made available to HyperCard to extend its built-in function set. External functions can be attached to a specific stack or to HyperCard itself. See also **external command.**

factor: A single element of value in an expression. See also **value.**

field: A type of HyperCard object; a container in which you type field text (as opposed to Paint text). HyperCard has two kinds of fields—card fields and background fields.

Field tool: The tool you use to create, change, and select fields.

formal parameters: See **parameter variables.**

function: A named value that HyperCard calculates each time it is used. The way in which the value is calculated is defined internally for the HyperTalk built-in functions, and you can define your own functions with function handlers.

function call: The use of a function name in a HyperTalk statement or in the Message box, invoking either a function handler or a built-in function.

function handler: A handler that executes in response to a function call matching its name.

global properties: The properties that determine aspects of the overall HyperCard environment. For example, userLevel is a global property that determines the current user level setting.

global variable: A variable that is valid for all handlers in which it is declared. You declare a global variable by preceding its name with the keyword `global`. Compare with **local variable.**

handler: A block of HyperTalk statements in the script of an object that executes in response to a message or a function call. The first line in a handler must begin with the word `on`, and the last line must end with the word `end`. Both `on` and `end` must be followed by the name of the message or function. HyperTalk has message handlers and function handlers.

hierarchy: See **message-passing hierarchy.**

Home cards: The first five cards in the standard Home stack, designed to hold buttons that take you to stacks, applications, and documents. Choose Home from the Go menu (or press Command-H) to get to the card in the standard Home stack that you've seen most recently. You can also type `go home` in the Message box or include it as a statement in a handler.

HyperTalk: The HyperCard built-in script language for HyperCard users.

identifier: A character string of any length, beginning with an alphabetic character; it can contain any alphanumeric character and the underscore character. Identifiers are used for variable and handler names.

keyboard equivalent key: A key you press together with the Command key to issue a menu command.

keyword: Anyone of the 14 words that have a predefined meaning in HyperTalk. Examples of keywords are `on`, `if`, `do`, and `repeat`.

layer: The order of a button or field relative to other buttons or fields on the same card or background. The object created most recently is ordinarily the topmost object (on the front layer).

literal: A string of characters intended to be taken literally. In HyperTalk, you use quotation marks (" ") as delimiters to set off a string of characters as a literal, such as the name of an object or a group of words you want to be treated as a text string.

local variable: A variable that is valid only within the handler in which it is used. (Local variables need not be declared.) Compare with **global variable.**

loop: A section of a handler that is repeated until a limit or condition is met, such as in a repeat structure.

message: A string of characters sent to an object from a script or the Message box, or that HyperCard sends in response to an event. Messages that come from the system—from events such as mouse clicks, keyboard actions, or menu commands—are called system messages. Examples of HyperTalk messages are `mouseUp`, `go`, and `push card`. See also **handler.**

Message box: A container that you use to send messages to objects or to evaluate expressions.

message handler: A handler that executes in response to a message matching its name.

message-passing hierarchy: The ordering of HyperCard objects that determines the path through which messages pass.

metasymbol: A word used in a syntax statement as a placeholder for an element that is different for each specific use of the statement. For example, the metasymbol *filename* is used to show where you put the name of a file you want a command to act on. In this book, metasymbols are shown in italics.

number: A character string consisting of any combination of the numerals 0 through 9, optionally including one period (.) representing a decimal value. A number can be preceded by a hyphen or a minus sign to represent a negative value.

object: An element of the HyperCard environment that has a script associated with it and that can send and receive messages. There are five kinds of HyperCard objects: buttons, fields, cards, backgrounds, and stacks.

object descriptor: Designation used to refer to an object. An object descriptor is formed by combining the name of the type of object with a specific name, number, or ID number. For example, `background button 3` is an object descriptor. Stacks do not have a number or ID number, so only the name can be used for a stack descriptor.

object properties: The properties that determine how HyperCard objects look and act. For example, the `location` property of a button determines where it appears on the screen.

online help: Assistance you can get from an application program while it's running. In HyperCard, online help refers to the HyperCard disk-based Help system.

operator: A character or group of characters that causes a particular calculation or comparison to occur. In HyperTalk, operators operate on values. For example, the plus sign (+) is an arithmetic operator that adds numerical values.

Paint text: Text you type using the Paint Text tool. Paint text can appear anywhere, while regular text must appear in a field created with the Field tool. Paint text is part of a card or background picture.

paint tool: Any HyperCard tool you use to make pictures. Paint tools include Lasso, Brush, Spray, Eraser, and many others.

painting properties: The properties that control aspects of the HyperCard painting environment, which is invoked when you choose a Paint tool. For example, the `brush` property determines the shape of the Brush tool.

palette: A small window that displays icons or patterns you can select by clicking. You can see two of the HyperCard palettes, the Tools palette and the Patterns palette, simply by "tearing off" their respective menus. To see the navigator palette, type `palette "navigator"` in the Message box. See also **tear-off menu**.

parameters: Values passed to a handler by a message or function call. Any expressions after the first word in a message are evaluated to yield the parameters; the parameters to a function call are enclosed in parentheses or, if there is only one, it can follow `of`.

parameter variables: Local variables in a handler that receive the values of parameters passed with the message or function call initiating the handler's execution.

picture: Any graphic or part of a graphic, created with a Paint tool or imported from an external file, that is part of a card or background.

pixel: Short for *picture element;* the smallest dot you can draw on the screen. The position of the pointer is often represented by two numbers separated by commas. These numbers are horizontal and vertical distances of the pointer from the left and upper edges of the card window, measured in pixels. The upper-left corner of the screen has the coordinates 0, 0.

point: (1) A location on the screen described by two integers, separated by a comma, representing horizontal and vertical offsets, measured in pixels from the upper-left corner of the card window or (in the case of the card window itself) of the screen.

(2) In printing, the unit of measurement of the height of a text character; one point is about 1/72 of an inch. When you select a font, you can also select a point size, such as 10 point, 12 point, and so on.

power key: One of a number of keys on the Macintosh keyboard you can press to initiate a menu action when a Paint tool is active. Power keys are enabled when you choose Power Keys from the Options menu or you check Power Keys on the Preferences card in the Home stack.

properties: The defining characteristics of any HyperCard object and of the HyperCard environment. For example, setting the user level to Scripting changes the `userLevel` property of HyperCard to the value 5. Properties are often selected as options in dialog boxes or on palettes, or they can be set from handlers.

Recent: A special dialog box that holds pictorial representations of the last 42 unique cards viewed. Choose Recent from the Go menu to get the dialog box. Also, an adjective describing the card you were on immediately prior to the current card, as in `recent card`.

recursion: The repetition of an operation or group of operations. Recursion occurs when a handler calls itself.

resource fork: The part of a file that contains resources such as fonts, icons, sounds, and so on.

regular text: Text you type in a field. You use the Browse tool to set an insertion point in a field and then type. Regular text is editable and searchable, while Paint text is not.

script: A collection of handlers written in HyperTalk and associated with a particular object. You use the script editor to add to and revise an object's script. Every object has a script, even though some scripts are empty, that is, they contain nothing.

script editor: A window in which you can type and edit a script. The title bar of the script editor describes the object to which the script belongs. You can use the Edit menu, the Script menu, and keyboard commands to edit text in the script editor. See also handler, object, and script.

search path: When you open a file from within HyperCard, HyperCard attempts to locate the stack, document, or application you want by searching the folders listed on the appropriate Search Paths card in the Home stack. Each line on a Search Paths card indicates the location of a folder, including the disk name (and folder and subfolder names, if any). This information is called a *search path*. Items in a search path are separated by a colon, like this:

```
my disk:HyperCard folder:my stacks:
```

Search Path cards: Three cards in the Home stack used to store information about the location of stacks, documents, and applications that you open while HyperCard is running. See also **search path.**

selection: A container that holds the currently selected area of text. Note that text found by the `find` command is not selected.

shared text: Field text that appears on every card in a background. Shared text can be edited only from the background layer. Text in shared fields cannot be searched.

source of value: The most basic HyperTalk expressions; the language elements from which values can be derived: constants, containers, functions, literals, and properties.

stack: A type of HyperCard object that consists of a collection of cards; a HyperCard document.

statement: A line of HyperTalk code inside a handler. A handler can contain many statements. Statements within handlers are first sent as messages to the object containing the handler and then to succeeding objects in the message-passing hierarchy.

static path: The message-passing route defined by an object's own hierarchy. For example, the static path followed by a message sent to (but not handled by) a button would include the card to which the button belongs, the background associated with that card, and the stack containing them. Compare **dynamic path.**

string: A sequence of characters. You can compare and combine strings in different ways by using operators. In HyperTalk, for example, `23 + 23` will result in `46`; but `23 & 23` will result in `2323`.

syntax: A description of the way in which language elements fit together to form meaningful phrases. A syntax statement for a command shows the command in its most generalized form, including placeholders (sometimes called metasymbols) for elements you must fill in as well as optional elements.

System file: Software your computer uses to perform its basic operations.

system message: A message sent by HyperCard to an object in response to an event such as a mouse click, keyboard action, or menu command. Examples of HyperCard system messages are `mouseUp`, `doMenu`, and `newCard`.

target: The object that first receives a message.

tear-off menu: A menu that you can convert to a palette by dragging the pointer beyond the menu's edge. HyperCard has two tear-off menus—Tools and Patterns. When torn off these menus are referred to as palettes.

text field: See **field.**

text property: A quality or attribute of a character's appearance. Text properties include style, font, and size.

tick: Approximately one-sixtieth (1/60) of a second. The `wait` command assumes a value in ticks unless you specify seconds by adding `secs` or `seconds`.

tool: An implement you use to do work. HyperCard has tools for browsing through cards and stacks, creating text fields, editing text, making buttons, and creating and editing pictures.

user level: A property of HyperCard, ranging from 1 to 5, that determines which HyperCard capabilities are available. You can select the user level on the Preferences card in the Home stack. Each user level makes all the options from the lower levels available, and also gives you additional capabilities. The five user levels are Browsing, Typing, Painting, Authoring, and Scripting.

value: A piece of information on which HyperCard operates. All HyperCard values can be treated as strings of characters— they are not formally separated into types. For example, a numeral could be interpreted as a number or as text, depending on what you do with it in a HyperTalk handler.

variable: A named container that can hold a value consisting of a character string of any length. You can create a variable to hold some value (either numbers or text) simply by using its name with the put command and putting the value into it. HyperCard has local variables and global variables. Compare with **constant.**

window properties: The properties that determine how the Message box and the Tools and Patterns palettes are displayed. For example, the `visible` property determines whether or not the specified window is displayed on the screen.

INDEX

" (quotation marks), in HyperTalk scripts, 187, 260
&, HyperTalk operator, 206
&&, HyperTalk operator, 242
( ) (parentheses), with HyperTalk functions, 169
* (multiply), HyperTalk arithmetic operator, 170
+ (add), HyperTalk arithmetic operator, 170
-- (double dash), in HyperTalk scripts, 187
- (subtract), HyperTalk arithmetic operator, 170
/ (divide), HyperTalk arithmetic operator, 170
? button, 28
^ (exponent), HyperTalk arithmetic operator, 170
~ (Tilde) key, 30, 36, 88
    with paint tools, 99
¬ (soft return), 187, 233

A

Abort command (Debugger menu), 212, 298
absolute links, 133
absolute reference, in linking buttons, 133
active window, 11
actual parameters, 317
add (+), HyperTalk arithmetic operator, 170
ADDmotion (Motion Works), 273
Addresses stack
    browsing through, 56
    and file server installations, 6
    and floppy disk installations, 6
    and hard disk installations, 5
adventure games, 121
Ahouse, Jeremy, 273

algorithms, 317
alignment, of text, 93
Amazing Paint (CE Software), 270
America OnLine, 283
animation
    adding to stacks, 192–201
    animation aids resources, 273–275
    with buttons, 207–210
    card-flipping, 192
    with icons, 203–206
    scripting, 201–203
Animation Help, 273
answer command (HyperTalk), 242, 247–248
Apple FDHD Superdrives, 6–7
Apple key. *See* Command key
Apple Scanner (Apple Computer), 272
Apple User Group Hotline, 283
applications, defined, xxi
Appointments stack
    browsing through, 47–49
    calendar buttons, 50
    and file server installations, 6
    and floppy disk installations, 6
    and hard disk installations, 5
    locating, 47
    returning to, 49
arithmetic operators, HyperTalk, 170
arrow keys, navigating with, 31, 36
Art Bits stack, 153–154, 155
ask command (HyperTalk), 246–247
asterisk button, 28

Atkinson, Bill, xx
audio, adding to stacks, 215–217. *See also* sounds
authoring user level, 71–72, 289. *See also* user levels
automatic backtracking, 239–240
automatic saving, 7, 55
    of graphics, 88

B
Back command (Go menu), 30, 32, 36, 88, 293
Background Art stack, 155
background buttons, 157
    building, 186–189
    defined, 317
    See also buttons
Background command (Edit menu), 73, 120, 293
background command (HyperTalk), 242
background
    adding fields to, 230
    benefits of, 121
    borrowing buttons in, 131–132
    borrowing, 155–159
    bullet chart, 182–184
    and card layer, xxiii, 120
    common (shared), 121
    copying current, 83
    creating new, 133–136
    creative graphics in, 181–182
    current, 318
    defined, 317
    drawing in, 123–128
    fields, defined, 317
    going into, 73
    as HyperCard object, 175
    of hypertext documents, 227, 228–229
    leaving, 136
    modifying, 70–71
    moving objects to, from the card layer, 128
    obscuring objects in, 136
    pictures, 317
    rearranging layers in, 189
    striped menu bar, xxiii, 73, 120
    viewing the script of, 192
    See also background buttons
backing up disks, 17–18
Backspace key, erasing characters, 45
backtracking, automatic, 239–240
backup copies
    of files, 7
    saving, 55
barn door close (visual effect), 111

barn door open (visual effect), 111
BASIC programming language, 174, 175
Berkeley Macintosh User Group (BMUG), 283
bg command (HyperTalk), 242
Bird Anatomy stack, 281
bit-mapped graphics, 85
    moving, 290
    stretching and shrinking, 124
    See also graphics
bits, defined, 85
bkgnd command (HyperTalk), 242
BMUG (Berkeley Macintosh User Group), 283
boing sound, 216, 275
boldface type, 234
    as used in this book, xxiv
Bomber stack, 281
Book of MIDI, The (OpCode Systems), 278
books on HyperCard, 284
boolean algebra, and marked addresses, 64
booting the Macintosh, 8–9
borrowing backgrounds, 155–159. *See also*
    background
borrowing buttons, 111–113, 131–132. *See also*
    buttons
Boston Computer Society Macintosh User
    Group, 283
branches (of tree structures), 226
    jumping between, 239
break points, in debugging, 210
Bring Closer command (Objects menu), 157, 294
Browse tool (Tools menu), 76
    defined, 317
    illustrated, 85
browsing
    with buttons, 28
    defined, xxii
browsing user level, 71. *See also* user levels
Brush shape... command (Options menu), 102, 298
brush shapes, selecting, 102
bugs, uncovering, 148. *See also* debugger
    (HyperTalk); Debugger menu; debugging
bullet charts, 181
    in background, 182–184
    creating, 185–186, 189–190
bulletin boards (BBS), 283
Bush, Vannevar, xxi
button animation, 207–210
button bar, in hypertext documents, 229–230
Button Info dialog box, 97
    Effect... button, 97–98
    Icon... button, 131

buttons
- animating with, 207–210
- background, 157, 186–189, 317
- borrowing, 111–113, 131–132
- browsing with, 28
- on buttons, 157
- in the card layer, 157, 317
- changing the visual effect, 132
- clicking, 25
- copying and pasting, 112
- creating, 95–96
- defined, 317
- deleting, 73–74
- described, xxii
- in dialog boxes, 14, 17
- hard-linking, 233–234
- hidden, 25, 34
    - revealing, 161
- hiding with buttons, 233
- as HyperCard objects, 175
- in hypertext documents, 227
- icons, 28, 32
- invisible, 106–108
- linking, 96–97, 146–148
- location of, 208
- looking under, 173–174
- and Macintosh menus, 24
- moving, 124, 208–210
- naming, 96, 107
- navigation, 28, 32
- and palette control, 32
- programming, 96
- resizing, 95
- scripting, 232, 237–238, 245–247
- testing, 98, 258
- transparent, 107, 141
- viewing the script of, 192
- *See also specific button*

Button tool (Tools menu), 71, 73
- creating buttons, 95
- defined, 317
- resizing buttons, 95

C

calculations
- HyperTalk, 170
- operator precedence, 170

calendar, updating, 48

calendar buttons, 50

Cancel button, in dialog boxes, 23

Canvas (Deneba Software), 271

card-flipping animation, 192. *See also* animation

Card Info... command (Objects menu), 178, 294

card
- adding, 57–58
- and background layer, xxiii, 120, 291
- buttons, defined, 317
- copying, 151–152
- creating illusions in, 191
- creating new, 130, 291
- current, 318
- customizing, 70–77
- defined, 317
- deleting, 58
- described, xxi–xxii
- displaying a sequence of cards, 171
- erasing painted contents of, 86, 290
- exits, 109
- fields, defined, 317
- finding, 59–60, 290
- flipping through cards, 161
- hot links, 244
- as a HyperCard object, 175
- layer, 120, 128
- linking buttons to, 96–97
- marking, 61–64
- moving, 161
- moving objects from, 128
- musical, 215–216
- numbering, 149
- order, 289
- pasting from the Clipboard, 152
- picture, defined, 317
- pixel grid, 208
- printing, 64–66
- reference, 235–237
- resizing, 34
- saving, 73
- selecting all graphics in, 128
- selecting size of, 83
- transparent graphics in, 142
- viewing the script of, 192

cartoon balloon button, 28

CD Audio Stack (The Voyager Company), 276

CD-ROM (compact disk read only memory), 276

checkerboard (visual effect), 111

checkpoints
- in debugging, 210–211
- setting/clearing, 212

choose message (HyperTalk), 173

Chooser (Apple menu), 66

chunk expressions, defined, 318

chunk (HyperTalk), defined, 241
chunks, defined, 317–318
Claris HyperCard package, 155, 261
Claris HyperCard Power Tools, 261
clickChunk function (HyperTalk), 241
clicking
    defined, 9
    double-clicking, 10, 24
    Shift-clicking, 16
clickText function (HyperTalk), 241
clip art
    borrowing, 153–155
    MacPaint files, 155
    sources, 155, 270–272
    using, 155, 269–270
Clipboard
    commands, 53, 58
    copying and pasting buttons, 112
    copying and pasting graphics, 98–100
    using, 53–55, 58
close box, 12
Close command (File menu), 12
closeStack message (HyperTalk), 217, 259
cloverleaf key. *See* Command key
cmdChar property (HyperTalk), 252
Command-1 (First), 30, 36
Command-2 (Prev), 29, 36
Command-3 (Next), 29, 36, 161
Command-4 (Last), 30, 36
Command-? (Help), 35, 36
Command-A (Abort), 212
Command-A (Select All), 16, 98, 146
Command-B (Background), 73, 121
Command-C (Copy), 53
Command-down-arrow (navigating stacks), 240
Command-D (Set/Clear Checkpoint), 212
Command-E (Eject), 17
Command-E (Scroll), 33, 36
Command-F (Find), 59–60
Command-G (Go), 212
Command-H (Home), 29, 36
Command-I (Step Into), 212
Command key, 29
    defined, 318
    stretching graphics objects, 124
Command-key shortcuts, specifying, 252
Command-K (Keep), 88, 122
Command-L (Next Window), 36
Command-M (Message), 31, 168
Command-N (New Card), 57
Command-N (New Folder), 16–17

Command-O (Open Stack...), 36
Command-Option (show buttons), 34, 36
Command-Option-Period, terminating scripts, 215
Command-Period (cancel current action), 36
Command-Period (terminating script traces), 212, 214
Command-Q (Quit HyperCard), 36
Command-R (Recent), 30, 36
commands
    Clipboard, 53, 58
    defined, 318
    dictionary of HyperTalk, 304–316
    external, 318
    and the menu bar, 10
    navigation, 28, 32
    summaries for all menus, 292–299
    summary of keyboard commands, 300–303
    summary of menu commands, 300–303
    See also specific commands
Command-Shift-O (open stack in new window), 36
Command-Space (hide/show menu bar), 34, 36, 134, 289
Command-S (Select), 98–99, 146
Command-S (Step), 212
Command-Tab (Browse), 98
Command-T (Text Style...), 92
Command-T (Trace), 212
Command-up-arrow (navigating stacks), 240
Command-V (Paste), 53, 54
Command-X (Cut), 53
Command-Z (Undo), 55, 87
Comment command (Script menu), 260–261, 297
comment markers (in HyperTalk scripts), 187, 260–261
    deleting, 260–261
comments
    defined, 318
    in HyperTalk scripts, 187
compact disk read only memory (CD-ROM), 276
Compact Stack command, 260, 292
compiled programming languages, 261
CompileIt! (Heizer Software), 280
compilers
    of programming languages, 261
    sources for, 280
Complete HyperCard Handbook, The (Goodman), 284
CompuServe, 283
computer programming. *See* programming
computer simulations, 121
concatenation, 242

conditional structures, 202. *See also* scripts
constants, defined, 318
constraint key, Shift key as, 62, 88, 124
containers, defined, 318
`container` variable (HyperTalk), 209
control structures, 202
    defined, 318
    See also scripts
ConvertIt! (Heizer Software), 281
Cooking with HyperCard 2.0 (Winkler/Knaster), 284
Copy command (Edit menu), 53, 293
copying
    cards, 151–152
    disks, 17–18
    fields, 74–75
    files, 15–16
    folders, 15
copyright laws, 261
Cosmic Osmo (Activision), 282–283
C programming language, 261
`create menu` command (HyperTalk), 252
current background, defined, 318
current card, defined, 318
current stack, defined, 318
cursor, defined, 50
Curve tool (Tools menu), 143
Cut command (Edit menu), 53, 293

D
database, HyperCard as, 44, 55–70
data files, defined, 44
data structures, reminder stacks, 240
dead ends, creating, 238
debugger (HyperTalk), 210–215
    debugging with, 214–215
    summary of keyboard commands and menu
      equivalents, 303
    turning off, 212
    See also Debugger menu
Debugger menu
    Abort command, 212, 298
    description of commands, 211–212
    Go command, 212, 298
    illustrated, 298
    Message Watcher command, 211, 298
    Set/Clear Checkpoint command, 212, 298
    Step command, 212, 298
    Step Into command, 212, 298
    summary of commands, 298
    Trace command, 212, 298

Variable Watcher command, 211–212, 298
    See also debugger (HyperTalk); debugging
debugging, 210–215
    defined, 318
    environment, 170
    examples, 214–215
    summary of keyboard commands and menu
      equivalents, 303
    See also debugger (HyperTalk); Debugger menu
default option, in dialog boxes, 17
Delete Card command (Edit menu), 58, 293
Delete key, 45
`delete menu` command (HyperTalk), 252
deleting
    buttons, 73–74
    cards, 58
    fields, 73–74
    files, 18
    folders, 18
    graphics, 152–153
    text, 52
delimiter, defined, 318
DeltaGraph (Delta Point, Inc.), 271
Deluxe Recorder (Electronic Arts), 277
descriptor, defined, 318
deselecting, 16. *See also* selecting
DeskPaint (Zedcor), 270
    clip art, 155
desktop, defined, 9
Desktop button, 22, 24
dialog boxes
    buttons in, 14, 17
    default option, 17
    defined, 14
    HFS navigation rules, 24
    locating files in folders, 22–24
    suppressing, 245
Dialoger Professional (Heizer Software), 279
digitizers, resources, 272–273
Director (MacroMind), 274
`disable` command (HyperTalk), 252
diskettes, defined, 5. *See also* floppy disks
disk icons, 9, 18
disks
    backing up, 17–18
    care of, 7, 8
    copying, 17–18
    ejecting, 12–13, 18, 22
    floppy, 5, 7, 8
    formatting, 13–15

disks *(continued)*
   hard, 5
   high density (HD), 6–7, 14
   initializing, 13–15
   locking, 13
   naming, 14
   one-sided, 14
   reinitializing, 14
   renaming, 15
   startup, 8
   two-sided, 14
   write-protecting, 13
dissolve (visual effect), 111
Distort command (Options menu), 139, 298
div (divide and truncate), HyperTalk arithmetic
   operator, 170
divide (/), HyperTalk arithmetic operator, 170
divide and truncate (div), HyperTalk arithmetic
   operator, 170
documents, defined, xxi. *See also* stacks
doMenu command (HyperTalk), 245
   quitting HyperCard, 249
double-click-dragging, selecting text, 53
double-clicking, 10, 24
double dash (--), in HyperTalk scripts, 187
down-arrow, of the scroll bar, 11
down-arrow key, 31, 36
dragging
   defined, 10
   selected graphics objects, 124
Draw Centered command (Options menu), 160, 298
Draw Filled command (Options menu), 103, 298
drawing
   in the background, 123–128
   curves, 143
   labels, 104–105
   lines, 85–86, 100–101
   ovals, 147
   polygons, 86–89, 103–104
   rectangles, 102–103
   summary of keyboard commands and menu
      equivalents, 302
   techniques, 100–108
   troubleshooting, 290–291
   in the wrong layer, 128
   See also graphics
Draw Multiple command (Options menu), 160, 298
Dream Machine, The (The Voyager Company),
   videodisc, 282
Drive button, 22, 24

Duplicate Icon command (File menu), 204, 295
dynamic path, defined, 318
dynamic presentations, creating, 180–210

E
EarthQuest (EarthQuest), 282
editing paint patterns, 136–137
editing text, 51–55. *See also* text
Edit menu
   Background command, 73, 120, 293
   Copy command, 53, 293
   Cut command, 53, 293
   Delete Card command, 58, 293
   Icon... command, 193, 293
   icon editor
      illustrated, 296
      summary of commands, 296
   illustrated, 293
   New Card command, 57, 97, 293
   Paste command, 53
   report version
      illustrated, 295
      summary of commands, 295
   Select All command, 16, 98, 146
   Select command, 98–99, 146
   summary of commands, 293
   Text Style... command, 92, 293
   Undo command, 54–55, 87–88
Editorial Advisor, The (Petroglyph), 282
Edit Pattern... command (Options menu), 136–137,
   298
Effect... button, 97–98
Eject button, 22, 24
Eject command (File menu), 13
ejecting disks, 12–13, 18, 22
electronic bulletin boards (BBS), 283–284
electronic music, 277–278
Electronic Whole Earth Catalog, The
   (Brøderbund), 282
Empty Trash command (Special menu), 18
endless loops, 215
end mouseUp message (HyperTalk), 175
Engelbart, Doug, xxi
Erase Disk command (Special menu), 14
Eraser tool (Tools menu), 86, 290
   and FatBits, 127
erasing
   all graphics on card, 86, 88
   painted graphics, 86–87
   See also deleting

error messages, viewing the script, 192
Esc key, 30, 88
Exit button, scripting, 247–249
exits, interactive, 247–249
exit statement (HyperTalk), 248–249
exponent (^), HyperTalk arithmetic operator, 170
Exposure (Preferred Publishers), 271–272
expressions
   chunk, 318
   defined, 318
   evaluating, 209
external commands (XCMDs), 261
   defined, 318
external functions (XFCNs), defined, 318
external hard disks, defined, 5
EZ Vision (OpCode Systems), 277

F
factors, defined, 318
FatBits, 125–127
   tips, 126–127
FatBits command (Options menu), 126, 298
Field Info dialog box
   checking for locked fields, 290
   illustrated, 183
fields
   adding to backgrounds, 230
   background, 317
   card, 317
   copying, 74–75
   creating new, 182–184
   defined, 44, 318
   deleting, 73–74
   editable, 71
   editing text in, 51–55
   entering text into, 50–51
   fonts in, 184
   as HyperCard objects, 175
   labeling, 75–77
   location, 208
   locked, 71, 290
   locking, 244
   moving backward through, 57
   moving between, 57
   moving from the card layer to the background
      layer, 124
   pop-up, 46, 231–233
   scrolling, 49
   searchable, 60
   summary of keyboard commands and menu
      equivalents, 301–302

   text, 50–55
   unlocking, 75–76
   viewing the script of, 192
field text, 91
   editing, 290
   fonts for, 184
   versus paint text, 129–130
   See also paint text; text
Field tool (Tools menu), 71, 74
   defined, 318
File menu
   Close command, 12, 292
   Duplicate Icon command, 204
   Eject command, 13
   icon editor
      illustrated, 295
      summary of commands, 295
   illustrated, 10, 292
   New Folder command, 16–17
   New Stack... command, 82, 122, 292
   Open command, 10
   opening stacks, 21–22
   Open Stack... command, 21–22, 36, 292
   Page Setup command, 66, 292
   Print Card command, 64, 292
   Print Report command, 66, 292
   Print Stack... command, 64, 292
   Quit HyperCard command, 36, 77, 292
   Save a Copy... command, 55, 292
   script editor
      illustrated, 297
      summary of commands, 297
   summary of commands, 292
files
   backup copies, 7
   copying, 15–16
   deleting, 18
   erasing, 18
   locating in folders, 22–24
   moving into folders, 17
   renaming, 15
file servers
   booting up on, 9
   defined, 5–6
   passwords, 6, 9
file server users
   customizing your work space, 19
   tips for, 5–6
Find button, scripting, 245–247
Find... command (Go menu), 293
   finding cards in stacks, 59–60

328   **Index**

Find... command (continued)
    and the message box, 32, 168
    tips for using, 60
find command (HyperTalk), variations, 242
Finder, 9
    working with files in, 15–16
First command (Go menu), 29, 30, 32, 36, 293
flexible disks, defined, 5. *See also* disks; floppy
    disks
Flip Horizontal command (Paint menu), 142, 299
floppy-disk-based system users
    customizing your work space, 19
    tips for, 6–7
floppy disks
    care of, 7, 8
    defined, 5
folders
    copying, 15
    creating new, 16–17
    deleting, 18
    double-clicking, 24
    locating files, 22–24
    moving files into, 17
    opening, 17
    organizing with, 16–17
    renaming, 17
Font menu, 293
fonts
    automatic substitution, 184
    defined, 93
    for field text, 184
    point size, 93, 128
    standard, 184
footnotes, in hypertext documents, 231–233
formatting disks, 13–15
Frame command (Special menu), 193
Freedom Trail, The (public domain), 282
Freehand (Aldus Corporation), 271
free space, eliminating, 260
function calls, defined, 318
function handlers, defined, 318
functions
    calling, 169, 318
    custom (programmer-defined), 253–254
    defined, 169, 318
    dictionary of HyperTalk, 304–316
    external, 318

G
general tools, 84. *See also* tools; Tools menu
GEnie, 284

get command (HyperTalk), 241
global keyword (HyperTalk), 246, 319
global properties, 202
    defined, 318
    See also properties
global variables
    defined, 246, 318–319
    displaying, 212
    See also variables (in HyperTalk scripts)
Go command (Debugger menu), 212, 298
go home command (HyperTalk), 174
Go menu
    Back command, 30, 32, 36, 88, 293
    Find... command, 32, 59–60, 168, 293
    First command, 29, 30, 32, 36, 293
    Help command, 28, 32, 35, 36, 293
    Home command, 29, 32, 36, 293
    illustrated, 29, 293
    Last command, 29, 30, 32, 36, 293
    Message command, 31, 32, 168, 293
    navigating with, 29
    Next command, 29, 32, 36, 293
    Next Window command, 32, 36, 293
    Prev command, 29, 32, 36, 293
    Recent command, 30–31, 32, 36, 289, 293
    script editor, 297
    Scroll command, 33, 36, 293
    summary of commands, 293
go message (HyperTalk), 177
go to next card command (HyperTalk), 213
graphics
    background pictures, 317
    bit-mapped, 85, 124, 290
    clip art, 153–155
    cloning, 124
    color, 270
    constraining with grids, 104–105
    copying and pasting, 98–100
    creating perspective in, 138–139
    creating titles, 128–130
    deleting, 152–153
    distorting, 139
    dragging selected objects, 124
    drawing curves, 143
    erasing, 86–87, 290
    FatBits, 125–127
    graphic tools resources, 269–272
    gray-scale, 270
    importing, 269–272
    moving from the card layer to the background
        layer, 124

graphics *(continued)*
    object-oriented, 290
    opaque, 142, 144
    painting techniques, 100–108
    paint patterns, 89–91, 136–137
    presentation, 181
    programs, 269–272
    rearranging, 152–153
    rotating, 139
    saving, 88
    selecting, 98–100, 98–99, 146
        all graphics objects, 146
        entire layer, 146
    shrinking, 124
    slanting, 139
    stretching, 124
    summary of keyboard commands and menu
        equivalents, 302
    tools resources, 269–272
    transparent, 142, 144
    troubleshooting, 290–291
    visual effects, 97–98, 111
Grid command (Options menu), 104, 298
grids
    constraining graphics with, 104–105
    turning on and off, 104
Group command (Style menu), 234
Guided Tour, of the Macintosh, 4

H
hand icon, resizing HyperCard windows, 33
handlers, defined, 319. *See also* function handlers;
    message handlers
Hand tool (Tools menu), 126–127
hard copy, creating, 64–67. *See also* printing
hard disks
    external, 5
    internal, 5
    passwords, 5
hard disk users
    customizing your work space, 19
    tips for, 5
hard-linking buttons, 233–234. *See also* buttons
hardware, sources of, 285–287
harpsichord sound, 216, 275
HD disks. *See* high density (HD) disks
headlines, in hypertext documents, 231–233
help, on-line, 28, 34–35, 319
Help command (Go menu), 28, 32, 35, 36, 293
Help Extras, 5, 6
Help stack, 35, 262

HFS dialog box navigation rules, 24
HFS (Hierarchical File System), 23–24
hidden buttons, 25
    finding, 34
    revealing, 161
    See also buttons
hide command (HyperTalk), 171
Hierarchical File System (HFS), 23–24
hierarchy, message-passing, 319
high density (HD) disks, 6–7
    identifying, 7
    initializing, 14
highlighting, defined, 9
Home button, 27
Home card/stack
    background layer, 120–121
    changing Home memory, 45–47
    defined, 319
    examples, 20–21
    and file server installations, 6
    and floppy disk installations, 6
    and hard disk installations, 5
    icons, 15, 25
    launching HyperCard, 20
    locating, 20
    and opening HyperCard, 44, 288
    resizing, 33–34
    returning to, 27, 28
    troubleshooting, 288–289
Home command (Go menu), 29, 32, 36, 293
Home menu
    illustrated, 294
    summary of commands, 294
hot text
    creating, 241–245
    in hypertext documents, 234, 239
    marking, 245
HyperAnimator (Bright Star Technology), 274
HyperCard 2 in a Hurry
    HyperCard version required, 4
    system software requirements, 5
    using this book, xxii–xxiv
HyperCard
    alternatives to, 280–281
    books about, 284
    as a database, 44, 55–70
    described, xix–xxi
    essentials of, xxi–xxii
    history of, xxi
    as a hypergraphics tool, 224
    as a hypermedia system, 224

HyperCard *(continued)*
  launching, 19–21, 44, 288
  learning, xxii–xxiv
  quitting, 36, 77, 249
  as a "software erector set," xx
  software and hardware sources, 285–287
  sources and resources, 269–287
  troubleshooting, 288–291
HyperCard AppleTalk Toolkit (APDA), 279
HyperCard CD Audio Toolkit (APDA), 276
HyperCard Developer's Guide (Goodman), 284
HyperCard Help, 5, 6, 35
HyperCard Script Language Guide: The HyperTalk
    Language (Claris Corporation), 262, 284, 304
HyperCard Serial Communications Toolkit
    (APDA), 279
HyperCard Stack Design Guidelines (Addison-
    Wesley), 284
HyperCard Tour, 5, 6, 24–27
HyperCard versions, 4
HyperCard Videodisc Toolkit (APDA), 277
HyperCom (Gava Corporation), 279
HyperDA (Symmetry Software), 278
hypermedia, 224
  defined, xxi
  See also hypertext
HyperMusic (Passport), 277–278
HyperSpeller (Foundation Publishing), 278
HyperTalk
  arithmetic operators, 170
  avoiding hazards of, 260–261
  calculations. *See* calculations
  compared to BASIC and Pascal, 175
  debugger. *See* debugger (HyperTalk)
  defined, 319
  described, xxii
  dictionary, 304–316
  functions. *See* functions
  interpreter, 261
  and marking cards, 64
  messages, sending, 168–169
  resources, 279–280
  visual effects, 188–189
HyperTalk Reference, 5, 6
hypertext
  defined, xxi, 224
  designing, 224–228
  hazards of, 244–245
  See also hypertext documents
hypertext documents
  automatic backtracking, 239–240

  backgrounds, 227, 228–229
  button bar, 229–230
  card design, 228
  example map, 226
  footnotes, 231–233
  headlines, 231–233
  hot text, 234, 239
  placing buttons, 227
  pop-up fields, 231–233
  reference cards, 235–237
  tree structure, 226–227
  user interface, 228
  See also hypertext

I
I-beam pointer
  illustrated, 50
  and the insertion bar, 51
icon animation, 203–206
Icon... button, 131
Icon... command (Edit menu), 193, 293
icon editor, 192, 193
  closing, 295
  illustrated, 195
Icon menu
  illustrated, 296
  summary of commands, 296
icons
  animating with, 203–206
  buttons, 28, 32, 132
  cloning, 203–204
  creating, 192–196
  disk, 9, 18
  dragging, 10, 15–16
  in the Home card, 25
  icon editor, 192
  icon view, 11
  navigation buttons, 28
  renaming, 15
  selecting, 9, 16
  stack, 20
  summary of keyboard commands and menu
    equivalents, 302–303
  See also specific icon
identifiers, defined, 319
`idle` messages (HyperTalk), 171
If Monks Had Macs (public domain), 282
`if` structures (HyperTalk), 179, 202
Illustrator (Adobe Systems, Inc.), 271
Image Grabber (Sabastian Software), 271–272

Import Paint... command, importing clip art, 155, 269, 292
initializing disks, 13–15
inserting text, 52
insertion bar, 50–51
  and the I-beam pointer, 51
interactive exits, 247–249
interactive fiction, 121
InterFace (Bright Star Technology), 274
internal hard disks, defined, 5
internal memory requirements, 7
interpreter (HyperTalk), 261
intersection, of subsets, 64
invisible buttons, 106–108. *See also* buttons
iris close (visual effect), 111
iris open (visual effect), 111
item (HyperTalk), defined, 209
Items menu, 295
  New Item command, 68, 295
It variable (HyperTalk), 241

K
Kay, Alan, xxi
Keep command (Paint menu), 88, 122, 299
keyboard, navigating by, 29–33
keyboard commands
  menu equivalents, 300–303
  summary, 36, 300–303
  See also specific command
keyboard equivalent key, defined, 319
keyboard shortcuts, 29. *See also* keyboard commands
keyDown system message, 172
keywords
  defined, 319
  dictionary of HyperTalk, 304–316
Kid Pix (Brøderbund), 271

L
labels, drawing, 104–105
Lasso tool (Tools menu), 98–99, 145
Last command (Go menu), 29, 30, 32, 36, 293
launching HyperCard, 19–21, 44, 288
layers, defined, 319. *See also* background; card
left-arrow button, 27, 28, 179
left-arrow key, 31, 36
light bulb button, 28, 46
Lighten command (Paint menu), 181, 299
LightningScan (Thunderware), 273

lines
  drawing, 85–86
  erasing, 86
  straight, 86
  thickness, 100, 102–103
Line Size... command (Options menu), 100, 298
linking buttons, 96–97, 146–148. *See also* buttons
links
  absolute, 133
  changing, 159–161
  checking the script, 178–179
  defined, xxii
  logical, 133
  two-way, 140–143
Links to the Past I and II (SMILE), 282
literal, defined, 319
local variables, defined, 246, 319. *See also* variables (in HyperTalk scripts)
location property, 208
locked fields, 71. *See also* fields
lock screen command (HyperTalk), 242
Lock Text option, for locking fields, 75
logical links, 133
logical reference, in linking buttons, 133
loops, defined, 319
loop structures, 202. *See also* scripts

M
MacDraw Pro (Claris Corporation), 271
Macintosh
  booting, 8–9
  Guided Tour, 4
  shutting down, 36
  startup disk, 8
  user friendliness, xx
MacPaint (Claris Corporation), 270
  clip art, 155
MacRecorder (Farallon Computing), 275–276
MacVision Video Digitizer (Koala Technologies), 273
"magic" command, resetting the user level, 72–73
Manhole, The (Activision), 282–283
maps (of stacks), 109, 113
  importance of, 150
  map tips, 149
margin bar, striped, xxiii, 73
Mark Cards command (Utilities menu), 61
marking cards, 61–64
  and boolean algebra, 64
  multiple criteria, 64
  See also card

me command (HyperTalk), 232
MediaTracks (Farallon Computing), 274
memex, described, xxi
menu actions, automating, 245
menu bar, 10
    hiding/showing, 25, 34, 134, 171, 217–218, 289
    modifying, 249–257
    specialized menus, 49
    striped, xxiii, 73, 120
menu commands, 36, 300–303
menu manipulation commands and properties, 252
menus
    custom, 249–257
    deleting, 250, 252
    disabling menu items, 252
    example menu-handling script, 256
    naming, 252
    pop-up, 23
    pull-down, 10
    specialized, 49
    summary of commands, 292–299
    tear-off, 84
    troubleshooting, 289
    writing manipulation scripts, 252–253
    See also specific menu
message box, 31
    as a calculator, 169
    defined, 319
    hiding/showing, 171
    and HyperTalk, 168
Message command (Go menu), 31, 32, 168, 293
message handlers, 175
    custom (programmer defined), 253–254
    defined, 319
message-passing hierarchy, defined, 319
messages
    defined, 319
    indenting, 172
    parenthesized, 172
Message Watcher, 170, 171, 211
Message Watcher command (Debugger menu),
    211, 298
metasymbol, defined, 319
MIDI (musical instrument digital interface), 277–
    278
MIDIplay (OpCode Systems), 277–278
mod (modulo), HyperTalk arithmetic operator, 170
mouse, using, 9–10
Mouse Droppings (Corvallis Macintosh User
    Group), 283
mouseEnter message (HyperTalk), 172

mouseLeave message (HyperTalk), 172
mouseLoc function (HyperTalk), 207
mouseUp message (HyperTalk), 175, 176, 254
mouseWithin message (HyperTalk), 172
MT-32 music synthesizer (Roland), 277
Multifinder, and RAM memory requirements, 7
multimedia computer applications, xx–xxi
multimedia makers, resources, 276–278
multiple-level sorts, 59
multiply (*), HyperTalk arithmetic operator, 170
music
    adding to stacks, 215–217
    electronic, 277–278
    See also sounds
musical instruments, digital, 277–278
Music Clips (OpCode Systems), 277
Music Data Company (Passport), 277
music stacks, examples, 281

N
name-and-address stacks, 57
naming
    buttons, 96, 107
    disks, 14–15
    everything, 260
    files, 15
    folders, 17
    menus, 252
    stacks, 84
navigating
    with buttons, 28
    by keyboard, 29–33
    with the Go menu, 29
    navigator palette, 31–33
    nonsequential, 239
    with the scroll window, 33–34
    summary of keyboard commands and menu
        equivalents, 300–301
    troubleshooting, 289
navigation buttons, 28, 32
navigator palette, 31–33
Nelson, Ted, xxi
nested if structures, 248–249
networks, booting up on, 9. See also file servers
network structures
    planning, 149–150
    versus tree structures, 227
New Background command (Objects menu), 133–
    134, 291, 294
New Button command (Objects menu), 95, 294
New Card button, 57

New Card command (Edit menu), 57, 97, 291, 293
New Field command (Objects menu), 182, 294
New Folder command (File menu), 16–17
New Item command (Items menu), 68, 295
New Report command (Reports menu), 67, 295
New Stack... command (File menu), 82, 122, 292
New Stack dialog box
  illustrated, 82
  options, 83
Next command (Go menu), 29, 32, 36, 293
Next Window command (Go menu), 32, 36, 293
nonsequential information, xx
numbers, defined, 319

O
object descriptors, defined, 319
object hierarchy, 176
object-oriented graphics, 290. *See also* graphics
object-oriented languages, 175
object properties, defined, 319
objects
  as components of stacks, 175
  defined, 319
  dictionary of HyperTalk, 304–316
  hierarchy, 176
  properties of, 202
  summary of keyboard commands and menu
    equivalents, 301
Objects menu, 289, 294
  Bring Closer command, 157, 294
  Card Info... command, 178, 294
  illustrated, 95, 294
  New Background command, 133–134, 294
  New Button command, 95, 294
  New Field command, 182, 294
  Send Farther command, 157, 294
  summary of commands, 294
on-line help, 28, 34–35, 319
on message command(s) message
    (HyperTalk), 175
on mouseUp handler (HyperTalk), 174, 175, 176
on OpenCard handler (HyperTalk), 205–206
on openStack handler (HyperTalk), 217
Opaque command (Paint menu), 142, 299
opaque graphics, 142, 144. *See also* graphics
Open command (File menu), 10
Open Stack... command (File menu), 21–22, 36, 292
openStack message (HyperTalk), 177, 217
operating system. *See* system files
operator precedence, in HyperTalk calculations, 170
operators, defined, 319–320

Option-Command, revealing hidden buttons, 161
Option-drag, to copy fields, 74
Option key, cloning graphics, 124
Option-Return (soft return), in HyperTalk
    scripts, 187
Options menu
  Brush shape... command, 102, 298
  Distort command, 139, 298
  Draw Centered command, 160, 298
  Draw Filled command, 103, 298
  Draw Multiple command, 160, 298
  Edit Pattern... command, 136–137, 298
  FatBits command, 126, 298
  Grid command, 104, 298
  illustrated, 298
  Line Size... command, 100, 298
  Perspective command, 138–139, 298
  replacing the Objects menu, 289
  Rotate command, 139, 298
  Slant command, 139, 298
  summary of commands, 298
Oval tool (Tools menu), 147

P
page layout
  changing, 68–70
  for printing, 66
Page Setup command (File menu), 66, 292
Paintbrush tool (Tools menu), 101–102
Paint Bucket tool (Tools menu), 90–91
painting properties, defined, 320
painting. *See* drawing; graphics; Tools menu/
    palette
Paint menu
  Flip Horizontal command, 142, 299
  illustrated, 299
  Keep command, 88, 122, 299
  Lighten command, 181, 299
  Opaque command, 142, 299
  replacing the Objects menu, 289
  Revert command, 88, 299
  Rotate Left command, 139, 299
  Rotate Right command, 139, 299
  summary of commands, 299
  Transparent command, 142, 299
paint patterns
  editing, 136–137
  pouring, 89–91
  See also Patterns menu/palette
paint text, 91–94
  defined, 320

paint text *(continued)*
    editing, 290
    versus field text, 129–130
    See also field text; text
Paint Text tool (Tools menu), 92
paint tools, 84–85
    in the background layer, 123
    defined, 320
    and FatBits, 127
    See also tools; Tools menu/palette
palette control buttons, summary, 32
palettes, defined, 320
parameters, 317, 320
parameter variables, defined, 318, 320
parentheses ( ), with HyperTalk functions, 169
Pascal programming language, 174, 175, 261
Passing Notes stack, 282
passwords
    on file servers, 6, 9
    on hard disks, 5
Paste command (Edit menu), 53, 54, 293
patterns. *See* paint patterns; Patterns menu/palette
Patterns menu/palette, 89, 299
    illustrated, 94
    replacing the Objects menu, 289
Pencil tool (Tools menu), 85
    and using FatBits, 125–127
perspective, creating, 138–139
Perspective command (Options menu), 138–139,
    298
phone dialer, using, 61
Phone stack, 61
Pickup command (icon editor), 192
picture element. *See* pixels
pictures, defined, 320
pixels, 85
    in a card, 208
    defined, 320
Play command, adding sound to stacks, 216–217
Plus (Spinnaker Software), 280–281
pointer
    I-beam, 50
    insertion bar, 50–51
    moving with the mouse, 9
pointing hand icon (Browse tool), 76
    illustrated, 85
points, defined, 320
point size of fonts, 93, 128
polygons
    drawing, 86–89, 103–104
    regular, 159

Polygon tool (Tools menu), 86–89, 103–104
    constraining, 89
pop card command (HyperTalk), 240, 241
pop-up fields, 46
    creating, 231–233
pop-up menus, 23
power keys, 298
    defined, 320
presentation graphics, 181
presentations, creating dynamic, 180–210
Prev command (Go menu), 29, 32, 36, 293
Print Card command (File menu), 64, 292
printing
    cards, 64–66
    controlling page layout, 66
    customizing, 65–66
    reports, 66–67
Print Report command (File menu), 66, 292
Print Stack... command (File menu), 64, 292
procedural languages, 175
programming
    defining the problem, 224–225
    stepwise refinement in, 226
properties
    defined, 320
    dictionary of HyperTalk, 304–316
    global, 202, 318
    of the HyperCard environment, changing, 174
    of objects, 202, 319
    painting, 320
    setting, 202
    text, 321
    window, 321
pseudocode
    converting to HyperTalk, 255
    defined, 251
pull-down menus, defined, 10
push command (HyperTalk), 240, 241
put command (HyperTalk), 209, 252, 253–254

Q
QuicKeys (CE Software), 278–279
Quit HyperCard command (File menu), 36, 77, 292
quitting HyperCard, 36, 77, 249
quotation marks (″), in HyperTalk scripts, 187, 260

R
RAM requirements, 7
Recent command (Go menu), 30, 32, 36, 289,
    293, 320
Recent dialog box, described, 320

recorders, sound, 275–276
records, defined, 44
Rectangle tool (Tools menu), 102
recursion, defined, 320
reference cards, in hypertext documents, 235–237
reference types, absolute and logical, 133
Regular Polygon tool (Tools menu), 159
regular text, defined, 320. *See also* field text; text
reminder stacks, 240
`repeat` structures (HyperTalk), 202, 206
Reports 2.0 (Nine to Five Software), 278
reports
    printing, 66–67
    summary of keyboard commands and menu
        equivalents, 302
    See also report templates
Reports menu, 295
    choosing report templates, 67
    New Report command, 67, 295
report templates
    choosing, 67
    creating, 67–70
    saving, 70
    See also reports
ResCopy (Maller), 275
ResEdit, moving resources, 275
`reset menuBar` command (HyperTalk), 252
resource fork, defined, 320
Resource Mover (Claris Corporation), 275
resources
    alternatives to HyperCard, 280–281
    animation aids, 273–275
    books on HyperCard, 284
    example stacks, 281–283
    graphic tools, 269–272
    for HyperCard, 269–287
    HyperTalk helpers, 279–280
    miscellaneous, 278–279
    multi-media makers, 276–278
    scanners and digitizers, 272–273
    sound resources, 275–276
    sources of software and hardware, 285–287
    user groups and bulletin boards, 283–284
Restart command (Special menu), 36
`result` function (HyperTalk), 242
`resumeStack` message (HyperTalk), 259
return-arrow button, 28
`returnKey` system message, 172
Revert command (Paint menu), 88, 299
right-arrow button, 27, 28
    scripting, 238

right-arrow key, 31, 36
Rotate command (Options menu), 139, 298
Rotate Left command (Paint menu), 139, 299
Rotate Right command (Paint menu), 139, 299
Rounded Rectangle tool (Tools menu), 104–105

S
Save a Copy... command (File menu), 55, 260, 292
saving
    automatic, 7, 55, 88
    backup copies, 55
    cards, 73
    graphics, 88
    report templates, 70
    stacks, 7, 55
ScanMan (LogiTech), 273
scanners
    importing clip art, 155
    resources, 272–273
Scrapbook, importing clip art, 155
Script... button, illustrated, 174
script editor, 174
    defined, 320
    editing techniques, 187
    File menu, 297
script editors, sources, 279–280
ScriptEdit (Somak Software), 279
scripting user level, 168, 289. *See also* user levels
Script menu
    Comment command, 260–261, 297
    illustrated, 297
    Set Checkpoint command, 210, 297
    summary of commands, 297
    Uncomment command, 260–261, 297
scripts
    conditional structures, 202
    control structures, 202
    debugging, 210–215
    defined, 320
    examining, 177–179
    example stack script, 255–256
    of HyperCard objects, 175
    "intelligent," 179
    loop structures, 202
    menu manipulation, 252–253
    repairing, 214–215
    script editors, 279–280
    shortcuts to, 192
    stepping through, 212–213
    summary of keyboard commands and menu
        equivalents, 303

scripts *(continued)*
  syntax, 187
  temporary, 257, 260
  terminating, 215
  testing, 257
  tracing actions in, 213–215
  variables, 206, 211–213, 246
script window, 174
  closing, 192, 212
  shortcut to get to, 177
scroll bars, 11–12
scroll box, 12
Scroll command (Go menu), 33, 36, 293
scroll down (visual effect), 111, 191
scrolling fields, 49
scroll left (visual effect), 111
scroll right (visual effect), 111
scroll up (visual effect), 111
scroll window
  opening, 33
  resizing HyperCard windows, 33–34
searchable fields, 60. *See also* fields
search path, defined, 320–321
Search Paths cards, defined, 321
Search Paths...Stacks card, 46
Select All command (Edit menu), 16
  selecting graphics, 98, 146
Select command (Edit menu), 98–99
  selecting graphics, 146
selecting, 10
  adding to a selection, 16
  defined, 9
  deselecting, 16
  graphics, 98–99, 146
  icons, 9, 16
  irregular areas, 99, 145, 146
  rectangular areas, 99–100, 146
  Select All command, 16
  shrink-to-fit, 145
  text, 53
  words, 53
Selection rectangle, 16
  selecting graphics, 98–100, 146
send command (HyperTalk), 254
Send Farther command (Objects menu), 157, 294
sequence buttons, scripting, 237–238
sequencer, music, 277
Set Checkpoint command (Script menu), 210, 297
Set/Clear Checkpoint command (Debugger menu), 212, 298
set cursor to watch message (HyperTalk), 174

set message (HyperTalk), 177, 202
Shared Text option, for text in fields, 75
Shift-clicking
  adding to a selection, 16
  selecting text, 53
Shift key, as a constraint key, 62, 88, 124
Shift-Tab, moving backward through fields, 57
show command (HyperTalk), 170–171
showing, summary of keyboard commands and menu equivalents, 301
shrink to bottom (visual effect), 111
shrink to center (visual effect), 111
shrinking graphics objects, 124. *See also* graphics
shrink to top (visual effect), 111
Shut Down command (Special menu), 19, 36, 77
shutting down the Macintosh, 36, 77
simulations, computer, 121
single-sided drives, 14
size box, 11
Slant command (Options menu), 139, 298
SnapJot (Trillium Software), 271–272
soft return (¬), 187, 233
software, sources, 285–287
software construction kit, HyperCard as, xx
software engineering, 109
sorting hierarchy, 59
sorting stacks, 59. *See also* stacks
sound recorders, 275–276
sound resources, 275–276
sounds
  adding to stacks, 215–217
  built-in, 216, 275
  memory requirements, 276
  sources for, 275–276
Special menu
  ejecting disks, 13
  Empty Trash command, 18
  Erase Disk command, 14
  Frame command, 193
  illustrated, 296
  Restart command, 36
  Shut Down command, 19, 36, 77
Special menu (icon editor)
  illustrated, 193, 296
  summary of commands, 296
Spelling Coach Professional (Deneba Software), 278
Spray Can tool (Tools menu), 113
Stack Exchange (Heizer Software), 283
Stack Info dialog box, 34
  checking free space, 260
Stack Overview card, 49

Stack Overview command (Utilities menu), 49
stacks
    adding animation, 192–201
    adding cards, 57–58
    adding sound, 215–217
    automatic backtracking, 239–240
    background information, 28
    backing up, 7, 260
    canned, 70–71
    closing, 254–255, 259
    creating new, 82–84, 122–133
    critiquing, 258–259
    current, 49, 290, 318
    custom stack menus, 250–257
    data structures, 240
    defined, xxi
    deleting cards, 57–58
    design, 151, 159
    eliminating free space, 260
    example script, 255–256
    exporting text, 49
    finding cards, 59–60
    finding key words, 28
    help, 35
    as HyperCard objects, 175
    importing text, 49
    keeping orderly, 161
    locating, 20, 46, 47–48
    maps, 109, 113, 149
    moving between cards, 27, 28–33
    music, 281
    name-and-address, 57
    naming, 84
    navigating, 28–35
    network structures, 149–150
    nonlinear structure, 161
    objects as components of, 175
    opening, 20, 21–22
    overview, 28
    planning, 149–150
    protecting, 250
    reminder, 240
    repairing, 149
    retracing your steps, 30
    saving, 7, 55
    sorting, 59
    sources for, 281–283
    stackware engineering, 109–113, 148–151
    starting, 122–123
    suspending, 250
    testing, 109, 243, 258
    viewing partial contents, 34
    viewing the script of, 192, 217
    visual effects, 97–98, 111
    working copies, 7
    wrap-around, 238
    See also specific stacks
stackware engineering, 109–113, 148–151
startup disk, 8
Step command (Debugger menu), 212, 298
Step Into command (Debugger menu), 212, 298
stepwise refinement, defined, 226
Straight Line tool (Tools menu), 86, 100
stretch from bottom (visual effect), 111
stretch from center (visual effect), 111
stretching graphics objects, 124. *See also* graphics
stretch from top (visual effect), 111
striped margin bar, xxiii, 73, 122
striped menu bar, xxiii, 73, 120
Studio/1 (Electronic Arts), 270, 274
Studio/8 (Electronic Arts), 271
Studio/32 (Electronic Arts), 271
Style menu, 293
    Group command, 234
    illustrated, 234
subtract (–), HyperTalk arithmetic operator, 170
SuperCard (Silicon Beach Software), 280
Superdrives (Apple FDHD), 6–7
SuperPaint (Silicon Beach Software), 270–271
    clip art, 155
suspended stacks, 250. *See also* stacks
suspendStack message (HyperTalk), 259
Swivel 3D (Paracomp), 274–275
Swivel 3D Professional (Paracomp), 274–275
syntax
    of HyperTalk scripts, 187
    of the HyperTalk visual effect
        command, 188–189
System clock, 169
system disks
    defined, 8
    for floppy-disk-based systems, 6
system files
    and hard disk installations, 5
    requirements, 4
System Folder
    on file servers, 6
    on floppy-disk installations, 6–7
    opening, 10–11
system messages, 170
    dictionary of HyperTalk, 304–316
system software, network, 6

T

Tab key, moving to the next field, 57
tear-off menus, 84
text
    alignment, 93
    boldface type, 234
    copying, 53–55
    cutting, 53–55
    deleting, 52
    editing, 51–55
    entering in fields, 50–51
    exporting from stacks, 49
    field text, 91, 129–130, 290
        fonts for, 184
    fonts, 93
    group text, 234
    hot text, 234, 239, 241–245
    importing to stacks, 49
    inserting, 52
    locking in fields, 75–76
    paint text, 91–94, 129–130, 290, 320
    pasting, 53–55
    point size of fonts, 93, 128
    properties, 321
    regular, 320
    selecting, 53
    styles, 93
    wrapping, 51
text fields, 50–55. *See also* fields
Text Style... command (Edit menu), 92, 293
textStyle function (HyperTalk), 241
Text Styles dialog box, 92–93
    illustrated, 92
the, with HyperTalk functions, 169
ThunderScan (Thunderware), 272–273
ThunderWorks (Thunderware), 272
ticks, defined, 321
Tilde (~) key, 30, 36, 88
    with paint tools, 99
time (HyperTalk function), 169
title bar, of windows, 11
titles, creating, 128–130
ToolBook (Microsoft), 281
tools
    defined, 321
    dictionary of HyperTalk, 304–316
    general, 84
    paint, 84–85
    summary of keyboard commands and menu
        equivalents, 301
    See also specific tool; Tools menu/palette

Tools menu/palette, 84, 293
    Browse tool, 76, 85
    Button tool, 73, 95
    Curve tool, 143
    Eraser tool, 86
    Field tool, 74
    general tools, 84
    Hand tool, 126–127
    hiding/showing, 171
    illustrated, 73, 84
    Lasso tool, 98–99, 145
    Oval tool, 147
    Paintbrush tool, 101–102
    Paint Bucket tool, 90–91
    Paint Text tool, 92
    paint tools, 84–85
    Pencil tool, 85, 125–127
    Polygon tool, 86–89, 103–104
    Rectangle tool, 102
    Regular Polygon tool, 159
    Rounded Rectangle tool, 104–105
    Spray Can tool, 113
    Straight Line tool, 86, 100
    tearing off, 84–85
Trace command (Debugger menu), 212, 298
tracing scripts, 213–215. *See also* scripts
Transparent command (Paint menu), 142, 299
transparent graphics, 142, 144. *See also* graphics
Trash, 9, 18
    ejecting disks, 18
    erasing files and folders, 18
Trax (Passport), 277
tree structures
    of hypertext documents, 226–227
    versus network structures, 227
troubleshooting, 288–291
two-way links, 140–143
typing, troubleshooting, 290
typing user level, 45, 71. *See also* user levels

U

UltraPaint (Deneba Software), 270–271
Uncomment command (Script menu), 260–261, 297
Undo command (Edit menu), 54–55, 293
    erasing graphics, 87–88
undo key, 30
union, of subsets, 64
unlock screen command (HyperTalk), 242
up-arrow, of the scroll bar, 11
up-arrow key, 31, 36
user groups, 283–284

user interface
  defined, 109
  of hypertext documents, 228
  user-hostile, 151
  using HyperCard to create, xx–xxi
user levels
  changing, 44–45, 218
  defined, 321
  removing the protective patch, 72–73
  resetting, 71–73, 289
  See also specific user level
user name, changing, 45
Utilities menu
  Mark Cards command, 61
  Sorting commands, 59
  Stack Overview command, 49

V
values, defined, 321
variables (in HyperTalk scripts), 206
  changing values, 211
  defined, 321
  global, 212, 246, 318–319
  local, 246, 319
  parameter, 318, 320
  viewing, 213
Variable Watcher command (Debugger menu),
    211–212, 298
Variable Watcher window
  showing/hiding, 211
  viewing variables in, 213
venetian blinds (visual effect), 111
videodisc players, 277
View menu, 11–12
`visible` property (HyperTalk), 233
`visual [effect]` command (HyperTalk),
    188–189, 213
visual effects
  adding to stacks, 97–98
  in HyperTalk, 188–189
  summary, 111
Voyager Video Stack (The Voyager Company), 277

W
`wait` command (HyperTalk), 206
"Where is___?", 23, 288–289
white paint, versus no paint, 105
Wild Things (Language Systems), 279–280
windows
  active, 11
  changing the view, 11–12
  closing, 12
    to save memory, 56
  defined, 10
  external, 32
  hiding/showing, 171
  location, 208
  opening, 10–11
  properties, 321
  resizing, 11, 33–34
  title bar, 11
wipe down (visual effect), 111
wipe left (visual effect), 111, 178
wipe right (visual effect), 111, 191
wipe up (visual effect), 111
`with` clause (HyperTalk), 252
`without dialog` command (HyperTalk), 245
words
  dictionary of HyperTalk, 304–316
  selecting, 53
working copies, of stacks, 7
work space, customizing, 18–19
wrapping text, 51. *See also* text
write-protection, of disks, 13

X
XCMDs (external commands), 261
  defined, 318
XFCNs (external functions), defined, 318

Z
zoom box, 12
zoom close (or zoom in) (visual effect), 111
zoom open (or zoom out) (visual effect), 111

Tools and Keyboard Modifiers

Tools	Click on tool	Double-click on tool	Drag with tool
Browse tool (turns to I-beam over unlocked fields)	selects Browse tool; used to click buttons, edit field text		selects field text
Button tool	selects Button tool; used to create, modify buttons		from middle moves button; from corner resizes button
Field tool	selects Field tool; used to create, modify fields		from middle moves field; from corner resizes field
Selection tool (marquee)	reveals paint menus	selects entire graphics layer	selects rectangular picture; moves selection
Lasso	reveals paint menus	selects all images in graphics layer	selects irregularly sized picture (shrink to fit); moves selection
Pencil	reveals paint menus	toggles FatBits on/off	draws fine line
Paintbrush	reveals paint menus	displays Brush Shapes dialog box	draws with selected pattern and brush shape
Eraser	reveals paint menus	erases entire graphics layer	erases graphics
Straight Line	reveals paint menus	displays Line Size dialog box	draws straight line
Spray Can	reveals paint menus		paints spray with selected pattern
Rectangle	reveals paint menus	toggles Draw Filled on/off	draws rectangle with selected line width
Rounded Rectangle	reveals paint menus	toggles Draw Filled on/off	draws rounded rectangle with selected line width
Oval	reveals paint menus	toggles Draw Filled on/off	draws oval with selected line width
Curve	reveals paint menus	toggles Draw Filled on/off	draws irregular curved shapes with selected line width
Regular Polygon	reveals paint menus	displays Polygon Sides dialog box	draws regular polygons with selected line width
Polygon	reveals paint menus	toggles Draw Filled on/off	draws irregular polygons with selected line width
Paint Bucket	reveals paint menus	toggles the display of the Patterns palette on/off	click to fill surrounded graphic area with pattern
Paint Text	reveals paint menus	reveals Paint Text Style dialog box	click to position pointer for typing paint text